MW01485897

Trilithon: The Journal of the Ancient Order of Druids in America

Trilithon:
The Journal of the
Ancient Order of Druids in America

Volume III
Summer Solstice, 2016

Copyright 2016 by the Ancient Order of Druids in America, Indiana, Pennsylvania.
(www.aoda.org)
All rights reserved.

ISBN-13:978-0692712733
ISBN-10: 0692712739

Colophon

Cover art by Dana O'Driscoll
"Spirit of Mugwort" (Painting channeled through meditation)

Designed by Paul Angelini using Adobe® InDesign.®

Herne's Oak, after Drawing by Mr. Stark.

A Treatise On The Identity Of Herne's Oak, Shewing The Maiden Tree to Have Been The Real One.
by William Perry, Wood Carver to the Queen, 1867

"Learn diligently what thou seest;
keep diligently what thou learnest;
and fear not to make known what thou knowest."

Triad from *The Druids and Theosophy, 1926, Page 205*

Contents

Letter from the Editor

Greetings everyone, and welcome to the Ancient Order of Druids in America's *Trilithon* volume 3! Three is a special number for Druids, and our third issue is certainly carrying on that tradition. First of all, I'd like to start with some announcements about the AODA, as this helps frame our issue this year.

The end of 2015 and beginning of 2016 have been a time of major leadership changes in the Grand Grove. John Michael Greer, who served as the AODA's Grand Archdruid for twelve years, has stepped down. Gordon Cooper, Archdruid of Fire for over a decade, has become our eighth Grand Archdruid. Further, Sara Greer, who served as Archdruid of Water and Siani Overstreet, Archdruid of Air, have also stepped down. I have been serving as AODA's chief editor for *Trilithon* and Grand Pendragon and have now moved into the Archdruid of Water position. Adam Robersmith, Druid Adept, is our new Archdruid of Fire. Finally, Paul Angelini, who has worked on the staff of *Trilithon* for the last two years, is now serving as the order's new Grand Pendragon. Because of these changes, we have devoted part of this issue to interviews with John Michael, Sara, and Gordon. We wanted to honor the work of of our Archdruid Emeriti and spend time getting to know our new Grand Archdruid. So we begin this issue with three interviews that explore their many contributions, histories, and knowledge.

Beyond our interviews, we are proud to be publishing a number of unique pieces of Druid scholarship. First is a segment of Adam Robersmith's Druid Adept project, titled "Grounding Through Heaven and Earth: An Introduction to the Nine Hazels Qigong." This piece is an adaptation of the traditional qigong movements to Druid practice, and, if I do say so myself, it is really enjoyable to practice! We also have the second installment of Tracy Glomski's "*Mabinogi* Skies" series that explores the astronomical aspects of the *Mabinogi*. It encourages us to look to the skies to connect to ancient wisdom and knowledge and offers an original scholarly interpretation based on astronomy. We also have "The Song of St. Margaret" by Christian Brunner, which translates and analyzes a poem from the remote areas of Switzerland and Austria and demonstrates its connections to ancient traditions. My own "Sacred Sites in America" reenvisions the sacred site for an American Druid context and suggests

ways of creating many different kinds of sacred sites. Daniel Cureton's "Saving Our History: Creating Pagan Archives" explores how to create digital and print archives of materials that can help establish a stronger history. Finally, Rick Derks shares his insights on staff creation.

We also have three pieces that have some connection to gardening and ceremony—Claire Schosser's "Ecology and Spirituality in the Vegetable Garden" provides insights not only on key gardening methods and her expert analysis of their efficacy, but also spiritual practices for the garden. Maxine Rogers shares her experiences in wassailing her apple orchard, and Will Harrington shares his own gardening insights. As a final offering for this packed issue, we are reprinting a lost Druid Revival pamphlet titled *The Druids and Theosophy* by Peter Freeman, which is not available anywhere else at this time.

As chief editor, I am truly delighted to see how our journal has grown over the last three years. Like an oak seed that has sprouted, each year grows stronger than the last, and this year, I am excited to offer you such a variety of pieces on Druid practice. I believe we are publishing some of the most interesting and engaging Druid scholarship and insights available anywhere.

I'd also like to acknowledge three people who have helped this journal take shape: Karen Fisher, who has been copy editing for us since the beginning of this journal, three years ago; Paul Angelini, who joined us last year on layout, and who did the full beautiful layout of the journal this year; and Kelly Trumble, who joined us as a copy editor this year. The AODA owes them much in the way of thanks for their service to the order!

Readers, I encourage you to consider submitting some of your own material in the coming months for our 4th issue, and to write to me at trilithonjournal@gmail.com with your thoughts and insights on our latest issue. And contributors to this issue or previous ones—thank you so much for making this journal what it is!

I want to conclude by saying that I think this is a very exciting time for the AODA. I encourage you to look forward to new offerings and material from the order in the coming months and years. In addition to this journal, we are now offering a regular newsletter (which you can subscribe to at this address: http://eepurl.com/bUMPPP).

Bright blessings to all—enjoy the summer sun and the blessings of the dew, the rain, the winds, the sea, and the land around us.

Yours under the sugar maples,
Dana O'Driscoll
Chief Editor, *Trilithon*
Druid Adept and Archdruid of Water, AODA

A History of British Forest Trees
by Prideaux John Selby, 1842

Trilithon Credits

Dana O'Driscoll *Chief Editor, Cover Art*

Dana O'Driscoll is the Chief Editor of *Trilithon: The Journal of the Ancient Order of America*, a Druid Adept in the AODA, and serves as the Archdruid of Water. She also is Druid grade graduate in the Order of Bards, Ovates, and Druids, a member of the Druidical Order of Golden Dawn, and a traditional western herbalist. Her AODA Druid Adept project explored the connection between druidry and sustainability and how to use permaculture design principles and community building to engage in druidic practice. By day, she is a writing professor and learning researcher; by night, an organic gardener, natural builder, mushroom forager, and whimsical artist. Dana is typically covered with paint, dirt, or both, and loves to sneak into the forest to play her panflute when other people aren't looking. Dana's writings can be found on the web at druidgarden.wordpress.com.

Karen Fisher *Copy Editor*

Karen M. Fisher is an Druid Apprentice in the Ancient Order of Druids in America and has been a pagan for over 30 years, most of which were spent on a Wiccan path. She is a professional freelance copyeditor for several academic publishers. She enjoys hiking and foraging and lives in a big old house in Pennsylvania.

Kelly Trumble, *Copy Editor*

Kelly Trumble, AODA Druid Apprentice, is an AODA office staff volunteer and an enthusiastic student of the Dolmen Arch magical system. In a past life, Kelly earned a PhD in eighteenth- and nineteenth-century British literature and taught writing and literature courses as an adjunct professor. Kelly currently lives in beautiful northern Michigan with her husband and son. She spends most of her time homeschooling her son, doing the occasional copy-editing, volunteering at the local library, and caring for her family, though she's been known to sneak in a little reading or puzzle-working if no one is looking.

Paul Angelini *Layout Designer*

Paul Angelini, native-Michigander and Druid Apprentice in the AODA, has been an assitant on the *Trilithon* staff for the past two years, and a member of the AODA since 2013. His passions include cyder making, permaculture design, used book stores, foraging for wild food and herbs, and the study and practice of the Western Esoteric Tradition. As Grand Pendragon of the AODA, Paul is commited to preserving the order's unique history and tradition for the benefit of generations present and future.

About The AODA

Founded in 1912 as the American branch of the Ancient and Archaeological Order of Druids, AODA is a traditional Druid order rooted in the Druid Revival of the eighteenth and nineteenth centuries, offering an opportunity for modern people to experience the teachings and practices of Druidry in today's world. We don't claim direct descent from the original Druids—the priestly caste of ancient Britain, Ireland, and Gaul, which went extinct around 1,200 years ago—and to be honest, we're skeptical of any group that does make that claim. Instead, like other modern Druid groups, the AODA evolved out of a 300-year-old movement, the Druid Revival, that found the fragmentary legacy of the ancient Druids a powerful source of inspiration and insight, and drew on a wide range of sources in shaping a nature spirituality to meet the challenges of today.

AODA understands Druidry as a path of nature spirituality and inner transformation founded on personal experience rather than dogmatic belief. It welcomes men and women of all national origins, cultural and linguistic backgrounds, and affiliations with other Druidic and spiritual traditions. Ecological awareness and commitment to an Earth-honoring lifestyle, celebration of the cycles of nature through seasonal ritual, and personal development through meditation and other spiritual exercises form the core of its work, and involvement in the arts, healing practices, and traditional esoteric studies are among its applications and expressions.

Its roots in the Druid Revival give the AODA certain features in common with esoteric societies such as the Hermetic Order of the Golden Dawn. It offers an initial ceremony of reception into the order, followed by three degrees of initiation—Druid Apprentice, Druid Companion, and Druid Adept—which are conferred upon completion of a graded study program. Its members have the opportunity to meet in local groups of two kinds, study groups and groves, and a Grand Grove oversees the order, charters study groups and groves, and manages the study program.

v

In keeping with the traditions of Revival Druidry, the AODA encourages its members to pursue their own spiritual directions within a broad common framework, and its approach to spirituality is personal and experiential rather than dogmatic. The initiation rituals and study program are prescribed, and AODA members are expected to keep four traditional Druid holy days, the solstices and equinoxes. Creativity and the quest for personal Awen—the inner light of inspiration—are among the AODA's central values.

The Gnostic Celtic Church (GCC) is an independent sacramental church of nature spirituality affiliated with the Ancient Order of Druids in America (AODA), a contemporary Druid order. Like many other alternative spiritual groups in American society, AODA—which was originally founded in 1912—developed connections with a variety of other compatible traditions over the course of its history. One of these connections was with the Universal Gnostic Church (UGC).

For more information about the AODA's study program, please visit:
http://aoda.org/curric.html

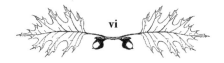

How to Join the AODA

The Ancient Order of Druids in America welcomes applications for membership from men and women of all spiritual, cultural, and ethnic backgrounds, age eighteen or older, who wish to create and follow a personal path of nature spirituality in the traditions of the Druid Revival.

By Mail: Send a letter of application to AODA, P.O. Box 1002, Indiana, PA 15701, USA. The letter should include your legal name, Druid name (if you have one), postal and email addresses, date of birth, an outline of your previous Druid studies if any, and anything you may want to say about why you wish to join AODA and what you hope to get out of it. Include a check or money order for US$50, payable to AODA.

Electronically: Please send a letter of application via email to info@aoda.org. The email should include your legal name, Druid name (if you have one), postal and email addresses, date of birth, an outline of your previous Druid studies if any, and anything you may want to say about why you wish to join AODA and what you hope to get out of it. Your membership fee of US$50 may be paid via PayPal; please have payment made to payment@aoda.org.

How to Contact the AODA

Trilithon Journal
> Contact the editor, Dana O'Driscoll, at trilithon@aoda.org

Contact the AODA
> Contact the AODA Grand Grove at info@aoda.org

Mailing address:
> AODA
> PO Box 1002
> Indiana, PA 15701

An Interview with Grand Archdruid Gordon Cooper

Interviewed by Dana O'Driscoll
Transcribed by Paul Angelini

Gordon Cooper became the 8ᵗʰ Grand Archdruid of the Ancient Order of Druids in America on December 21ˢᵗ, 2015 after the Grand Archdruid Emeritus John Michael Greer stepped down after 12 years of service. We caught up with Gordon to hear about his journey in the AODA, learn more about him, and hear about some of his upcoming plans for the order.

Dana: What drew you into Druidry initially?

Gordon: It helps to realize the term Druidry was *not* in active use in the 1960's and 70's. I never actually heard the word until OBOD's revival. However, the first time I was cognizant there *were* other Druids was on Autumn Equinox of 1976, at about 6:30pm in the evening. That was the day I checked into the domicile of the Defense Language Institute in Monterey, California. In the room across from mine were a handful of people bent over a map with the logo "Outdoor Adventure" on it that were rolling a whole bunch of really strangely shaped dice. Over the next 2 days, one of the people in the group said "I'm going to tell you secrets you probably shouldn't know. One of them is that person X is a witch, OK, and that they want to be a Druid." So that was my introduction to the fact that such people existed.

Dana: And then how did you end up being a Druid yourself?

Gordon: Wow! That's a little more complicated.

Dana: You can give us the short version if you want.

Gordon: I never self-identified as a Druid until the middle-to-late 90's, because I thought it was presumptuous. However, at the point where OBOD members began referring to me as a Druid, I decided that, at least in this case, consensus wins. And I was a Druid because they *said* I was.

Dana: So then what about your membership in the AODA? Tell us about that. How long were you a member? When did you join?

Gordon: Let's see.... Before there was the AODA, there was a plan. And the plan was called druidwisdom.com, and it was going to be an alternative Druid group that John Michael [Greer], Sara [Greer], and I bought the domain name for in the summer of either 2002 or '03. Then just *after* that time, JMG had been contacted by the surviving members of AODA, so what was going to be Druidwisdom.com essentially had its energies put into the revival of the AODA. I think I joined in year two, and I put some very specific conditions on my joining, mainly regarding membership and financial transparency, given that I've seen more than a few national groups *completely* implode over these issues. My observation is that the only way you can *really* interact *legitimately* with your own community is by being transparent as possible with these things.

Dana: So you were an Archdruid pretty early after JMG became the Grand Archdruid?

Gordon: Yes. Yes I was. And this was coming not very many years after I'd helped Philip rewrite the Bardic Grade Gwers. I probably published or put out *at least* 150,000 words around what became known as "CR" [Celtic Reconstructionism], and starting in the early 80's, I had begun to put together the notion of spirituality is more closely tied to the biome that you lived in than a theoretical calendar that a group of people threw together one evening as an excuse for more parties in a year. So these are issues that I've really been following and working on since 1983.

Dana: So a very, very long time?

Gordon: Not long enough, but yes.

Dana: So now that you've become our Grand Archdruid, what plans do you have for the Order?

Gordon: Continuing to grow, create new materials, foster the creation of art, foster and encourage a sense of community, not in the mode of churches, but of special interest groups. I mean, really, if a group of gamers can get together every Tuesday night for 3 hours for a session of D&D, there's no good reason that small groups of people interested in Druidry couldn't get together once or twice a month just to have dinner, a meditation, and exchange poetry and some pickup music.

Dana: What do you see right now as AODA's greatest strengths?

Gordon: We're in a *very* unique position, because we're a hundred years old—and we're only a few years old. We are climbing up close to a thousand members without any real advertising—that speaks to the strength of the materials that are available through AODA. Past that, the Fraternal Lodge element within it is deliberate. Why? Because it *works*. The lodge system has had *centuries* in which to get refined, which is not to say it cannot be abused or become abusive. *Anything* put together by human beings can be messed up. But, that said, the lodge system of checks and balances help to really, really minimize certain kinds of conflict in ways that consensus-based organizations simply *cannot do*.

Dana: I'm thinking of my experience in joining the AODA ten years ago. I didn't really have a strong sense of just how good our magical system really is. I was wonder if you could speak a little about that?

Gordon: I'm not the person to ask, because over the course of my magical life, I have learned at least *6 different systems* for dealing with energy and its manifestations. To be honest, it requires a great deal of emotional effort to keep them straight. There is such a thing sometimes as too much on your plate. Back in the middle nineties, when I was helping develop the materials for what would become "CR", I was meditating one day and all of a sudden the 4/5/6 elements collapsed into a bundle, and I was left with 3 realms—Sea, Earth, and Sky. So I sort of have to do other magical paradigms through a filter of the 3 realms. I know of more than one way the Earth energy systems are *interpreted*, so again, there are multiple manifestations. What I do like about AODA, is that it has a coherent system and approach. Its open-ended, though. It can be extended.

Dana: I think a for lot of us who have worked our way through curriculum early on are now are finding ways to extend that, and I think *Trilithon* is doing a nice job in showing just how these things can be extended in different ways.

Gordon: Yes. Something that is important to realize is that spiritual groups, if they're worth anything at all, are living entities. As one sobering example, 40 years ago there was an OBOD ceremony that called on Archangels! They don't do that anymore. Things change, which does not in any way invalidate the previous practices. Its not where people are standing right now, though that said, if there was a Druid in OBOD who wanted to work with Archangels, I am certain there'd be no issues at all with that.

Dana: Can you tell us a little bit about some of your other projects or creative arts, things that you do?

Gordon: I am a photographer. I work with *actual* silver halides, i,e, *film* that is exposed through a lens, capturing an imagine. I've been serious about my own black and white work for just over 20 years now. I do my own processing myself for black and white. Color I send out to a lab in California—color requires the use of *really, really* toxic bleaches which I simply cant be exposed to. I'm starting to place art in bookstores and other places this year (I sent you a couple of examples of my work last week, I believe). I shoot 4x5 in a WWII Press Camera, 2 1/4 x 2 1/4 in a pair of Rolleicords older than I am, and a pocket sized Rollei 35S, along with a handful of last generation point and shoot 35mm film cameras that cost about five dollars now, in box with paperwork. A markdown of 80%.

I learned photography in the Fauntleroy Creek Watershed in West Seattle, which is just this *magical*, little out of the way watershed park. Its an *incredible* place. 3 years ago I did a series in the Mohave desert, I need to have the color images from that re-scanned and corrected because one of the cameras I was using didn't have an ultra-violet filter, so *all* of the color is washed out. Luckily, I have reference pictures so I can manually correct colors.

I'm an amateur radio operator, KE7RYM, though largely non-practicing because I'm five-hundred-and-ninety feet from an AM transmitter which causes *all* sorts of problems. My focus is on getting an FM meteor detection system up and running this autumn, along with some antennas for picking up East Asian Shortwave broadcasts.

I spent 5 years in college studying as an indoor disciple of a family Chinese martial arts system. I'm a full instructor in the Hsin Lu Tao system. I have hopes of going back to the Mother school in El Paso later this year in training. I do have some training equipment here, of course lacking partners you have to improvise—*a lot*. I collect odd, out of the way things in the way of history, for example a book on developing the True Will, written around 1895 by Thomas Inch, a professional British Strongman.

I've read paragraphs from Inch to people who are Thelemites, and they just assumed it was something of Crowley's that was unpublished. Years ago, Dee Seton-Barber gave me this *wonderful* approach that I've always found to be of value. She said, "Gordon, if you look at people, and you look at situations, you will never understand what is going on until you grasp what the *connections* are—not the *differences*, but the *connections*, subtle or otherwise. And I have found that to be *really* profound and quite true, and its taken me *all* sorts of wonderful places. I mean, being in the sub, sub basement of the University of Washington, Suzzallo Library, and finding a book on boxing, bayonet fighting, and grenade throwing for children from 1917.

Dana: Wow!

Gordon: Yes, wow indeed. It turns out that many, many *many* of the New Thought texts on yoga and magnetic healing or breathing were translated into Chinese in the 1930s where they became foundational Nei Gung texts *there*. Yes, grinding off the serial numbers and recycling something is an *old* and venerable occult practice. It's fascinating. Dion Fortune's teacher borrowed a great deal of material from Atkinson. Atkinson derived his base from New Thought, magnetic healing, and spiritualism, while of course not admitting that's where he was getting it from.

Dana: So these things happen often, certainly.

Gordon: *Daily!*

Dana: So what is you favorite tree?

Gordon: The frenelopsids. Aka Frenelopsidaceae, probably the first major trees (coniferous in this case) to have been pollinated by insects.

Dana: Okay. What is that?

Gordon: A now-extinct Order of trees from the Triassic and Jurassic.

Dana: Awesome. Awesome. You know its funny because I asked you, and John, and Sara for that answer and everyone of you had to sort of pause and think about it. Do you have any wisdom you wanna share with our members? Or bits of advice?

Gordon: Always leave a party wearing the same clothes you showed up in.

Dana: [laughs] Do you have anything you want to add that we didn't touch on that you would like to discuss?

Gordon: AODA has been a hell of a ride, and I only expect it to get better. Ross Nichols knew and believed that Druidry was part of an ongoing process that manifests in linear time. He didn't realize it, but he was in effect discussing Process Theology. Judy Harrow, one of my good friends introduced me to this concept about 20 years ago, and I have found Process Theology to be quite applicable to the many Independent Sacrality Movements we have, with Druidry, Wicca and modern NeoPaganism being well known members of this clade, though there are many others.

As we change, so change our interactions with the world, visible and Otherwise. I don't think it is something we should be afraid of, but it is something we need to be cognizant of.

My favorite Grail story over the last 30 years has come to from the Lancelot-Grail Cycle, which was a direct inspiration for Thomas Malory's Grail work.

In this cycle, the Grail is being sought in desert city, occupied not just by Christians, but by Muslims. The image of a city in the desert running low on water, running low on food, and *desperately* looking for a way to restore the land strikes me as a perfect paradigm for our situation today. We're not just running out of fossil fuel, we're running out of fossil *water* even faster. The Ogallala Aquifer in the Midwest, and the Hueco Bolson in Southwest Texas are being drawn down to nothing. There is no *plan*. I mean, if you look at *any* of the existing documents from government agencies, there is simply no plan around what to do when they draw it down to salt water.

This is *scary*—or it should bc. I would also say that this is a time of *extraordinary* opportunity. Yes, things are very bad, and I *completely* acknowledge that. But by the same token, those situations are capable of calling out of us as individuals, and even as ad hoc communities what is best, and what is necessary. The difference, as my good friend Helen pointed out many times, between being poor and *poverty* is the *attitude* with which you live. Poverty is such a devastating emotional state that it *precludes* joy— being poor doesn't. That is not a small distinction to be made. I would advise people, as I did in my wildcrafting article[1] to step out of of the car, off the road, and see whats out there, because it certainly *does not* correspond to the reality that is hawked on the nightly news. Its all different. Its sometimes worse, sometimes better, but there are depths to be found and participated in. And reality, as my Spiritualist teachers have often said, is a full-contact sport—best you learn to duck or put on helmets. And I would say that my voice is probably about gone for the day.

Dana: Well, that's actually the end of the interview, Gordon so that's perfect. Thank you so much.

Congratulations again to Grand Archdruid Gordon Cooper—we look forward to many years of his leadership and guidance!!

---

1   http://aoda.org/Articles/Wild_crafting_the_Modern_Druid.html

Interview with Grand Archdruid Emeritus John Michael Greer

Interviewed by Dana O'Driscoll
Transcribed by Paul Angelini

John Michael Greer (JMG) became the seventh Grand Archdruid of the Ancient Order of Druids in America and served the AODA for 12 years in that office. He stepped down on the Winter Solstice of 2015. We spent time talking with JMG about his history as a druid, his experiences as the Grand Archdruid, and the new things he's working on since his retirement from service to the AODA.

Dana: What drew you into Druidry?

JMG: That's going to require a long, complex, and ornate answer. When I was in my teens, I had, as many people did in those days, this vague sense of something out there magical, and interesting, and cool, that maybe had something to do with Druids, and maybe had something to magic, or witches, or I wasn't really sure what. It was something that differed as far as possible from the ghastly sort of suburban existence that I had to live at that time, growing up in a slowly imploding family in the south Seattle suburbs. And so I was interested for a while in what was known of the Druids; there was very little to be had in those days—again, this is back in the Seventies. OBOD was in abeyance at that time after the death of Ross Nichols; the handful of other groups that were out there that were doing Druidry were doing it int a very quiet way, and so often you had to know somebody to even know they existed. So I read a bunch of books and filed the information.

The first magical material that got into circulation that was of any quality, and had any relation to what I wanted, had to do with the Golden Dawn tradition of Hermetic

occultism. That's what I found, and that's what I plunged into with all of the enthusi-asm you would expect from a geeky teenager—which of course is saying something. And, so I did Golden Dawn, and more Golden Dawn, and still more Golden Dawn. In the course of the process, some decades later, I ended up starting a magical lodge in the Seattle area with an older and very experienced Golden Dawn occultist, and also with my wife Sara, who was at that point was very active in that tradition as well.

And one of the people that the older occultist in question brought into the lodge was an old friend of his, a member of OBOD; this was the late Corby Ingold, who just passed away a little while ago. Corby Ingold was not interested in recruiting, but he wasn't particularly secretive, and he talked a little bit about OBOD. Now, what would it have been, maybe five years before any of this got started, *The Book of Druidry* had been published, edited by Philip Carr-Gomm, and I had glanced at it but not actually pursued it; there was a zing, but I thought, "Druidry, okay that was the stuff I was really interested in as a teenager, but I'm doing Golden Dawn stuff now."

At any rate, one thing led to another, I got to talking with Corby about OBOD, and said "You know, I could see myself doing this." I was feeling a need to branch out from from the sort of strict focus on Golden Dawn magic I had at that time, and I decided to glance at OBOD, and I ended up enrolling in OBOD. I proceeded to spend five and a half years slogging my way through OBOD's really very good correspondence course, and finally became a Druid Companion, with the fancy certificate on the wall and everything. I found that work extremely interesting. And that led me into other modes of Druidry, and probably into questions that you haven't asked yet. But that's basically how I stumbled my way into Druidry. It was part of a process of looking in other directions, past the Golden Dawn. I ended up doing a lot of different magical things, everything from radionics to old-fashioned Renaissance astrological magic, with a good bit of traditional Southern hoodoo and conjure magic in there as well. Unlike most of the others, Druidry did not simply become a sideline—something I learned from and then moved on past. It became something much more central, to the extent that it eventually displaced my interest in the Golden Dawn tradition for a while.

Dana: Right, so I guess then the next question is what drew you initially into AODA?

JMG: The kind of chapter of accidents that, if you tried to put it into a novel, you'd get a note back from the publisher saying this is completely implausible—that's usually

the way these things happen. So I finished my OBOD studies, I look into a couple of other Druid groups. I was briefly involved in Ár nDraíocht Féin, ADF, which was kind of a mixed experience, frankly. Then I ended up finding this rather interesting little book, I think was called *American Druid Traditions*, or *American Druidry*, something like that. It was by a little knock-off press, back before the print-on-demand revolution, where there were not yet millions of little bitty presses out there, but this was by a little bitty press. It had a little summary of all kinds of different Druid Orders, it was written by a Celtic Reconstructionist who was very enthusiastic for Druid groups that were Celtic Reconstructionist, and very down on those that weren't. And tucked away in the back there in the list of American druid orders, it had a reference to something called the Ancient Order of Druids in America. The author didn't like it at all; he said it's stuffy, it's fraternal, it's like Freemasonry, and it's nothing like as nasty toward the Christians as it should be. So I knew immediately I would like it.

And so I sent off a letter. Distant sound of crickets. I sent off another letter. No more. I did as much searching as I could do. The Internet was getting underway at that point, I didn't have an account but I could go down the library and use it. I kept on drawing one blank after another. And then this is where it gets absurd, okay? In the meantime, while all this other stuff was going on, I had gotten involved in the American Tarot Association—I was doing a lot of Tarot in those days, especially meditative work, pathworkings, this kind of stuff. And because that work got into some things that nobody else was doing, Sara and I were both invited down to a Tarot Conference in Portland, Oregon. And we went down to Portland and this is where we both met the inestimable John Gilbert, who has a rich and complex reputation in the magical community. I happened to mention the AODA thing to him, and he said "Did you know that I am the secretary?" and I said "No—you're kidding!" No, he was, in fact, the secretary. So we got to talking—we talked in person, we talked on the phone, we exchanged a lot of e-mails (I had gotten an email account by then), and I talked to some of the other old members. It turned out the Ancient Order of Druids in America was a handful of people, scattered across the country by that point. There were fewer than a dozen, all of them were way past retirement age, and here was this mostly defunct Order, and I learned a little bit about it. And my response was, "Wow! This is sounds really cool! I'd like to learn more about this, would you consider telling me more?" And so we talked some more. And by that time I was going "Wow! This is really cool! Have you considered blowing the inch of dust that's gathered on top of this off and doing something with it? Because I think really think people would be interested. I certainly am." And not that long after, I was going "You want me to *run it*?!"

Because what happened was that they sat down together, the old members—actually, they did it on the phone. But they called around and decided if AODA was going to do anything but fall over dead, since I was the only person who had expressed any interest in it decades, I was the one chance they had. They knew about my books, they knew about my work in the Golden Dawn tradition, they knew that I had helped revive a couple of failing fraternal lodges in Seattle. And so they said "Hey, you know, maybe the Gods or something have sent this crazed youngster to us to apply shock paddles to the prostrate body of the Order and see what happens." And so, about five months after I first contacted AODA, and three months after I became a member, I suddenly found my backside planted in the Northern Chair as the seventh Grand Archdruid of the Ancient Order of Druids in America, and then, of course, I had to find out what it was that had just been dropped into my lap, because I still only had fairly vague ideas, based on what I had gotten from conversations. So it was very much a matter ending up in charge of AODA, and then finding out why it was interesting. (Laughs) I really didn't have a lot of choice. The thing is, there was a lot of really neat stuff, and I proceed to spend much of the next twelve years, again, blowing the layers of dust off, gradually collecting old documents, piecing together fragments, and figuring out what this thing was, what it had been.

Dana: So, then, when you came to the Order, it seems we were missing a lot. I'm wondering about how much you had to reconstruct, and how we ended up with the rituals, and the initiations, and all of the things that we have now?

JMG: Some of the core rituals, for example the Sphere of Protection, I got from John Gilbert intact. Certain other rituals that he and a couple of the other people had, I got by way of some long phone conferences—they were not written down. Back in the day, it was always done by memory. And so what happened was that John would sit down on the phone with a couple of other people, and they'd remember as much as they could. And they sent me the lengthy draft, and I proceeded to work with it. John wrote a set of new lectures, which I ended up rewriting very considerably.

The real challenge here was one that very gradually sunk in, which was that there was an issue that nobody was quite willing to talk about. And the issue was that I'm a regular Freemason, and most of the other people, the old members of AODA, belonged to one of the irregular jurisdictions of Freemasonry. There were several different organizations that AODA was connected to, and one of them was an irregular branch of

Freemasonry. And it was only over a period of some years that I realized that the old AODA rituals had borrowed heavily from Masonic symbolism and so on, to an extent that you really couldn't do them if you were a regular Freemason, not without violating your obligations. And so there were things that had to be quietly deleted when I came in. They did most of the deletion, I did a little bit more with their approval, but the core symbolism, the basic structure of the rituals and so on, that wasn't affected. That was all as it came to me from the old guard. Now, I proceeded to elaborate on that. Everything that's in the *Druid Magic Handbook*, for example, is me going through the material and saying, "Wow, here we have these neat ritual structures—let's do things with them." The Grove opening and closing, that's traditional. It's only been very mildly modified.

Dana: Are you talking about the solitary version, or the others?

JMG: All of them.

Dana: Okay. So all of the grove openings and closings came to us.

JMG: All of those came to us. And there were a range of other scrips and scraps—lots of scrips and scraps. And then there was all the stuff that started landing in our mailbox once I became Grand Archdruid. Back in the late 90's, AODA had had a little bit of an explosion. They'd had a political crisis, and the then Grand Archdruid quit and tried to dissolve the Order, which he did not have the power to do, not without the unanimous consent of the other Archduids, which he didn't have. But a lot of people quit, and a lot of stuff had gotten lost then. A lot of people had gone to ground in various places. But when word got out that there was a new Grand Archdruid, people started mailing and emailing the AODA address saying, "Here's some stuff you ought to have." And I got the most amazing things in the mail, stuff that nothing to do with AODA in many cases, but also a bunch of stuff that did.

And so some of that became raw material for AODA. I mentioned earlier that AODA ran with a number of other organizations, and there was a lot of common ground. There a lot things that were shared, and so I was able to say "Okay, here is this piece that still survives in the Order of Spiritual Alchemy, and it obviously fills a place where there is a gap in our system (makes sound of a cork popping) so we pull it out of the one, and pop it into the other—with appropriate symbolic changes. So it

was—I'm going use a fancy word your deconstructionist readers will like—there was a lot of bricolage involved. There was a lot of piecing together, a lot of mosaic work. I didn't have to invent very much. I drew in some things from *Barddas*, because it was very clear for a number of reasons there was a very strong Welsh Druid connection going on there. An example—when I became an Adept, a third degree Druid in the old AODA system, I had communicated to me "The Grand Druid Word." I had to explain to them, "Well, this may be profoundly secret here, but it's something that everybody in all the other Druid groups chants out loud all the time—Awen." But in AODA this was the Grand Druidical Word, which it is in a number of other traditions of Welsh Druidry. So there definitely was this Welsh stuff going on here, there definitely was some material from Barddas. And so I borrowed stuff from there, but I really invented very little.

Dana: So, in what ways do you think the Order has grown or evolved in the time that you were Grand Archdruid?

JMG: Well, of course the obvious thing is we have gone from fewer than a dozen members to more than 900. We have a bank account now, with plenty of money in it. We have a publishing program—practically everything except our initiation rituals is public, readily available, and is influencing a lot of people. The Druid Revival, the broader tradition of which AODA is a part, used to be something people look down their nose at: "Oh those horrible, fake meso-Druids." And we've gone from that, to the point that some of the people that used to say that most loudly are now surreptitiously borrowing details from our study program. How could the trailing edge become the cutting edge? And yet we are.

These days AODA is a force to be reckoned with. It's a serious presence. A lot of people know about it. *The Druidry Handbook*, which was introductory first degree manual I wrote for the order, is one of my best selling books and is very widely available. People cite it, people quote it, people use it who have no connection to AODA, so the ideas are out there. The order's really gone from being a prostrate body on the floor desperately needing shock paddles, to being up there playing the fiddle and dancing in the midst of the ceilidh.

There are some issues that need to be solved—we don't have a lot of local groups. I'm not all sure that some of the the adaptations the curriculum went through were really

a good idea, and the new administration will need to take steps as 2017 approaches, the next of our septennial program reviews, but I really think I accomplished what I wanted to accomplish, which was getting AODA up off the floor and turning it into a lively, viable, populous, prosperous Druid Order—at this point, based on conversations that I've had with Druids in several other organizations, it's one of the two or three largest in this country.

Dana: What do you consider to be your greatest contribution to the AODA?

JMG: Publicity. Which is really a mutual thing, because AODA gave me what in the publishing business is called a "platform." "Why do you want to read this person's books?" That's a platform. As in, "I'm an Archdruid, therefore you need to read all my books on Druidry and all my books on ecology." It was a huge sales benefit for me, but at the same time, as I became a very well-known figure, and not just in the Druid scene, everyone was going "Okay, what's this organization he heads?" And it was really quite funny, because people from all the different fields where I write, and many that I don't, would come to AODA from all kinds of places. There was publicity on the one hand, the other thing is doing my level best not to get in the way.

Most leaders fail by getting in the way, by trying to make everything go through them. I was the Cheerleader in Chief, and a lot of very gifted people came and contributed, and did remarkable things for the Order. I basically walked around and nodded and smiled and attracted folks to the crowd. There were other things that I think that I contributed, but primarily I functioned as a colorful figurehead who had no difficulty prancing about in a funny hat. A lot of people in the occult community are either very shy of publicity, or very bad at it. It's either "I don't want to talk to anybody," or what have you, or it's "I AM THE GRAND EXALTED PANJANDRUM, AND YOU SHOULD KISS MY FOOT!!". Neither of those go over well. And so, AODA and I were able to mutually promote each other, and bring the Order to the attention of people who could join it, who could enrich it, who could make it turn into the happening thing it is now—and I really think that's the major contribution that I made.

Dana: So what is your favorite AODA moment?

JMG: I don't know that I can answer that question, there's just so many.

Dana: Could you share one or two?

JMG: I'm gonna pass on that one. Its just not a thing of moments, it's a thing of textures, and of many different experiences, all of which went into the process of twelve years galumphing about in a funny hat.

Dana: Where do you see the Order heading next?

JMG: That depends completely, totally, and utterly on where Grand Archdruid Gordon Cooper takes it next. One of the reasons why I felt it was a very good time for me to step down is precisely that I'd done with the Order roughly what I wanted to, and if its going to grow and not just spin its wheels in the same place, its needs to head into new directions. Gordon has his own ideas. Some of the other members of the Grand Grove have their own ideas—that's good. And, as long as nobody tries to force the Order into a narrower channel, I think it will probably go marvelous places—I for one very much look forward to seeing where Gordon's going to take things.

Dana: What are you planning next?

JMG: I have no shortage of things to do! To begin with, back in 2013, with the publication of my book *The Celtic Golden Dawn*, I quietly founded a magical order, the Druidical Order of the Golden Dawn. It works with the system that was taught in that book and in the series of sequels that are currently under development. It's a fusion of Druidry and the Golden Dawn, just like it sounds. There were, back in the 1920s and 1930s, a number of orders in England and elsewhere that fused the two traditions. As far as I know, next to none of their papers survived, so I had to reverse engineer the thing and come up with something that used Golden Dawn techniques and Druid symbolism. As for the Order, the DOGD, my thought in putting it together was "Okay, this is worth the gamble, lets see if it goes anywhere." Obviously, it's not the kind of very broad organization that AODA is, which has opened up in so many different angles and directions—its a very specific, very tightly focused group of people who are working a specific system of Druidical magic, but at that, it's got a bunch of members, it's chugging away merrily, we have a good email list, which is only open to members, by the way, so don't everyone run off and try to join—you'll just get an irritated e-mail. At any rate, the Druidical Order of the Golden Dawn can use a bunch of my time at this point.

I have a range of further practices that I have been developing. I have a large book on the Druidical Cabala, which is in process. I have done a bunch of work on the old Welsh Bardic alphabet, the Coelbren[an earlier version of this was published in *Trilithon Vol II*--ed], feeding that into the Druidical Cabala, Druidical magical practice, and soon, so there's that—that's thing one.

Thing two is my problem child, the most problematic of my creative problem children, *The Sacred Geometry Oracle*. It was produced some years ago by a publisher I will not name, who made a complete mess of it—but it's being reprinted, finally, the way I would like it. That was originally meant to be the anchor of a system of Druid practice, based on sacred geometry. Again, that's going to be a specialized taste, but it's one of my major interests. So I've been dusting all that off, gradually putting the necessary books and other resources out there so that that can get going. Sacred geometry has really been the red-haired stepchild of modern esotericism. It's an incredibly rich field, full of symbolism, full of amazing teachings, and yet it's been either ignored completely, or its been consigned to the space lizard brigade—the people who are convinced that if you stare at these strange diagrams, aliens from space will make you immortal, or some such rot. It deserves much better. So *The Sacred Geometry Oracle* will be published in 2016, the first of a series of books that will eventually expand that into a full system of Druidical spirituality.

The third thing—a long time ago in a galaxy far, far away, when I was a young whippersnapper getting involved in occultism, I dabbled in astrology, and I said, "This is enormously complex. This is the kind of thing I want to get into when I am middle-aged—right now I want to do ceremonial magic!" I'm middle-aged now, and so I've started learning astrology—actually I'm well along, I started studying astrology intensively about six years ago. But that is becoming an increasingly focal part of my own studies and practices. It's a lot of fun, there's a lot to learn, and I have a lot of work I want to do in that field.

And finally, speaking of things set down many years ago and picked back up again more recently, I originally wanted to write science fiction and fantasy, but couldn't break into print; I got absolutely nowhere with that for decades. All of a sudden that's changed. I have several books in print in that field and several more on the way; I have a career shaping up as a science fiction and fantasy author, and I want to be able to put some time into that, insofar as I can squeeze it in among all the other things.

I have no shortage of things to do, now that I have fobbed off the funny hat onto the intrepid Gordon Cooper.

Dana: Do you have any parting wisdom to share with members of our Order?

JMG: I don't know that I have any particular wisdom at all, parting or otherwise. I will pass on, however, the single best piece of advice that I received at any point in the process. This happened in 2003, after Sara and I went to Britain, on the invitation of Philip Carr-Gomm—I was that year's OBOD Mount Haemus Scholar. And we had a wonderful time, and we came back, and it was not long after I got back that it became clear to me what was about to happen in AODA. And so I contacted Philip, and basically said, "PHILIP, HELLPP!!" After all, he was the only other person I had ever encountered who suddenly been pitchforked into the headship of a mostly-defunct Order, and told "Hey, kid, see what you can do." And his response was absolutely perfect—he said, "John, the one thing you must always be sure to do is have fun!" And I have. And it seems to have worked. Therefore, since I have no idea whether I have any particular wisdom of my own, but I can certainly plagiarize Philip here, and encourage everybody—"Have fun!" If you don't, you're wasting your time.

Dana: What is your favorite tree?

JMG: Whichever one I meet next.

Dana: Is there anything else you'd like to share?

JMG: One of the things that made AODA so interesting to me, and so confusing to everybody else, is that it doesn't fit the stereotypes. It is not a Neopagan organization; it dates from before Neopaganism. AODA was a going concern when Gerald Gardner was still tending rubber plantations in Sumatra—yes, I know that Wicca dates goes back to the dawn of time, but the dawn of time in this case was about 1947. AODA doesn't fit current pop-culture categories, and that caused people a certain amount of confusion. In the course of getting to know the AODA tradition, it really sank in that one of the main reasons that I like the AODA is that it doesn't correspond to the stereotypical categories, and that's a plus because many of those stereotypical categories suck. People say, this is Pagan, this isn't Pagan, and what does this actually do, besides brandishing a label for people to fight over? Nothing that I can see. And so I appreciated the fact

that AODA provides a place where people of all religious opinions can practice nature spirituality together, so long as they are willing to treat each other with courtesy and respect and show respect for our distinct traditions of symbolism and practice.

The fact is that AODA isn't a Neopagan order, that it's doing its own thing, something that's at a 45-degree angle to the conventional wisdom. What's more, it doesn't have to be your only commitment, and for most members it isn't their only commitment. All of these had a lot of people scratching their heads going "Uhhh..... Uhhh....." There's an enormous amount of talk about diversity these days, but it's remarkable how rarely that works out to a diversity of choices. We may all be different, but for some reason we're all supposed to choose the same things. And in the alternative spirituality scene, there's a great deal of peer pressure to conform to a sort of lowest common denominator stereotype of what nature spirituality and Druidry have to be. I got plenty of pushback on that, for twelve solid years, people trying to insist, "Well, you're a Druid order, you've got to worship the Goddess!" My answer—"Which one?"—is not a response they like. "You're a Druid Order, you've got to be involved in this or that political cause." "No we don't do politics, that's our tradition." "You're a Druid Order, X, Y, Z." There were all kinds of things like that. I really think one of the gifts AODA has to offer, one of the things it gave me, and I think gave many other people as well, is precisely that it doesn't fit the stereotypes, and it gives people the space they needed to refuse to fit those stereotypes themselves, to do something new, or old, to do something that isn't what everyone else is doing. And I really hope it continues to provide that inestimable service to Druids for the next hundred-and-some years.

An Interview with Archdruid Emeritus Sara Greer

Interviewed by Dana O'Driscoll
Transcribed by Paul Angelini

Sara Greer served the AODA as Archdruid of Water for 9 years. She stepped down from her role at the Fall Equinox in 2015. We spoke with Sara to hear more about her experiences in serving the order for over a decade, in learning more about her and her path. We honor and thank Sara Greer for her tireless work for AODA.

Dana: What drew you into Druidry?

Sara: Well, JM[G] and I, as part of work we were doing with the ceremonial magical adept that he mentioned earlier [see JMG's interview, page 8], were part of a study group that was working with R.J. Stewart's underworld material. Stewart was coming to Seattle to give a presentation, and a bunch of people from our study group decided to go to the presentation. We went with our friend (the adept). An old friend of his, Corby Ingold, was also there, so our friend introduced us to Corby, and we ended up becoming friends with him as well. The more Corby talked about OBOD, and about Druidry, the more I started thinking this was something that connected to a part of who I am, because from my earliest childhood I have always loved the world of nature.

As a 3 or 4 year old, when most kids that age can't sit still, I would spend hours laying on my stomach in the grass, watching bugs walk back and forth, and looking at the little tiny plants that will grow in a lawn. I was always up in a tree. I was climbing trees, and I would climb rock outcroppings over the river near where I lived even though I couldn't swim. Luckily I never fell! If there was a thunderstorm in the middle of the

night, my parents would get up, because they would find me sitting out on the porch watching the thunderstorm in my little nightgown.

So I was really drawn to the idea that nature could be viewed as something that was not merely important, but also sacred. For some reason, that idea had never crossed my awareness before; I had never encountered the idea that nature could be sacred in any other context. Possibly in part that was because I was raised Catholic. During my childhood, the church was being torn apart by the sequels of the Second Vatican council in 1962, and people were dropping out, and people were schisming away. They were introducing guitar masses that basically completely diluted the message of the church without providing anything else. The idea of connection with the environment that the activists of the 60's tried to bring into a religious context was lost on the Catholic Church, which just kind of went "Huh? What? Huh? Go away." And so I had never run into that before encountering some of the things Corby had to say about Druidry, and the Druid Revival.

There was also a personal connection, in that when I started looking into this, I realized that the Welsh Druid Gorseddau,1 Gymanfoedd Ganu, and other cultural festivals[1] came out of the Druid Revival. A lot of people in the early Druid Revival were Welsh people who were trying to preserve their traditional forms of poetry, song, literature, and what have you in the face of the encroaching English culture. And so my family had actually been involved in competing in these various contests, you know, playing music, performing poetry, etc. This was part of my mother's family's cultural heritage. Since I was raised to be very much aware of the Welsh background of her side of the family, because both of her parents had emigrated from Wales, it was still very close in my childhood. That was also something that interested me, and OBOD of course is part of the Druid Revival, and that was the Druid Order Corby was a part of.

And so I came to the conclusion that Druidry was a natural choice for me, and JMG had been initiated into OBOD at Imbolc-- I can't remember whether it was 1992 or 1993.

Footnote [1]: Welsh Gorseddau (singular: Gorsedd) are cultural gatherings where people perform and compete in traditional Welsh arts --- poetry, music, dance, etc --- using traditional Welsh forms and the Welsh language. For the most part, these are held only in Wales. Gymanfoedd Ganu (singular: Gymanfa Ganu) are gatherings for the purpose of singing traditional Welsh songs and hymns, usually in the Welsh language. Gymanfoedd Ganu are held all over the world in places where Welsh immigrants settled and formed communities, but over time they have become less common outside of Wales.

JMG: It was 1993, and I was initiated at Beltane, and you came in at the Solstice.

Sara: I thought I came in at Lughnassadh.

JMG: No, you came in Lughnassadh, that's right.

Sara: He was initiated at Beltane, and I was initiated at Lughnassadh. And I really, really enjoyed being part of OBOD, and being a Druid. That worked with something in me and in my nature that was not satisfied by ceremonial magic, because ceremonial magic has its really good points --- it's not a bad system at all --- but done by itself without any leaven of nature spirituality, it is, for me, unbalanced. And so Druidry was the natural balancing point for the ceremonial magic.

Dana: So then, moving from OBOD into AODA—how did that happen?

Sara: Meeting John Gilbert is how that happened. We went down to a Tarot conference in Portland over Labor Day weekend in 2001, and we met John Gilbert and a number of other really interesting people. John Gilbert really, I think, is the last of the old-time 1950's-style occultists. He has an amazing range of initiations, he has studied more things than you would believe, he has a great deal of knowledge, and, as was common of people of his generation, he joined a number of different occult Orders. Many of these Orders, as time went on and their members got older and older, ended up with sort of a lot of cross-membership and propping each other up. They were all in the same part of Colorado, which is where he lived at that time. And he ended up basically being the secretary of the different Orders, with a file cabinet full of briefcases, each one of which had the core material for one of these organizations. AODA was one of those organizations. He was basically single-handedly keeping a bunch of these things propped up, and keeping some of the others propped up with the assistance of the same 8 or 10 elderly people. John Gilbert was the youngest of them and when we first met him, he was about 62 or 63. He was the youngest living member in all of these different groups.

So I talked to him quite a bit about AODA, as JM did, and JM joined and really liked it, and basically, I decided that, as things came together, I would also join. It took me a little longer to join than I had originally expected, because I ended up having a major health crisis, but also we ended up relocating out of Seattle, and so a whole bunch of stuff kind of got in the way of my actually being able to do anything with the

AODA material other than be a member. Even though I joined fairly early on in 2003, I didn't effectively start working with AODA until we relocated to Oregon in 2004. Before that I wasn't doing much beyond really basic reading and that kind of thing. So that's what got me into AODA. (And, of course, I'm still a member of OBOD.)

I really liked the fact that AODA is a multi-faith organization. It's not a church exactly, its a multi-faith religious body and you can bring whatever religious beliefs you have to it, and it makes it clear that Druidry is a philosophy that is relevant to pretty much any spiritual path that's compatible with it. So essentially, it's a very fluid and accepting approach. I had been for a while a member of a another Druid Order, which I won't name, which wants to the One True Holy Apostolic Roman Catholic Church of Druidry, and since I was raised Catholic, I very quickly came to the conclusion that I do not want an organization which is going to dictate what members are permitted to think, and do, and believe. I wanted to be part of an organization that was going to say "What you think and believe is important, and you can bring that here, and it's okay so long as you can play well with others in the process." So I really liked that element of AODA.

Dana: What was AODA like before you were an Archdruid? I want to know more about what was the work of it back in that time period.

Sara: I did not actually become an Archdruid until about a year after JM did.

JMG: It was pushing 2 years because you became an Archdruid after Kathy stepped down.

Sara: That's true, yes.

JMG: You were brought into the Grand Grove as the Pendragon.

Sara: I was the Pendragon originally. I was functioning as the Almoner (treasurer), but I think I held the title Pendragon (secretary), because the duties of the Officers of the Grand Grove are flexible according to the needs of the Order.

So by the time I was brought in as an Archdruid, JM had already done quite a bit of revival work. We had a number of members. We had, I think, about 30 or 40 members by that point, maybe as many as 60. We had several people who gotten First

and Second degree by transfer credit, were working on their Third degrees, had study group charters, and were working on Grove charters. The Order had already survived its first major crisis under JM's leadership with an officer of the Grand Grove basically blowing out and destroying a bunch of records and things in the process, and so it was quite clear AODA was an up and coming thing and was gonna make it.

So the picture had actually changed a fair amount in that 2 years, in large part due to JM's hard work, also due to a lot of work that John Gilbert was doing, because once he had a sense that JM was really getting things revived, he basically went around beating the bushes for AODA and telling people about it. Things were really on the upswing and there was a lot of hope, and a lot of energy coming into the Order, so I became an Archdruid in a different Order in a sense, than JM did.

Dana: In what ways has the Order grown and evolved in the time you were an Archdruid?

Sara: It has changed enormously. It has been a place that a lot of people could come and they were welcome, and feel that they had a place that they could talk about things without getting bullied and hazed. One of the things that happened during my Archdruidship was that we put in civility policies on all of the email lists of the Order. We had been having tremendous problems with trolls joining the email list and basically doing the internet equivalent of a drive-by shooting, sending out several posts talking about how horrible, and evil, and vile, and nasty, and gross, and disgusting, and fake we were. The person who had been managing the email list had not really been effectively controlling that, and I had seen another Order have similar problems and had figured out, watching what they were doing (because I was a member of their email list), some things that I thought would work. Those of us that were running the list (I was one of them and there were a couple of other people) basically put together a policy and took it to the Grand Grove, requiring that other people's beliefs be treated seriously, even if you disagree with them, and having a set of policies in place for how to moderate, ban, etc people who were causing trouble, and what causing trouble constituted, how that was defined, versus what was considered appropriate and reasonable; questioning, asking for explanations, and so on.

And so we evolved a place where people could actually come and talk about different opinions and ideas in a civil fashion and not get flamed, and that was very important

for a while. The email lists have dropped off in activity, but that seems to be part a of a larger cultural shift. Most of the email lists I've been involved in have had a similar drop off. People are chatting Facebook and Twitter now, instead of on Yahoo, Liveournal, and other places like that. But while the list was really a seriously growing concern, which was about 8 years, we got a lot of positive feedback from people because they could come there and talk, and generally AODA has tried to be a place where people can be themselves while sharing certain types of experiences.

So we have at this point a very wide variety of beliefs and opinions and approaches to life among our membership, and I think that's a very good and healthy thing. We've become a very diverse organization. Most of our members are really good at playing well with others and handling dissenting opinions with respect, and actually being willing to talk to and listen people who have different ideas and approaches, rather than just say "There's something wrong with you because you believe that." And that's something that I think is really good.

Dana: So what you consider to be your greatest contribution to the AODA?

Sara: The nuts and bolts of every day, behind the scenes management. When I was first brought into the Grand Grove, I started running the books, and I was the one who put everything into Quickbooks, and started putting in on some kind of formal basis. At that time, basically soon after I came on, once I became an Archdruid, I was working with Kellas, our Pendragon Emeritus, who did a tremendous amount of work for years. I think it was 5 or 6 years. She just worked her butt off for the Order. We would not have gotten as far as we did without her. She did an amazing amount of work, and she was really, really good at dealing with all of the many questions and concerns that come to the office email every day. She and I are very good friends, and we work together really well, so the two of us worked as a team to basically get the behind the scenes stuff stable and organized and operating fairly smoothly. We came up with a system for keeping track of who joined the Order, have they paid yet, who asks who which questions to get stuff answered as promptly as possible, and making sure that the records were as correct and complete as we could make them, and stuff like this. When she had to step down, I basically ended up handling both the books and the secretaryship (until we got some volunteers to help). Some of the mechanisms she and I put in place were not needed during that period, but basically we put the day-to-day running of the Order on an even keel and kept it there, and that made it

possible for JM to focus on other things like reconstructing AODA's actual traditions and stuff like that.

Dana: What is your favorite AODA moment?

Sara: As JM said, I don't think that its really a matter of moments so much. In my case, I think my favorite thing has been seeing one person after another go, "Oh my goodness! I've been a Druid my whole life! Can I join your group?" and come in and find their feet, and find the path they want to tread as Druids, and just go for it. I've seen so many people just really blossom doing that, and I think that is my favorite thing about AODA. It was just having had the chance to spend 5 years as the Secretary (because that's how was long I was doing or managing the secretarial duties after Kellas stepped down), seeing that happen to person after person after person.

Dana: Where do you see the Order heading into the future?

Sara: I have no idea, but I'm looking forward to seeing where it goes. I think that Gordon and the other Grand Grove Officers have some really good ideas, and I'm looking forward to seeing what gets implemented, how the curriculum gets updated, and where things go from here, because I think there's the potential for a lot of really positive growth.

Dana: What are you planning next?

Sara: I have experienced a great deal of personal change, especially over the last couple of years. Particularly in the 3 months since I actually stepped down, with my father's passing, and also the death soon afterwards of a very old friend, Corby Ingold —in fact my mentor and initiator in Druidry—and various other changes. I really am not quite sure where I'm going next, but I'm going to be able to take more time again to spend time in nature, to work with the trees, and the sun, and the moon, and the stars, and the river, and the hills, and just participate in the living world with fewer burdens and cares on my shoulders. I'm looking forward to having more time and energy for some creative projects that have been moving kind of slowly, because I've spent the last couple of years basically handling my father's affairs, and handling his care, and that's no longer an issue since he's passed away. So I'm going to be spending

the next few months just kind of resting and being outside, and working with my creative hobbies, and just kind of putting myself back together.

Dana: Do you have any parting wisdom to share with members of the Order?

Sara: One of the most common misconceptions I encountered as an Archdruid was the idea that to be a Druid, you have to "go back to nature", and going back to nature involves having to go buy a farm in the country and grow all your own food and live off the grid. Baloney! One of my favorite pieces of wisdom with regard to going back to nature was a quote from the inimitable Orion Foxwood, who at a Pantheacon lecture said something along the lines of "When somebody tells me they're gonna go back to nature, my response is 'Honey, who told y'all could leave?!?'" We are part of nature. We are natural beings. We are part of the living world. Everything we do connects to nature one way or another. People talk about buildings as being "unnatural." Well, there are lots of animals in nature that build structures. Termites come to mind, and lyre birds who build these elaborate grass nests, and there are various other kinds of creatures, prairie dogs and beavers and what have you.

Another thing that I experienced at Pantheacon with R.J. Stewart was when he was giving a lecture and he talked about how people talk about how it's terrible and unnatural for pagans to gather in a hotel. His response was, approximately, "Where you do think the materials that this hotel was built out of came from? They came from the Earth. Yes, they have been changed, some of them beyond recognition, but they came from the Earth. Let's start this event today by reminding this building that it is of the Earth, and reminding ourselves that this building is of the Earth. We are not apart from nature just because we are sitting inside a building." And that's very important.

It's also very important to remember that your backyard, and the sky over your house or apartment, and the birds that sit on your windowsill, and the opossums that rummage through your garbage are all part of nature. You're not away from nature anywhere, ever on the face of this Earth. And I think one of the reasons why so many cities are so ugly and dirty and blighted is because people don't remember that its part of nature, and they don't care about it, and they don't try to take care of it. So, remember that nature is everywhere, everything, and don't create the false dichotomy of what is nature and what is not nature. You can be a Druid anywhere. You can be a Druid in a one bedroom apartment in the middle of Manhattan, you can be a Druid

in the middle of the Sonoran desert, you can be a Druid on top of Glastonbury Tor, you can be a Druid sitting down in a sushi restaurant in Tokyo – you can be a Druid anywhere, because nature is everywhere.

Dana: What is your favorite tree?

Sara: Big-leaf maple.

Dana: Is there anything else you would like to add to the interview, or share with the members?

Sara: Remember that Druidry that is not just a religion, it's also a philosophy, and in spite of the fact that modern philosophers have turned philosophy into something that is petrified and largely irrelevant, philosophy is by nature flexible, and it deals with the realm of experience, and things that we all go through every day of our lives. Remember that Druidry is infinitely flexible. Don't try to petrify it, and don't try to try petrify yourself within it.

Grounding Through Heaven and Earth: An Introduction to the Nine Hazels Qigong

by Adam Robersmith

Adam Robersmith, AODA Druid Adept and Archdruid of Fire, is a clergyman ordained as a Druid Priest and Unitarian Universalist Minister. He works in the parish and privately as a spiritual director, specializing in formation: the ways in which people develop in their spiritual lives and practices, whatever their understanding of the universe may be. This article is adapted from his 3rd Degree project, entitled The Nine Hazels: A Druid Qigong, *which includes a practice manual and video of the full qigong set. The first triad of movements will soon be available as a short supplemental curriculum from the AODA, as he figures out the best way to teach the full set to people across the country. You may find him online at* www.oakandthorn.com *or knitting, reading, walking, or wishing he had more time for his garden and art near his home in Chicago, which he shares with his partner and dog.*

Much has been written and said about the dichotomy of body and spirit—physicality and energetics—in our broader Western culture. In my work as a Druid and spiritual director, I have seen a pair of concurrent needs: the teaching of energetics/magic that can draw on both imagination and kinesthetic learning as well as a need to support bodily awareness and health. Many of us struggle with time enough (or discipline enough) to practice any one thing deeply, much less exercise and magic. In Druid fashion, I have sought a third thing that could unite both of these into a useful, practical, manageable whole. My experience with qigong and Taoism led me to create a qigong form that would support the learning of basic Western magical

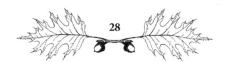

energy practices, provide health benefits, and encourage a sense of embodiment as a spiritual, magical, natural being.

Nine Hazels[1] is a Druid qigong. It uses nine traditional or modified traditional qigong movements in a new sequence in order to give the practitioner both a good practice for the body and a system for developing awareness of Western magical/energetic skills. Both Druidry and Taoism encourage practitioners to better understand the subtle energies of existence and bring them into healthy expression through practices—magic and qigong—that help us intentionally engage the material and spiritual aspects of our lives. Each of the Nine Hazels is a qigong movement linked with a particular energetic/magical skill so that the action of the body supports the awareness and practice of the skill. In this article, we will explore these energies and how they are related to the Third Hazel, the skill of grounding, supported by the qigong movement called Heaven and Earth.

The Energies of Existence: Where Druidry and Qigong Meet

Facing the sky, I feel the sun warming my skin, the wind moving past, rain falling as thirst-quenching drops upon me. I see the stars and the moon in their slow progression above. The heavens offer a sense of goodness that I take in through life-giving light, darkness, wind, and rain. Opening to these gifts, I also find myself drawn out toward the expansive cosmos into unimaginable vastness, into peace, into utter blessing.

Under the soles of my feet, I feel the earth as both soil and stone. My toes can feel the give of good topsoil, the gritty slip of sand, the sharp and skitter of gravel and scree. I sense the stability that the bedrock offers, the interplay of solidity and gravity that keeps me on the surface of the earth. Connecting with the ground, I know myself to be part of this ancient earth, its history, cycles, and slow changes, a long and abiding presence.

And then, in between, are all of us living things, occupying a middle space that is vital, flowing, growing, and moving. The plants, the animals, the fungi, and the

---

1   The name refers to the Irish lore that the hazel is a potent source of wisdom. Each skill and movement is one kernel, one hazelnut, of wisdom. For an example, see the myth of how Fionn MacCumhal became wise from a taste of the wisdom in hazelnuts eaten by a salmon. Furthermore, qigong sequences often have symbolic or descriptive names, such as "Eight Brocades" or "Five Animal Frolics." Who am I to break with tradition?

single-cells all are receiving what is offered by heaven and earth and then trans-forming those elements through every moment of living. Paying attention to what is above and what is below reminds us of our connection to all other inhabitants of this world, with whom we share air and soil, imagination and place. Feeling the wind or the ground reminds us of our existence right here and right now; we are not just observers in this world, we are the creations of it. Accordingly, many cosmologies consider the sky and the ground as parents, mother and/or father of all life. We exist as we do because of the interaction of what is materially above us and below us. Many of these cosmologies also posit that the energetic above and below—the spiritual above and below—have an equal or greater role to play in our in-between existences.

Druid Revival and Taoist cosmologies both use a lower/middle/upper framework to explore existence and everything within it. Using the visionary (if ahistoric) work of Iolo Morganwg, Druidry arising from the Druid Revival imagines the cosmos within a framework of *calas* (stone), *gwyar* (water), and *nwyfre* (sky). These three elements are more than just their material forms. They also correspond to the body, the blood/life, and the mind; form, process, and vision; and matter, energy, and spirit. All things can be understood as the interplay of these elements. The Taoists also use a three-part framework, understanding a dynamic harmony in between yin and yang. Yin corre-sponds to the earth, darkness, below, the body, and *jing* (the essence of the body, such as sperm or egg). Yang corresponds to heaven, light, above, the spirit, and *shen* (the most vast and transcendent part of oneself). The dynamic harmony of life gives rise to the created middle, humanity, breath, our heart-mind (the unity of emotion and intelligence), and *qi* (the energy of our living bodies through time and space). *Jing*, *Qi*, and *Shen* are referred to as The Three Treasures, lifting up their importance for health and vitality.

Comparison of Taoist Cosmology and the Druid Elements[2]

	Taoism	Druidry
Upper	Heaven	*Nwyfre* (Sky)
	Yang	Vision
	Spirit	Mind
	Shen	Spirit
		Solar Current
Middle	Humanity/Life	*Gwyar* (Water)
	Dynamic Harmony	Process
	Heart-Mind	Life/Blood
	Qi	Earthly Energy (heat, light, etc.)
		Lunar Current
Lower	Earth	*Calas* (Stone)
	Yin	Form
	Body	Body
	Jing	Matter
		Telluric Current

These two systems are not identical. They come from different places and times, arising from different cultural and spiritual contexts. Their ways of imagining the universe do not overlap perfectly, yet they share some commonalities. Neither system sees the levels as progressively "better," instead recognizing the importance and value of each in relation to the others. The lower aspects are material, physical, bounded, and formed. The middle aspects are energetic, flowing, alive, and changing. The upper aspects are spiritual, visionary, boundless, and formless. As creatures of the middle, we engage with both what is above and below; we (and all of life) are spirit, matter, and the processes that hold them together. Druidry and Taoism also understand the body

---

2   There are more detailed descriptions of the three Druid elements in *The Druidry Handbook* by John Michael Greer (pp. 60-62) and Taoist/Chinese cosmology, particularly The Three Treasures in *The Healing Promise of Qi* by Roger Jahnke (pp. 60-67) as well as *Tai Chi: Health for Life* by Bruce Frantzis (pp. 194-196) and *Opening the Energy Gates of Your Body* by Frantzis (p.25).

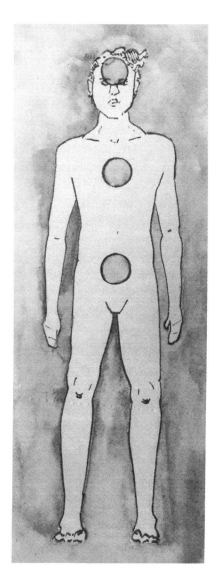

Figure 1

to have three main energy locations along the core of the torso. Taoism calls them the lower, middle, and upper dantian. Druids call them lower, middle, and upper cauldrons or the womb, heart, and head energy centers.[3] [Fig. 1]

The energies that Nine Hazels develops are called *qi* in Taoism and *nwyfre* in Druidry. As you can see in the table above, *qi* and *nwyfre* are located in different levels of their respective cosmologies; however, in practice, both names refer to energies that we can experience through our senses and imaginations. Using the congruities between Druid magic and Taoist qigong, we can adapt and create disciplines of energetic awareness and physical health centered in our living bodies. Qigong, meaning *energy practice*, is a term that includes many different forms and styles of movement and stillness. The National Qigong Association notes that "all styles have three things in common: they all involve a posture, (whether moving or stationary), breathing techniques, and mental focus."[4] The various forms and styles of qigong address a variety of needs, abilities, and end goals – some focus on physical health, others on mental or emotional balance, and still others on spiritual care and growth. Some qigong is related to the work of martial arts, training the practitioner in both physical and energetic defense and attack. Other qigong focuses more specifically on the circulation of energy through the body for health and balance.

---

3   There are more detailed descriptions of these energy centers in *The Druid Magic Handbook* by John Michael Greer (pp. 191-195), *The Healing Promise of Qi* by Roger Jahnke (pp. 63-65), and *Opening the Energy Gates of Your Body* by Frantzis (p. 138-139, 238-239).

4   From the NQA website: http://nqa.org/about-nqa/what-is-qigong/

Magic, which I think of as *energy work,* takes a wide variety of forms and requires mental focus for effective practice, too. Magic seeks to affect the inner and outer worlds through the direction of energy and alteration of patterns and interconnections. Some magics are defensive, offensive, or protective; some are healing and balancing for an individual, a community, or the earth; some are aimed at shaping who we are and will become. In our Druid and neo-Pagan traditions, certain energetic/magical skills have become commonly understood as foundational for the magical practitioner, including centering, grounding, shielding, projecting, and receiving. Much of our Western magic is performed through the imagination as connected to energy; ritual, rather than exercise forms or postures, is one common way we embody our energy work.

Movements and postures, like those of qigong, offer us a way other than ritual or spellcraft to develop our energetic and magical awareness. By choosing movements and postures that relate to specific kinds of magic/energy work, we can practice these skills in a way that becomes natural in mind and body and has the added benefit of supporting bodily health. Not every Druid practices magic, of course, but all of us engage with *calas, gwyar,* and *nwyfre* simply as embodied beings. We are connected to the material and spiritual worlds—to heaven and earth—as a part of the flow of life. Whether we seek to practice magic or not, anything we can do to increase our understanding of existence and the health of our beings is wise and worth doing.

The Third Hazel: Grounding through Heaven and Earth

Grounding, the act of connecting your own energy directly to another (far larger) source of energy, is the first practice that I actively developed as I began my exploration of energy and magic. It's the most comforting and nurturing magical practice I know. When I feel disconnected from magic, nature, or myself, it is the practice to which I return. When I am feeling weary or drained, grounding brings me strength. When I feel most isolated or overwhelmed, even if it is difficult, I attempt to ground. The fundamental task of grounding is consciously choosing to be connected with the energy of things beyond and generally far larger than yourself. In grounding, we remind ourselves that we are not alone and experience that by exchanging energy with that to which we are connected, drawing or giving enwergy as needed.

Sometimes called rooting or earthing, grounding is often done as a connection to the earth in tai chi and in western magic, but it isn't limited to earth alone. One can ground (connect directly and deeply) to earth, water, air, or fire; to sun, moon, or stars;

the ocean, a mountain, or the wind.[5] Contemporary practitioners of western magic who learn this skill often follow a tradition of beginning with earth, water, air, and fire. Each of these elements is a distinct and specific thing and is also energetically so immense that our needs and uses of it cannot (generally) damage that element. Equally important, the larger and more primordial the thing to which one connects, the more likely it is that its energies will be neutral to beneficial for the magician and the magic. The purpose of grounding is to correct imbalances in the self and connect in healthy ways to the world around us. Grounding to a particular stone, living being, or other finite creation has great risk for the finite creation and for the practitioner as well.[6] I do not encourage this kind of grounding, lest you create further imbalance or harm for yourself or anything else.

There are many ways to use your imagination to support the practice of grounding. Let's begin with grounding to earth. Many people use their senses as a template and guide for the movement and connection of energy. You can envision a link between your lower dantian (see Fig 1) and the center of the earth, for example, or a great tree root moving through the earth from your pelvis or your feet. You can extend your energy beyond yourself, using the imagination of touch to reach down into the earth until you meet a welcoming and healthy-feeling connection. Try listening for the sound of the earth – the tone, vibration, pulse, or melody – and then bring your own energy into compatibility with it, either as rhythm or pitch, in unison or harmony. You might taste or smell the earth until you find the energy that is pleasing or right. You might use your sense of balance, feeling beyond yourself until you reach the place that feels balanced and stable.

Grounding to earth can easily be a practice that takes days, weeks, or months to grasp. You may need many attempts in order to sense the connection that you have

---

5   Do not attempt to ground to a deity! Inviting that kind of energy to run directly through oneself is perilous without the proper preparations, not to mention the permission of the deity. Ritual, prayerful presence, or even spiritual union with a deity is not the same as grounding to an energy or place.

6   Some of us wear or carry stones or other talismans to help us stay grounded throughout the day, which can be very useful. (Hematite, for example, is an excellent stone for helping one to ground.) Such things help us stay connected to the earth or other greater source of energy, but we are not connecting to and drawing on only them. Instead, they act as a support or conduit for the larger connection. Grounding to an individual stone, for example, can drain its energy or put too much into it; neither is good for the well-being of the stone.

made. Then, beyond that initial exploration, you could spend years sensing nuance after nuance. Since this is a lifelong practice, though, I recommend that you don't wait until you feel like you know everything about grounding to earth before attempting something else. When you have gotten comfortable with grounding to your first element, then try another. When I began my exploration of grounding, I started with earth. After earth, I chose air to try. I originally attempted to use the same method as I had with earth, but discovered that air did not work the same way for me. I had to spend some time thinking about how I would sense this new connection. My method of grounding relies on touch first and vision second – I feel my energy extend or shape itself, but I can then envision what that looks like. To connect with the earth, I feel my energy moving beyond the shape of my body to interact with the energy of the ground deep beneath me. To connect with the air, I had to feel something lighter, more gossamer and fine extending into the winds and space above me. Over time, as I developed my ability to connect to water, fire, stars, and so on, I had to seek out my own instinctive ways of creating links.

Now, using the first method that comes to your mind, try to create this kind of connection yourself. After that, try other methods, too. Take some notes about what feels easy, good, wrong, or simply ineffective. Your ways of sensing these connections need not be—will not be!—exactly the same as mine. You can take these suggestions as something to try first or just as ideas to help you find your own points of departure. There is no *you must do it this way* in learning to ground, other than *you must be wise and safe, grounding only to those things that you can trust completely and are so large that you cannot harm them.*

Another way in which to explore the skill of grounding is through practicing Heaven and Earth qigong. There are many different specific movements called "Heaven and Earth," but they all share a bodily extension upward and another downward, reaching toward the heavens and toward the earth. This particular version activates the three dantian/energy centers along the center line of the torso as the arms also reach downward and then upward tracing the shape of a tree, from roots through trunk to branches and back.[7] The movement begins and ends by focusing your attention on the lower dantian, which is the body's safest center in which to store and draw the kinds of energy qigong develops. (See Fig. 1.)

---

7   You'll find a companion video showing this movement at https://youtu.be/5gTwI0SPEqA.

Before you begin the movement, you also need to know how to contract and expand your body. To expand, make your arms, legs, and spine straighten and extend outward while inhaling. This action will create cause your body to take up more space and more room for air in your lungs. This is like allowing a spring to expand, releasing the energy it stores when it is held small. To contract, bend your arms and legs as well as round your spine slightly, drawing inward while exhaling. This action will cause your body to take up less space and have less room for air in your lungs. This is also akin to contracting a spring, such that it holds energy for expanding within itself. When you are ready, do the movement as outlined and pictured here.

1. Stand at rest with your knees slightly bent (neither locked nor crouching) and with your torso neither slouching, nor at-attention stiff, with your hands crossed over your lower dantian.
2. Move your hands out to your sides, palms down, and then contract while bringing your hands and arms downward in a circular way, as though you are scooping up a pile of leaves or laundry.
3. When your hands meet facing upward in the middle of the lowest point of the circle, begin to straighten your legs and spine.
4. Draw your hands upward in front of the center of your body, carrying what you have gathered until you reach the lower dantian, then move your hands outward once again, this time facing upward. Your hands should be fully separated by the time they reach your middle dantian.
5. Circle your hands outward in an upward reach, expanding your body to the sky. Bring your hands together over your head as though you are gathering winds or clouds.
6. When your hands meet facing downwards in the middle of the highest point of the circle, bring your hands down the center of your body to your lower dantian, and either repeat the movement starting with step 2 or return to the position you began with in step 1 to conclude your practice.

As you are moving, follow the vertical motion of your hands with your eyes, looking along the center line of your body. Use your peripheral vision to follow your hands when they are to your sides. As you follow your hands with your eyes, be careful not to bend your neck too severely. If and when you bend your neck, raise your head as though there were a string attached to the crown of your head pulling upward and opening the space in your vertebrae. Ideally, it should feel like you are stretching your neck, lifting your head even as you bend it.

Step 1

Step 1, pt 1

Step 1, pt 2

Step 3

Step 4

Step 5, pt 1

Step 5, pt 2

Step 6

<u>Above Images:</u>

The author demonstrating the sequence of movements.

Growing the Tree of Wisdom: Practicing the Third Hazel

I am energized, alive, connected to the world beyond me, and settled within my own being. Whether in motion or stillness, I am present to this place and moment. The elements, the stars and planets, the energies of existence are all available to me as sustenance and inspiration. I am of the earth and of the spirit and my life brings them into dynamic harmony.

When I am at my best, this is how I feel: both settled in myself and embedded in the all-that-is. I reach this way of being through creativity, contemplation, ritual, observing the natural world, and qigong, too. Performing Heaven and Earth offers me a way to be both attentive and open, connecting my inner and outer worlds. Of course, that's not always the way it works. Sometimes I can't find the right time or place. Sometimes I feel uninspired or uninterested. Sometimes my mind, heart, or body just won't remain focused and my practice is a struggle. There are things that we can do to help make practice easier, more effective, and more enjoyable—most of them are answers to the questions *when, where,* and *how?*

It may be easier to describe the right place and time in which to practice than to actually find the right situation, but it is better to practice in an imperfect place and time than to wait until you have the ideal circumstance. Most practitioners say that the best time to practice qigong is in the morning, before your day begins in earnest. Making your practice an early part of your day means that you're less likely to get caught up in other things and forget. The energy of the morning hours is also generally appropriate for qigong and for Heaven and Earth in particular. If, however, this isn't possible for you or if you need to wait until the afternoon, that's fine! Practice whenever and wherever you're able – do not wait for perfection.

Look for a place that is flat and relatively without distractions. Do not practice with the computer or television on. Turn off the ringer on your phones, turn smartphones and tablets off or at least face down, or better yet, leave them in another room. Face a direction that allows you to keep your eyes open without being distracted by too many interesting things at which to look. I generally like to face north, because I enjoy that energy. You may face whatever direction feels best or is least distracting. Practicing outdoors can be enjoyable when the temperature is right, the winds are pleasant, the sun isn't glaring into your eyes, and the area noise isn't too annoying. If anything about practicing outdoors makes it difficult, especially while you're first learning, stay inside. When you reach a point where being outdoors is a joy rather than a pain, enjoy practicing in the fresh air.

In order to get the most from Heaven and Earth, be aware of both your inner attitudes and outer actions. When you begin the form, take the starting posture deliberately and slowly. Do not rush into movement. If you approach qigong from a need to be quick about it or from too much agitation, it will not be especially effective. Instead, use this as an opportunity to take extra time in calm and peace. In addition, many of us have a tendency to close our eyes when we want to be calm or focus closely on an intent or a movement. For this practice, you should keep your eyes open to help you keep your balance and see how you are moving. Energetically, this is important as well. The eyes are a place of interconnection with the energy outside the body—no matter how good or poor your eyesight is, keeping your eyes open will allow for better energetic connection through the movements.

With any movement or exercise, it is important to pay attention to the limitations and abilities of your body. If you cannot stand or stand for long, you can do the upper body movements while seated. If you are unable to bend your spine or move an arm as far as the movement indicates, you can adjust the movements to meet the abilities of your body. Do your best to match your opposite sides and movements. We all have imbalances in the strength and flexibility of our bodies. Don't worry if they aren't perfectly matched. Perfection is not the point! Instead, follow the lead of your more limited side. If your body will only turn so far to one side, do only that much on the other. If you can only raise one arm so high, raise the other one no higher than that.[8] In many cases, it is possible that the qigong will help to create greater strength, flexibility, and balance as you practice over time. Tai chi and qigong teacher Bruce Frantzis advocates the 70% rule: Only do 70% as much as you are capable of doing.[9] If you follow this for the degree to which you extend or contract as well as for the number of repetitions you do, you will be less likely to injure or exhaust yourself. Moreover, by practicing at 70%, your 100% capacity will grow, and your 70% will become correspondingly more capable over time.

Many of these guidelines for qigong also hold true for grounding. First, don't overdo it! Too much energy flow before you have developed your skill can result in exhaustion, odd sensations, terrible headaches, or other experiences that do not feel safe. The 70% rule is useful here, but I would suggest even doing far less than 70% when you are just beginning to ground. Be cautious! Be tentative! Allow yourself to move forward with

8   Should you have limited mobility on one side of your body, follow the wisdom you have learned from other forms of exercise and the way in which your body does move.

9   See *Opening the Energy Gates of Your Body* by Frantzis (pp. 28 & 35).

small steps until you feel truly confident in your ability to manage the kinds of energy to which you are connecting. Next, find places and times in which to practice that are comfortable, encourage the kinds of connection you want to make, and lack distractions that will draw your attention from the experience of grounding. The experience can be quite subtle and you will need all your focus to learn the skill. Alternately, you may have a breakthrough that feels overwhelming; in that case, you should be in a safe and calm environment as well. Finally, perfection is not the point. Take care of your own well-being and think carefully about the well-being of the rest of the cosmos in your practice. We learn as much from our mistakes and failures as our successes. Pay attention, practice often, and your skills will grow!

References

Greer, John Michael (2006). *The Druidry Handbook.* San Francisco: Weiser Books.

Greer, John Michael (2007). *The Druid Magic Handbook.* San Francisco: Weiser Books.

Frantzis, Bruce (2006). *Opening the Energy Gates of Your Body: Chi Gung for Lifelong Health.* Berkeley, CA: Blue Snake Books.

Frantzis, Bruce (2006). *Tai Chi Health For Life.* Berkeley, CA: Blue Snake Books.

Jahnke, Roger (2002). *The Healing Promise of Qi.* New York: Contemporary Books, McGraw-Hill.

Ecology and Spirituality in the Vegetable Garden

by Claire L. Schosser

Claire Schosser earned a B.S. and Ph.D. in chemistry more years ago than some of today's Druids have been alive. These days she prefers to practice science in such places as her garden and the local streams. Since she began practicing Druidry, she has opened to the possibility of enjoying a spiritual as well as a scientific relationship with the place in which she lives, a few miles from the confluence of the Missouri and Mississippi Rivers in the greater St. Louis, Missouri, metropolitan area. She is a Druid Apprentice in AODA.

As Druids we might be drawn to vegetable gardening. Growing vegetables in our backyards can lighten our burden on the earth by allowing us to eat vegetables whose sources of energy are the sun, soil, and rain plus our labor instead of the fossil fuel-powered machinery, ammonia fertilizers derived in part from natural gas, and the huge trucks and refrigerated storage required to carry vegetables from agribusiness fields to distributors, retailers, and finally to our table. Knowing this, Druids in the AODA may choose to grow vegetables as one component of their Earth Path activities.

By no means is this the only reason to grow some of our own vegetables. Unlike the case with agribusiness, where vegetables often must be harvested underripe to withstand the stress of shipping and the many days between harvest and consumption, gardeners can harvest vegetables at their peak in flavor and eat them shortly thereafter or preserve them for eating later on. We can grow varieties with particular attributes important to us, such as those used in an ethnic or regional cuisine or for special occasions. We can choose vegetables that grow the best in our particular climate and soil,

that are especially sweet or tender, or that have a flavor we like that is not present in the few varieties grown by agribusiness.

Our vegetable garden can also help us attune to the seasonal cycle where we live. We can watch how our vegetables grow and develop and how they interact with soil, rain, wind, sunlight, and insects and other wildlife. We might use our vegetable garden as a way to deepen our understanding and practice of ecology, as I have done. If we choose this path, our vegetable garden could become an Ovate Exploration for the grade of Apprentice or the focus of Ovate work for the grades of Companion or Adept in the AODA.

In addition, when we eat vegetables that we grow, we are taking in energy from the land on which we live. We become part of the land as the land becomes part of us. Thus growing vegetables can be part of our Druid path of spiritual engagement with nature as she expresses herself through our garden and our garden then expresses itself in and through us.

More than twenty years ago, long before I embarked on the path of Druidry, I began growing vegetable gardens with some of the popular methods of backyard vegetable gardening. Since then, I have kept records on the inputs I have added, the area devoted to each crop, and the weights of the crops I harvest each year. By the time I performed my self-initiation as a candidate in the AODA in late 2012, yields were decreasing for most crops I grow, and the garden suffered from increases in pest and disease pressures. I was concerned about this trend and began to search for information on ecology as it applies to vegetable gardening to help me understand what was happening. By that

time, two backyard gardening books written by Steve Solomon, one focused on older gardening methods (Solomon, 2005) and one focused on soil mineral levels and how to balance them effectively (Solomon with Reinheimer, 2013), came to my attention and have become the ecological basis of my gardening practice. In 2015 I also began to explore spiritual work with garden plants and seeds. I will discuss what I've learned in the hope that it will aid Druids and others interested in growing vegetable gardens in tune with ecological processes and the more subtle energies and spiritual aspects of gardening.

Vegetable Plant Ecology

To understand how to provide for the needs of vegetable plants, it is helpful to know their ecological role and the interactions that they enter into with the other plants, the animals, and the soil of the place where they grow and with the natural processes present during the growing season. Ecologists use a concept called succession to understand how the kinds of plants that occur together in a particular area change with time. Plant succession is the progression of a group or community of plants from early or pioneer stages to an end or climax stage, dependent on climate and soil (Jacke with Toensmeier, 2005). The early or pioneer stage is created through a disturbance of some kind that kills or removes some or all of the plants that used to exist in that area. The plants that grow after the disturbance occurs follow a pattern that is similar in locations with the same kind of soil, bedrock, climate, and weather. That pattern is plant succession. Succession uses seeds and plants already in the soil or brought there from outside the area by wind, water, or animals (including humans) to form a new plant community that undergoes changes in plant composition and distribution over time. As I meditated on the concept of succession, I realized that a succession process governs the plant community we attempt to create in our backyard gardens over the course of a single growing season, similarly to the way it does in an abandoned field over the course of many years.

In order to create a vegetable garden, we remove the previous plant cover in some way, for instance by digging or tilling it in or by mulching over it. All of these activities count as a disturbance to an ecologist. Once that disturbance occurs, the process of succession begins. If we understand how succession affects our backyard gardens during the course of the growing season, we can better direct the succession in ways that will favor the plants we want for that space over the plants that might otherwise be present.

What happens after you create the disturbance that becomes your vegetable garden depends on the details of the disturbed area. Do you dig or till in the previous plant cover, or sheet mulch over it? What kinds of seeds or roots exist in the soil that can grow into plants, and what are the weather conditions and the time of year? What are the physical and chemical characteristics of the soil? Do you add anything to the soil, such as compost or soil amendments? What seeds or plants do you add at the time of the disturbance or later on, and if the latter, how much later? What seeds might be brought into the garden from outside it by wind, water, or animals other than yourself? What will grow and how soon it grows depends on these factors as well as rainfall, day length and whether it is increasing or decreasing, and temperatures.

If you disturb the soil during the growing season in your area and then leave it bare, as long as there is sufficient soil moisture and there are seeds or rhizomatous roots in the soil bank or they are brought into the site from outside sources, you will soon find plants growing on it. In Missouri where I live, these plants will typically be annual and perennial grasses and weeds. By rapidly putting down roots to catch and hold minerals and sending up their green bodies to catch and transform sunlight, these plants cover and protect the soil, reducing the potential for wind and water to erode it, and begin to reestablish the cycles that keep minerals, other nutrients, and soil microorganisms within the soil to nourish the plants and the animals that feed on them (Jacke with Toensmeier, 2005). If we were to allow these weeds to remain, as they repaired the soil over a period of years they would yield (succeed) to plants more suited to the changed conditions. During the several months of our backyard gardens, we need to concern ourselves with the plants or seeds that we add, along with the roots and seeds already in the soil that can grow in that period of time and any others that find their way into the garden from outside it, and with how all these plants compete for water, light, and nutrients as discussed below.

We also should consider if our potential vegetable garden space has enough organic matter and other nutrients required for our desired plants to develop properly. Organic matter is the food source for soil microorganisms that work in concert with plant roots to supply some of each other's needs. Plants also require certain chemical elements (which are usually called nutrients or minerals in gardening books) to be present in the soil in order to grow. These are categorized as major, minor, or trace nutrients depending on the relative amounts needed. While individual vegetables have some-what different nutrient requirements, they all fall within a rather narrow range. From

the gardener's standpoint, the most important thing to know is that if any one or more of these is present in less than the amount the plant needs to grow its best, the vegetable plant will not reach its full potential of size or nutrient density. A soil test will provide information on the amount of organic matter present and the levels of at least some of the nutrients needed by plants to grow. Basic soil testing, which should include organic matter level and the amount of all of the major nutrients and some to all of the minor and trace nutrients, is available to gardeners in the United States through the agricultural extension service of the state in which they live.[1] I'll mention two other soil testing services below.

Most of the vegetables that we grow are refined versions of weedy plants that pop up in disturbed places (Solomon, 2005).[2] Many of them, such as lettuce, beans, sweet corn, and cucumbers, are annual plants: They grow, set seed, and die within a year or less. Many other common vegetables, such as onions, kale, carrots, and beets, are biennial plants: They begin their growth in spring, summer, or fall, survive the following winter as green plants or dormant roots, then regrow, set flowers and seed, and die the following spring or summer. They are also well suited to grow in a disturbed area but tend to grow less rapidly during their first growing season compared to annual plants. Only a few common garden vegetables are perennial plants, capable of living a few to many years, and some of them, such as tomatoes and peppers, are killed by frost and thus are grown as if they are annuals in vegetable gardens in temperate climates (Ashworth, 1991). Most perennial plants do not find freshly disturbed soil to their liking. They will tend to take hold and grow once the annuals and biennials have restarted the nutrient cycles and added their decayed bodies to the soil as organic matter and mulch.

Since most of our vegetable crops are annuals or biennials partial to disturbed areas, they are best suited to life in soil that has been dug or tilled just before they are planted, as long as it has enough organic matter and nutrients for them to grow. (Temperate perennial vegetables such as asparagus or rhubarb and tropical perennial vegetables such as peppers, eggplants, and tomatoes are ecologically suited

1   To find an extension office for your state, go to USDA, Partners and Extension Map (http://nifa.usda.gov/partners-and-extension-map) and click on your state. Below the map you'll find a list of the extension offices in your state. Click on one of your state's extension offices and search for "soil test."

2   Carol Deppe (2010, pp. 13–14), "Covenant: The Contract Between the Domesticated Plant and Her Gardener" also makes this point in an amusing and insightful way.

to a sheet-mulched garden, since it mimics the increased levels of organic matter at the surface and in the soil that are found later in the successional cycle when perennials become common. However, the tropical perennial vegetables we grow have been selected to do well under the same bare-soil conditions that favor annual and biennial vegetables.) As noted above, the soil may harbor other seeds and roots that can grow rapidly in our gardens, and some may be brought onto the site as the garden grows. Those unwanted plants, which gardeners call weeds, may be removed in various ways. By doing so, gardeners allow the plants or seeds they add to the garden to use as much of the nutrients present in the soil as possible for themselves. However, the vegetables we plant may come into competition with each other if their roots or bodies touch, so it may be necessary for gardeners to remove some of the desirable plants while still young in order to allow the ones that remain to reach their full potential, a process called thinning. If the entire vegetable plant is removed for kitchen use, that act of harvesting creates another area of bare soil, which then begins the succession process again. Plants that are removed from the garden take with them all the nutrients that they absorbed from the soil to create their bodies. Thus vegetable gardens require occasional and intelligent intervention on the part of the gardener to create disturbances, add the plants or seeds they desire, manage nutrient levels and replenish them as necessary, and act to remove interfering plants and harvest the desired plant at the proper time. A gardening method that works in concert with these ecological realities will enable us, the gardeners, to grow and eat healthy, nutrient-dense food while respecting the needs and lives of all the participants in the garden system.

Ecological Analysis of Three Backyard Gardening Methods

One of the realities a first-time gardener confronts is a bewildering array of information on how to grow vegetables. Popular gardening magazines, state extension services, and backyard gardening books all offer advice to the novice. I will begin by assuming that you wish to garden following nature's lead as much as possible. This narrows down the choice to those methods that are based on organic gardening principles.

You may choose between a row-based system similar to that used on farms (this might be the system advocated by your state extension service) and a system in which the plants are arranged in a bed, as many backyard gardening books describe. When I began gardening, we lived on a tiny city lot, so I chose to grow vegetables in small beds and now grow them in larger beds on our suburban lot. The three systems described

below are all based on growing vegetables organically in beds three to five feet wide. This is a sensible choice for people who are growing food on a backyard scale for themselves and their families.

Square Foot Gardening

The first gardening system I tried was the square foot gardening system, developed and popularized by Mel Bartholomew (1981, 2013). I worked from the 1981 edition, which directed me to dig up about six inches of soil, mix into it two-inch-deep layers of peat moss, vermiculite, and compost, and enclose the resulting garden bed with six-inch-wide boards of rot-resistant wood. I made the beds four feet wide and ten feet long and hammered in nails on each edge to mark out one-foot widths for the planting grid.

Bartholomew (2013) has changed the method somewhat since I used it. First the gardener builds a box from six-inch-wide untreated wood or plastic lumber. The box is four feet wide and long. After laying the box down on a weed mat or landscape fabric, the gardener purchases or makes from components a soilless mix consisting of equal volumes of peat moss, vermiculite, and blended compost. The gardener dumps this mix into the box, moistens it thoroughly, and attaches to the edges of the box a grid that marks the planting surface into squares one foot on each side, hence the method's name. Then the gardener plants vegetable seeds or seedlings in each square according to directions in the book. The garden amounts to a very large and shallow container planting. With proper timing of planting and with watering when needed, little more care is required, especially during the first year if weed seed–free compost is used in the soilless mix. The neat appearance and ease of plant layout and garden care have made this method popular, according to Bartholomew.

How does it stack up against the ecological and practical realities of vegetable gardening? By minimizing the competition of unwanted plants from the soil under the bed and incorporating some nutrients and a high level of organic matter into the soilless mix, this method potentially allows for good yields of vegetable plants, assuming the vegetables are planted at the right time and spacing and cared for properly after planting. Beginners, gardeners who want to grow small numbers of vegetable plants for fresh eating, those with tiny yards or little time to spend on gardening, or those who want a neat and tidy garden might find this method attractive. It might also be good for gardeners with poor or no soil or soil contaminated by industrial chemicals,

or who live in areas with cold, short growing seasons. In these cases, vegetable plants will grow better in the warmer soilless mix of the framed beds than in the unimproved soil under the bed, and they will not be affected by any contaminants in that soil.

However, the method has ecological and practical disadvantages. To begin with, the shallowness of the soilless mix causes problems for deep-rooted crops like carrots (Bartholomew (2013) suggests making a small, deep version of the box for these crops) and may lead to too much competition among even properly spaced plants under conditions favoring rapid plant growth. The soilless mix will not have a good nutrient balance if the compost used in it is not nutrient balanced (this is why Bartholomew (2013) suggests using a blend of different brands of compost, but that does not itself guarantee that the blend will be nutrient balanced). It may become depleted of nutrients without the gardener knowing it, especially after the first few years of use. The frame makes it difficult to cultivate (disturb) the soil near the edges when it is needed. The frame can provide a good environment for certain garden pests to live and make it difficult to control them, and weeds can be hard to remove near the frame if they are able to root through the weed mat or they enter the garden from bird feces or other outside sources. In hot, dry weather the mix in the frame will dry out rapidly, necessitating frequent watering, while in cold weather the mix will freeze more rapidly than the soil under it, killing plants in the raised bed sooner than if they had been planted in soil. Finally, the frame and soilless mix are costly, and the soilless mix includes peat moss, a natural material being harvested faster than it replenishes itself. When I wanted to expand the size of my garden but did not want to pay for the wood and materials for the mix, I stopped gardening by this method and chose instead to garden with the soil that I already had.

GROW BIOINTENSIVE **Method (HTGMV)**

The GROW BIOINTENSIVE method of vegetable gardening was developed by Alan Chadwick and refined by John Jeavons (2012) and others. This method is aimed at gardeners who want to produce as much as possible of their own food and the organic materials that keep their gardens producing well from year to year. The book that describes this method, *How to Grow More Vegetables* (hereafter HTGMV after the book title), was first published in 1974. I began working with the method in 1999, when the book was in its fourth edition. The method as described in the eighth edition, the one on my bookshelf and that I reference here, is very little changed from the fourth edition.

In this method the gardener begins by removing the sod or weeds from the area to become the garden bed, then adds compost and any other soil amendments indicated and digs those deeply into the soil. The soil surface is then smoothed out and planted as desired. Gardens grown according to HTGMV consist of beds about three to five feet wide and as long as the gardener likes; beginners might start with a small bed, say three to four feet long and wide depending on how far they can reach (you should be able to easily reach the middle of the bed when you are planting from one edge), and expand by lengthening the bed and/or adding more beds as they gain experience and interest.

One of the unique aspects of HTGMV is that it advocates double digging the soil if possible to a depth of two feet, which is supposed to allow plant roots to grow deeper into the soil. Another unique aspect is that the beds are planted on a hexagonal grid, with the plants closer together than is typical for gardens planted in rows or by the square-foot method. HTGMV claims that the hexagonal planting grid allows for maximum yield (defined as pounds of food obtained per 100 square feet of bed space) and reduces weeding and water use compared to other gardens of the same size as the desired plants grow large enough to shade the soil surface.

In all, HTGMV includes eight different aspects. Besides the two already mentioned (deep soil preparation and intensive planting), the others are growing compost crops so the garden meets its own needs for fertility; making and using compost from those crops to maintain organic matter and fertility from year to year; using companion planting to improve the growth of crops planted near each other; growing high-calorie crops to provide as much as possible of the gardener's food in a small space; and using open-pollinated seeds so the gardener can save and replant seeds from year to year. When all of these practices are used together, the garden becomes a whole, sustainable system, the eighth and final aspect (Jeavons, 2012).

This method has some ecological advantages over the square foot method for people who have enough soil to grow a garden and whose climate is not too cold during the growing season. Because of the deep soil preparation, deep-rooted crops can grow well. Because the soil in the beds is connected to the soil around and below them, the beds dry out less rapidly and stay warm longer in cool weather. Because the beds are not enclosed, the entire bed area can be worked to amend the soil and remove weeds. HTGMV recommends having the soil tested and includes a set of suggested amendments to

remedy any deficiencies found, so it acknowledges that nutrient deficiencies might be present and should be addressed for optimum plant growth. HTGMV describes how to grow compost crops within the garden area and make compost from them to provide for the garden's organic matter and at least some of its fertility needs. And it has some practical advantages over the square foot method as well: Because HTGMV provides information on potential yields, a gardener can weigh the harvest and calculate the yields obtained to see progress or the lack of it over the years, and HTGMV gardens are less costly to establish and maintain than square-foot beds, especially if the only amendment the gardener adds each year is homegrown compost.

However, HTGMV has some ecological and practical disadvantages that revealed themselves to me over the years that I practiced this gardening method. Because I kept records on each variety of crop I grew each year, I had enough information collected by 2012 to know that most of my crops were yielding less each year instead of the same or more, despite my consistent practice of crop rotation, suggesting that the garden soil was becoming more rather than less unbalanced over time, even though I added the recommended amount of homemade compost each time I planted a crop. The hexagonal planting grid took more time to plant than the square-foot grid. Because the HTGMV method grows plants in soil, weeds happen, and it was quite time consuming to hand-pull weeds as the method recommends. It was also difficult to work in the narrow paths between beds because plants at the edges of the bed hung their bodies well out into the paths. Those plants tended to get squashed before they could be harvested. Finally, starting root crops in flats and transplanting them to the garden, as the method recommends, took too much time and resulted

in poorly shaped roots, while direct seeding those crops on freshly dug beds resulted in poor seed germination.

Gardening When It Counts/The Intelligent Gardener (GWIC/TIG)

In 2013 I began to experiment with a different method of backyard vegetable gardening, described by Steve Solomon in two books. In *Gardening When It Counts* (GWIC), Solomon (2005) suggests that intensive planting methods such as HTGMV might not work as well as their proponents claim because the vegetable plants are too crowded, thus competing with their neighbors and making it difficult to weed between them. Solomon advocates using row-based layouts within beds (the rows are along the short dimension of the bed for small crops or along the long dimension for large crops) and larger space between plants to accommodate their root systems and allow each plant to grow to its full potential. He also shows us a way to direct-sow seeds that restores capillarity (the ability of water to move around and between grains of soil) within the row after bed preparation and thus promotes seed germination and rapid seedling growth.

The Intelligent Gardener (TIG; Solomon with Reinheimer, 2013) addresses soil nutrient levels and how these interact with plants to produce nutrient-dense plants for the gardener to eat. While information on how to balance soil nutrient levels for optimum plant growth and nutrition has been available within the holistic farming community for some time, TIG to my knowledge is the first source to bring it to the attention and full use of backyard gardeners.

In 2013, the first year I amended the soil following the recommendations in TIG but used most of the same spacings for vegetables that I had used in the past, I noted a few instances of increased yields and a few varieties that tasted better. But the biggest change was a reduction in insects and diseases that had been plaguing my garden for several years (Schosser, 2013b). After rereading TIG in early 2014, I added enough agricultural lime to remedy all of my soil's calcium deficiency and enough gypsum (calcium sulfate) to remedy all the sulfur deficiency. I did this because the soil test results had revealed that my soil had an excess of magnesium relative to calcium, and TIG suggested this was the most effective way to bring that ratio to the proper value (Schosser, 2014a). I made one more change: I reduced the amount of oilseed meal I added compared to 2013. The oilseed meal provides food for microorganisms. The waste products of the microorganisms then provide nitrogen in a form available to plants

(Solomon with Reinheimer, 2013). Now that the rest of the minerals were coming into better balance, I reasoned, I might be making more potent compost, which would better supply my plants with the nitrogen they needed.

The 2014 garden results and end-of-season soil testing showed that while the calcium and magnesium in my soil were now properly balanced, few of the yields improved and some decreased. After I posted the results on my blog (Schosser, 2014b), a gardening mentor contacted me to share information that he felt would improve my garden in 2015. First, now that the levels of calcium and magnesium were well balanced, he suggested that I should address the ratio of manganese relative to iron. Although the test results suggested both elements were in excess, he felt that for the amount of iron in my soil, the manganese level was too low and I should add a bit in 2015 to see if it had any effect. More importantly, however, he noted that because of the long, hot summers where I live, many crops needed more oilseed meal than I applied in 2014 to fully supply their needs for nitrogen, and because I have little clay in my soil to retain some of the minerals over the full season, the long-season, high-demand crops should receive a mineral boost during the season. He suggested reformulating the amendment mix accordingly and to side-dress the high-demand crops with it about every six or eight weeks (Schosser, 2015a). So I used the reformulated blend before planting each bed in 2015, and I made two other changes as well: I increased the spacing for some crops to be closer to that recommended in GWIC, and I kept up with hoeing in 2015 to reduce weed competition, at least until the crops were big enough so that weeds had little effect on them.

As it happened, I did not side-dress any of the crops that I should have during 2015. I had not factored in the extra oilseed meal I'd need into the amount I ordered at the beginning of the season, so I ran out of it around the time that I should have side-dressed. I had only ordered enough to use for the new plantings, not for side-dressing. Even so, yields of the crops I care about the most stayed the same or went up (in some cases, went up by large factors); insect and disease pressures remained low; and taste of all crops stayed the same or improved, dramatically in some cases such as for turnips, which were very sweet with no harsh taste or bitterness at all (Schosser, 2016).

I think there are ecological reasons behind my success with the approach developed in GWIC/TIG compared to HTGMV. Recall the ecological nature of vegetable plants,

most of which are annuals or biennials that grow rapidly following soil disturbance. This is why gardeners and farmers dig or till before planting crops: Removing the existing plant cover creates bare soil that allows fast-growing annual and biennial vegetable seeds and plants (and weeds) to establish themselves and grow rapidly. While it also aerates the soil, thus allowing plant root systems to grow faster than they otherwise would, it is the bare soil that is the primary benefit to digging or tilling the soil.

HTGMV does not, in my opinion, fully understand how to promote the growth of vegetables over weeds. The hexagonal planting grid used in HTGMV makes it impossible to use a hoe to remove weeds when vegetables are planted six inches or less apart, and HTGMV advocates pulling weeds by hand for all planting distances. To do this, the bed must be quite moist, which may require the gardener to water prior to weeding. Weeding beds planted by HTGMV is tedious work that must be done on hands and knees in a cramped, narrow row between beds. I found it impossible to weed without squashing desired plants at the edges of the beds. By contrast, using the GWIC system of rows separated by twelve inches or more makes it possible to weed using a hoe while standing. By choosing a dry, sunny day and hoeing when the weeds are still quite small, it is sufficient to slice off the aboveground portion to set the weeds back relative to the vegetable plants. Doing this a few times gives the vegetable plants' roots enough time to monopolize the soil even if some weeds remain. Moreover, the thickness of soil that is disturbed by the hoe is no longer in capillary contact with the soil beneath it. This creates a dust mulch that reduces the sprouting of weed seeds in that layer (it is too dry for that) while allowing the vegetables access to water in the soil underneath the dust mulch. In contrast, because the full thickness of the soil needs to be moist to pull out the entire weed when gardening by the method in HTGMV, other weed seeds may sprout if the vegetables are still small (Schosser, 2015b). I spent more time weeding beds when I grew by HTGMV than when I grew by GWIC.

When using the HTGMV method, the soil can dry out rapidly after digging a bed, which makes it difficult for small seeds placed in the hexagonal grid pattern to germinate and grow. HTGMV advocates starting almost all vegetable seeds in flats and then transplanting seedlings from the flats into beds, even deep-rooted plants such as turnips and beets, which are usually direct-seeded. I found it extremely tedious to transplant the many tiny seedlings I wanted to grow, and the long, fine roots often bent

or broke in the process. In contrast, GWIC shows us an easy way to mark out planting rows while at the same time restoring capillarity to the soil in the rows, allowing the seeds in the rows to germinate and grow well. While I did some hand weeding in and near rows of small, slower-growing seedlings and some thinning as the seedlings became overcrowded, it was faster and easier to do both of these tasks than to plant flats, transplant seedlings, and hand weed around them when I planted beds using HTGMV's hexagonal grid. I only had to hand weed once or twice before the GWIC rows were clear enough of weeds and the desired plants large enough to see and avoid so I could weed standing up with a hoe.

What about long-term sustainability? One of the reasons HTGMV was so attractive to me and to many other gardeners is HTGMV's claim that by using all of its techniques together, with all wastes recycled and enough organic matter grown to ensure that the garden can produce enough compost to create and maintain sustainable soil fertility, HTGMV can create soil rapidly and maintain its fertility (Jeavons, 2012). Phrased this way, it seems to imply that compost should be sufficient to produce and maintain soil fertility. But later on, in the fertilization chapter, HTGMV acknowledges that outside inputs will be needed for a period of time, until the soil nutrients have been balanced through competent soil analysis followed by the application of the appropriate quantities of organic fertilizers (Jeavons, 2012). Because TIG also addresses nutrient balancing through soil testing, the addition of amendments, and the preparation and use of compost, either approach could be used. Some people might prefer the approach in HTGMV because little mathematics is required of them; the soil testing service recommended by HTGMV performs this task for the most part.[3] Because TIG delves deeply into soil mineral balancing, it is a longer and more difficult read than HTGMV. Unlike the soil testing service recommended by HTGMV, the soil testing service TIG recommends reports the levels of the various minerals found in the soil but not how to balance them properly.[4] Thus TIG provides a list of possible amendments and shows the reader how to calculate the target level of each mineral for different types of soil and how to determine which amendments to apply and how much to use to achieve the target

---

[3]   Timberleaf Soil Testing, 39648 Old Spring Rd., Murrieta, CA 92563, 951-677-7510 (http://www.timberleafsoiltesting.com/).

[4]   Logan Labs, PO Box 326, Lakeview, OH 43331, 1-888-494-SOIL (http://www.loganlabs.com/).

level for each mineral. For anyone who is not scared off by the mathematics involved (and anyone comfortable with manipulating fractions and decimals knows enough math to do the calculations) or the soil chemistry discussion, TIG's approach will lead to a better understanding of the soil and how to bring it to a good mineral balance. I found it far more interesting and understandable than the sketchy treatment of soil in HTGMV, though my training as a chemist may have something to do with that. And using the information and techniques in TIG has had the result Solomon said it would: After three years of using TIG I am now applying fewer amendments to my soil than it needed at the start while yields have stayed the same or increased.

Overall, then, I find that GWIC and TIG combined allow me to grow a garden that is as productive or more than the gardens I grew by HTGMV while requiring less time to prepare, plant, and maintain. This is because GWIC and TIG together mesh better with the ecological needs of vegetable plants and the practicalities of working in my garden than does HTGMV.

Blessing the Plants and Seeds

Because of my scientific training, I find it easy to relate to my garden as the subject of a scientific investigation. However, as my practice of Revival Druidry has strengthened and deepened, I have become aware of the possibility for a different kind of relationship with my garden. First, remembering that the seeds and plants are alive, I want to acknowledge and honor them for their gifts. Second, if I take seriously the possibility of the existence of beings or powers that are other and more powerful than humans, and if one or more of those beings expresses it/themselves through my garden, then it follows that a practice of acknowledgment of and gratitude toward such being(s) is most appropriate. Sara Greer's (2014) article on devotional practice was particularly helpful in bringing this possibility to my attention. In 2015 I began to practice a simple blessing ritual whenever I planted seeds or seedlings in the garden as a way to begin coming into relationship with these beings or natural forces.

Sources of inspiration for the blessing that I developed were John Michael Greer's (2006) remark that we can learn the art of the fusion of telluric and solar currents from watching a plant grow, and the Sphere of Protection (SOP) ritual of the AODA (Greer, 2007). Here is the basic form of the blessing:

May you feel the breeze around your body,
The warmth of the sun on your leaves,
The raindrops falling on and around you,
And the soil firm and fertile against your roots.
May the telluric current provide the power for you to grow
And the solar current show you when and how to grow
So you may combine these into the Green Ray of growth and fruitfulness

After I planted seeds or seedlings, I stood near them and recited the blessing. I didn't memorize the blessing, which made the ritual more awkward than it might otherwise have been, but it always incorporated the seven elements of the SOP in the same order and similar wording as given above. This usually completed my garden work for that day. In some cases I did not remember to bless the seeds or seedlings till the next morning after planting them. I did not attempt to do a scientific experiment with the blessing, such as saying it to certain plants but not to others. That was not its purpose. Its purpose was to connect my life more closely to that of the garden plants, the wider ecosystem of which the garden is a part, and the subtle energies and beings not acknowledged by scientific materialism. I saw it as an act that balanced the scientific with the sacred.

Because I did not bless the plants "scientifically," I cannot say with any level of certainty what, if any, effect the ritual may have had on them. I do feel the ritual had a positive effect on me: Because of it, I felt more closely connected to the plants and to

the subtle energy of the garden than I had before. And I have a sense that the garden in some way responded positively to it.

Beginning or Extending Your Gardening Practice

For those of you who have not grown vegetables before but are inspired to try gardening, I suggest you begin by asking yourself where you might be able to grow your garden and what the current conditions of that location are. If you don't have any land on which to garden, or the land you do have is too shady for vegetables or the soil is unsuited to that use, you might do an Internet search for community gardens in your area that you could join. Community gardens often offer small raised-bed gardens to their members. In this case, the square foot method makes sense, and you can begin by reading the book. You'll need to supplement the book with information that is specific to your area, which the community garden should be able to provide. It might even offer workshops on garden topics.

Do you have a small sunny area available for a garden and soil that is not too shallow or rocky to dig or till? In this case, you might start by reading both HTGMV and GWIC to see which might fit best with your situation and interests (and to notice where they disagree). Both HTGMV and GWIC are adequate basic guides for beginners, but you'll want to supplement whichever you choose with local growing information such as your last spring and first fall frost dates, varieties that do well in your area, and suggested times for planting various crops. You can learn some of that from your state extension service or from community gardens or other local gardening organizations as well as from local gardeners.

If you are already growing vegetables but are dissatisfied with your results, read whichever of HTGMV or GWIC/TIG appeals more to you. Then start using the method, following directions as closely as possible.

Whichever gardening method you choose, make time to observe your garden as often and carefully as you can, to learn how nature expresses herself through it. This will teach you much about garden ecology and help to satisfy the nature observation requirement of AODA's Earth Path. Reading books on ecology such as *Basic Ecology* (Buchsbaum & Buchsbaum, 1957) or gardening books with discussions on ecological concepts useful to gardeners (Jacke with Toensmeier, 2005; Carroll & Salt, 2004) will help you understand what you are observing. They may lead you to fine-tune your

method to local conditions or change to a method better in tune with your garden's ecological nature, as I have described above. You might find my blog post on science as dialogue (Schosser, 2013a) helpful in keeping the kind of records that will help you learn how the method you choose is working for you and your garden.

With so little experience in the spiritual aspect of gardening myself, I hesitate to offer much guidance in this effort. If you'd like to add a blessing practice to your gardening as I have, you could develop a blessing of your own, or you might use Dana Driscoll's (2015) three-element blessing or the one I describe above. I think the best way to go into a blessing practice is with curiosity, respect, and openness. Otherwise I look forward to learning more from my garden and from others with much more experience in this way to work with nature.

References

Ashworth, S. (1991). *Seed to seed.* Decorah, IA: Seed Saver Publications.

Bartholomew, M. (1981). *Square foot gardening: A new way to garden in less space with less work.* Emmaus, PA: Rodale.

Bartholomew, M. (2013). *All new square foot gardening: The revolutionary way to grow more in less space.* Minneapolis: Cool Springs.

Buchsbaum, R., & Buchsbaum, M. (1957). *Basic ecology.* Pittsburgh: Boxwood.

Carroll, S. B., & Salt, S. D. (2004). *Ecology for gardeners.* Portland, OR: Timber.

Deppe, C. (2010). *The resilient gardener: Food production and self-reliance in uncertain times.* White River Junction, VT: Chelsea Green.

Driscoll, D. (2015, December 5). Sacred gardening through the three Druid elements—designing sacred spaces and planting rituals [Blog post]. Retrieved from http://druidgarden.wordpress.com/2015/12/05/sacred-gardening-through-the-three-druid-elements-designing-sacred-spaces-and-planting-rituals/

Greer, J. M. (2006). *The Druidry handbook: Spiritual practice rooted in the living earth.* San Francisco: Red Wheel/Weiser.

Greer, J. M. (2007). *The Druid magic handbook: Ritual magic rooted in the living earth.* San Francisco: Red Wheel/Weiser.

Greer, S. (2014). Devotional practice. *Trilithon, 1,* 52–66.

Jacke, D., with Toensmeier, E. (2005). *Edible forest gardens, vol. 1: Ecological vision and theory for temperate climate permaculture.* White River Junction, VT: Chelsea Green.

Jeavons, J. (2012). *How to grow more vegetables (and fruits, nuts, berries, grains, and other crops) than you ever thought possible on less land than you can imagine.* Berkeley, CA: Ten Speed.

Schosser, C. L. (2013a, May 9). Science as dialogue: What my garden and I are discussing in 2013 [Blog post]. Retrieved from http://livinglowinthelou.blogspot.com/2013/05/science-as-dialogue-what-my-garden-and.html

Schosser, C. L. (2013b, December 14). What my garden told me: Results of the 2013 garden dialogue [Blog post]. Retrieved from http://livinglowinthelou.blogspot.com/2013/12/what-my-garden-told-me-results-of-2013.html

Schosser, C. L. (2014a, February 4). What the soil told me in 2013, and my response [Blog post]. Retrieved from http://livinglowinthelou.blogspot.com/2014/02/what-soil-told-me-in-2013-and-my.html

Schosser, C. L. (2014b, December 10). What I learned from my garden in 2014 [Blog post]. Retrieved from http://livinglowinthelou.blogspot.com/2014/12/what-i-learned-from-my-garden-in-2014.html

Schosser, C. L. (2015a, January 20). A tale of two gardening methods [Blog post]. Retrieved from http://livinglowinthelou.blogspot.com/2015/01/a-tale-of-two-gardening-methods.html

Schosser, C. L. (2015b, June 1). An ecological look at vegetable gardening systems [Blog post]. Retrieved from http://livinglowinthelou.blogspot.com/2015/06/an-ecological-look-at-vegetable.html

Schosser, C. L. (2016, January 14). What I learned from my 2015 garden [Blog post]. Retrieved from http://livinglowinthelou.blogspot.com/2016/01/what-i-learned-from-my-2015-garden.html

Solomon, S. (2005). *Gardening when it counts: Growing food in hard times.* Gabriola Island, BC: New Society.

Solomon, S., with Reinheimer, E. (2013). *The intelligent gardener: Growing nutrient-dense food.* Gabriola Island, BC: New Society.

Revitalizing Your Orchard with a Wassail Ritual

By Maxine Rogers

Maxine Rogers is the President of the Denman Island Garden Club because they couldn't find anyone else to take the job. She was a Community Garden Coordinator in Victoria where she fixed a lot of hoses. After a passionate youth spent scuba diving off Vancouver Island, working as a Reserve Medic in the Canadian Army, playing rugby, alpine skiing, sailing and getting a degree in Spanish from UVic, she developed chronic fatigue syndrome and retired to a small farm. She leads a fascinating existence on the farm with her long-suffering husband, a flock of milk sheep, geese, chickens, ducks rabbits, a large garden and an orchard. She paints and writes when she gets the time. She is currently studying as a candidate for Druid apprenticeship. She has never had this much fun with religion before.

I have a small farm in the Northern Gulf Islands on British Columbia's coast. The first European settlers here were Orkney Scots, and they covered the island in hundreds of different varieties of apples with very distinct flavors, as well as pears, plums, and some excellent walnuts. That was over a century ago, and many of their orchards are still productive. The walnuts they first planted now dwarf the three-story houses they tower over.

Our summers are usually long and fairly dry and our winters mild and wet. The soil varies from clay to gravel and sand. Nevertheless, the apples seem to like it here. The old apple trees are all standards, the largest size of apple tree.

Size of the tree is determined by the root stock, and the settlers did not think they could have too many apples. Most modern orchards are of dwarf trees because they are easier to care for but do not last like the big standards. The dwarf trees are only good for about thirty years, and of course they do not bear as heavily as the standards.

There are a few families descended from the original settlers here, but they are a bit standoffish with people from away. I do not know what traditions they brought with them from Britain, and such traditions would have varied depending on which county or indeed country they were from in Britain.

Before the advent of very cheap fuel, the apples of our islands satisfied the whole province and were transported by rail over the Rockies to the far-off Prairie Provinces. As fuel prices rise and the Canadian dollar falls, imported American apples will become very expensive; our apples will once again be an economic and culinary necessity. It is time to consider our orchards a blessing again.

Rituals of blessing the land and the flocks are ancient and are so important to agriculture and rural life that Christianity held to all the ancient festivals by different names. These rituals guided the work of the year so everything would be done in the correct time. In farming, timing is everything. I actually had a very well-educated young lady ask me if I had a computer program that told me what to do on my farm. No such luck!

Religious festivals gave farmers an insight into their work as a spiritual endeavor. These festivals gave them something to look forward to and a date to get the relevant work done so that they will not be disgraced by, for example, not having the orchard pruned when their friends came to Wassail.

Traditional agriculture was not about making money; it was about making the land healthy and fertile, and the people were part of the land. These festivals and traditions also engaged the support of the Gods by whatever name they were called.

So the many ancient festivals of blessing of the land, the harvest, and the flocks and herds are proper holy days for Druids to celebrate if they coincide with your climate and agricultural calendar. I think even Druids who live in urban areas will benefit from learning and celebrating such rituals.

Let's get back to my farm and our apples for a bit of context. We planted a little mixed orchard when we moved here six years ago. We now have a good crop of apples, cherries, pears, and plums, plus more exotic persimmons, figs, and hazelnuts. But the old-timers were right; you can never have too many apples.

Christmas With The Poets, A Collection of Songs, Carols, and Verses, 1852

We preserve apples by canning sauce, drying apple rings, and fermenting the juice to make cider and wine. The old-timers used to boil the juice down at a ratio of seven quarts to one for apple syrup and nine quarts to one for apple molasses. We wrap apples in sheets of newspaper and store them in the cold workshop to preserve them for fresh winter eating. We share our apples with our beloved dairy sheep, our rabbits, and our chickens. An apple a day keeps the veterinarian away.

So apples are a source of delight, wealth, and health for us. I am a new student of Druidry, and I heard about the custom of Wassailing the orchard. I was drawn to Wassail our orchard here. This custom comes from southwest England, one of the most delightful places on Earth, and part of my family comes from there. It seemed

so right for me to celebrate Wassailing, as if it was something I had done for hundreds of years and then forgotten about.

The word "wassail" is very old English, and it means, "Be thou healthy!" It was used as a toast, and the reply was, "Drink Hail!" meaning, "drink health." Have you ever wondered why we call a wish combined with a drink a toast?

The custom comes from Wassailing. Pieces of buttered toast were soaked in the mulled cider and hung on the branches of the senior apple tree in an orchard. Another custom was to Wassail people and then serve toast on top of the hot cider to be eaten.

The day for Wassailing is January 17th, old Twelfth Night. Twelfth Night means the twelfth night after Christmas in the Julian calendar; however, I suspect the custom is much older than Christianity. January 17th is an excellent day to Wassail orchards because this marks the time to get all your orchard work done before the 17th, while the trees are still dormant.

Orchard work around Wassail primarily includes pruning. Apples like to be winter pruned while they are dormant, and in a mild climate such as Denman Island British Columbia or Devon, England, you risk hitting a warm patch if you leave it later than the Wassail date of January 17; pruning apples in bud is bad for the trees.

We rarely have snow, so in January we can rake up all fallen leaves if we have not yet done so. Various diseases, and especially insect pests, overwinter in the fallen leaves. I compost the leaves after allowing the hens to shred them and eat the coddling moth caterpillars. The soil under the drip line of the trees can be limed. Our soil on the West Coast is very acid, so we have to lime a lot. You may not have to lime if you live east of the Coastal Mountain Range. A dressing of composted manure should be spread under the fruit-tree's drip line, but that should wait until spring.

The most important chore in the winter orchard is to get the pruning done. Any dead wood must be cut out. The same goes for weak or crossing branches. Growth on top of the branches should be pruned off as this is not a good place for a fruiting spur. The fruit would hang against the branch and be abraded by rubbing on the branch. Branches should grow out from the center and not be allowed to grow back into the

center. Clip long spindly branches back to a downward facing bud. All this makes it easy to thin the fruit and to harvest it.

Any fruit tree can be trained into a good strong shape by tying a small rock into a cloth and hanging it by a piece of bicycle inner tube to the branch to train it down. If you stand with your arms held straight out from your shoulders, you will have the angle you are hoping to train the branch into.

Once you have all the work done, the orchard is ready to Wassail. The Ancient Romans had a saying, "The Gods can only help you if you put yourself in their path." The Gods can bless an orchard but cannot compensate for a lazy orchardist.

I picked the eldest apple tree to Wassail, but it could also be the central tree, the biggest tree, or the favorite tree. I performed a Grove Opening and had written a mediation and an invocation to the Goddess Pomona. Pomona is the Roman Goddess of orchards. She is a sweet young girl, and you can recognize her by the basket of fruit she is carrying and the curved pruning knife she holds in her right hand. I saw her come to my orchard ready for work with the skirt of her long tunic tucked into her belt and her hair held back in a practical braid.

This is the meditation I wrote:

"The orchard sleeps and the sun is low in the sky. The day is short and the night is full of brilliant stars. In the heart of winter, we wake the apple trees and beseech them to delight our hearts with a sea of pink and white blossoms in the proper season. Now, we have cleaned the orchard and pruned the graceful trees. When the geese fly home and lambs dot the pasture, buds of leaf and blossom will swell on the branches and autumn's bounty will begin."

This is the invocation I wrote:

"On this day, I invoke Pomona, the cheerful girl, spirit of abundance and content. Pomona, who blesses the orchard and guides the hand of every devout orchardist. Pomona, Pomona, Pomona, join with me in the most sacred apple grove. Be benevolent and propitious to me and to my orchard. Grant me your blessings and receive my thanks and love in return. Watch over this grove and the trees of this island in the turning of the year's wheel now before us."

Of course, the beauty of Druidry is that you can invoke whatever entity you like or none at all. I merely mention Pomona because I think her very fit for the job and worthy of veneration. After the invocation, I drank the health of my trees and my Goddess and offered them some of the hot mulled cider. I asked the trees to bear well and to stay healthy and thanked them for the previous harvest. I soaked the two slices of homemade bread, toasted and buttered, in the cider and hung them on the freshly pruned branches of the central apple tree. The toast is to nourish the tree spirits and the wild birds, of course.

I sang a variation of the traditional Wassail song: "Apple tree, apple tree, we all come to Wassail thee. Bare this year to fill our farm with good cheer. Hats full, caps full, three-cornered sacks full. Pantry full, cidery full and a little heap under the stars."

I am no singer, and I could not find a tune that really worked so I just did my best. The little heap under the stars strikes me as important. We should share some of our bounty with wild creatures and not be greedy.

I did all this a bit inexpertly, but it was my first time. Next year, I plan to invite some friends to make noise to bring the trees out of dormancy and to chase away evil spirits. The noise making and, in some cultures, the striking of the tree trunks and branches is meant to wake the trees to get on with their important work. I do not like the idea of striking the trees, but I think banging spoons on pots can do no harm. Then we will give a feast of rabbit Pomona, apple crumble, and more mulled cider.

The recipe for rabbit Pomona calls for one jointed rabbit, but you could use a chicken or duck cut up. A quarter cup of olive oil to toss the meat in, salt and black pepper, nine fresh bay laurel leaves and three, six, or nine apples cored depending on how many guests you have. Each person should have their own apple. Bake this in a covered roasting pan at 350 degrees for 2 to 2 1/2 hours.

For the cider, heat a cup of water, 3 whole cloves, 3 allspice buds, 3 split cardamom pods, 3 cinnamon sticks, and the juice of an orange and a lemon in a saucepan with half a cup of honey. When this is hot and the flavors are blended, add two bottles of cider and heat to quite warm, but do not boil the alcohol out. Happy Wassailing!

The Consecrated Garden

By William Herrington

William Herrington (druid name: White Feather) has been a member of AODA for almost two years and has successfully completed his Candidate year. He is a student of JMG's Dolmen Arch course and will soon be starting on Grade 4. He has also finished one of the three core modules in the Florida Master Naturalist Program (FNMP), offered by the University of Florida. He is a hands-on type of druid, and can often be found barefoot in his small "No-Till" garden, dressed in ragged shorts and t-shirt with an old Ruger sixgun on his hip, and much dirt on his hands.

This essay is dedicated with inexpressible gratitude to my teachers,
John Michael Greer and
George E. Mattson.

Consecrate: Dedicate to a sacred purpose.

I have enjoyed small-scale gardening for many years. Growing edible flowers, vegetables, and herbs using traditional methods rewards me with fresh produce for the table and valuable quiet time. I believe many of my fellow gardeners would agree.

It was during one of these quiet times that I realized gardening, from a different perspective, could do something much more than that, could become what it was always meant to be—a sacred communion with the natural world, an act of prayer physically expressed. This idea is not new. I've come to learn that it is common among many indigenous cultures, though it's now lost for the most part among the shining machinery and glittering lights of our modern age. How sad it is that we've worked diligently to perfect the method and forgotten so much of the meaning.

To be successful in the truest sense, a garden must nourish the spirit as fully as the body. Mine did not, and in knowing it did not I found the need for reconciliation, a path by which to make my practice whole.

In the ancient Druid tradition I sought answers in nature's example, and they weren't difficult to find. The first epiphany was simply that nature did not employ the unnatural. I abandoned synthetic chemical fertilizer. The second epiphany was that nature never took without giving. Observing this, I realized that the chemical fertilizer was only necessary because by repeatedly tilling the soil I was depleting the natural food web and then had to artificially replenish it. This was solved by adopting a no-till method, which incidentally reduced my input of manual labor by about 75 percent. Rather than tilling, I applied generous amounts of compost and mulch to the surface, thereby building soil fertility. Last, I noticed that plants did not naturally grow in segregated groups of individual species, but in wild conglomeration. I introduced companion planting to my garden, and a wonderful thing happened. I found myself working in a harmonious communion with nature. Soil, plants, and gardener worked together for the benefit of all and the detriment of none.

The Song of St. Margaret: How Alpine Goddess Worship Survived Centuries in a Simple Farmer's Song

By Christian Brunner

Christian F. Brunner was born in Austria and lived there for more than thirty years before he moved to the United States in 1997. In his teenage years, he started to research ancient and contemporary indigenous methods of alternative healing, and practiced with a group of pagan naturopaths in Vienna for several years. This practice, based on folklore and customs of the Alps, has been the core of his work for more than two decades, and eventually led him to Druidry. Now he is a Druid member of the Order of Bards, Ovates and Druids, working on becoming a tutor and Druid celebrant. Christian is also the author of three books in German: a novel, a cookbook for the eight festivals of the year, and a study of Alpine lore and customs, which is now also available in English under the title Mountain Magic: Celtic Shamanism in the Austrian Alps *(at* www.lulu.com *and other online bookstores like Amazon.com and Barnes and Noble).*

There are three tasks of the Druid:
to live fully in the present, to honor
tradition and the ancestors, and to hear
the voice of tomorrow.

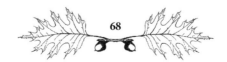

This well-known triad tells us much about the expectations we should have of a Druid, no matter the degree. It is not always easy to fulfill any of these objectives individually, and it can become really difficult to combine all three of them at the same time. In this article I'd like to contemplate an old song rooted in ancient Celtic lands, singing of the fears of its makers, ancestors to some of us, during times of change and turmoil. What we consider history, our past, was their present. This little gem thus connects us directly to our pre-Christian forebears and thus, as we will explore, deeply with the land. It does so even though the song was created not in ancient but in medieval times, for it is a lament about what was then "the old ways" already; it evokes a time when it was the Goddess who made the land fertile through pagan ritual and who gifted her people with magic. When we discover the song's linguistic and geographic origin, we will learn of its Celtic roots, and by digging further we'll find a truly magical core of the story. We will also lift the veil that disguised the main character well enough that women working in the fields in the high mountains of the Alps could sing it without fear of being persecuted by Christians, both Catholic and Protestant. While all this took place in the heart of Europe centuries ago, we'll also see that the story is relevant to our own time. And as we listen to the voice of the future, we may just realize that little has changed since our ancestors' traditions were jeopardized by religious righteousness. But maybe, if we work a little magic described in the song, we still can make our present and our future a better place.

Social Studies: Who Sang the Song and Where?

"La Canzun de Sontga Margriata," which means "The Song of St. Margaret," is composed in Raetho-Roman, a language still spoken in some very remote areas of Switzerland. Raetho-Roman, also sometimes referred to as Romansh, belongs to the Roman language family, and replaced a hybrid tongue formed from Roman Latin, Celtic, and some very old forms of High German. Raetho-Roman is named after the Celtic province of Raetia, itself named for the Celtic Raetii tribe. As shown in Figure 1, the province covered a section of the Alps where we now find the Austrian provinces of Tyrol and Vorarlberg, South Tyrol (now a part of Italy), the Italian province of Trentino, the western part of the Veneto region, and finally the Unter-Engadin, the lower (i.e., *unter*) section of the Swiss part of the Inn valley today. In the Inn valley, Raetho-Roman is still spoken. Even the valley's name hints at this old language, for *En*, the first syllable of Engadin, is Raetho-Roman for the river Inn. To the north, Raetia stretched all the way to Lake Constance and the Danube. The Helvetii, the Proto-Swiss so to speak, lived to the west of the Raetii, and in the east we find the kingdom of Noricum, with

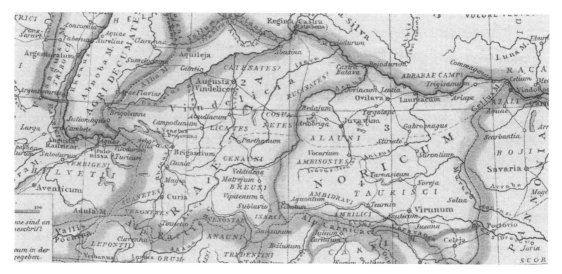

<u>Figure 1:</u>

The province of Raetia, from a historical map. Droysens Historischer Handatlas, 1886. Public domain from Wikipedia (https://de.wikipedia.org/wiki/Raetia#/media/File:Droysens_Hist_Handatlas_S17_Germanien.jpg)

Hallstatt right in the center of it. Although the earliest culture we identify as Celtic is named after this quaint little village, Hallstatt was not the main city of the realm. The capital of Noricum is believed to have been the city of Noreia, mentioned in lore, but—officially—not yet found. There is, however, promising evidence that the city has been discovered very recently, as erosion has uncovered vast amounts of remains such as pottery and weaponry in an area of Austria long believed to be the capital of the kingdom of Noricum, where I was born and raised. Horse enthusiasts may also know of the breed Noriker or Noric Pinzgauer, once known only as the Pinzgauer, which is named for the kingdom. The current name is a nineteenth-century invention, driven by the Celtic revival. Still, the breed itself originates from the area that was Noricum.

The Raetii themselves were a conglomerate of a number of Celtic tribes and non-Celtic folk, most prominently the Ladin people with their mythological forbears, the Fanes (Wolff, 1913). They are believed to have been a matriarchal society (Göttner-Abendroth, 2005) who inhabited the fertile valley of the river Po in northern Italy originally. Their folk poems sing of their attempts to hold the Celts at bay, who entered the Po valley from their home in the Danube valley to the north. These poems are full of magic and well worth reading, even though the Fanes vanished, as they assimilated with the Celts eventually.

Similar to other Celtic provinces right along the northern border of the early Roman Empire (before the Romans waged their wars beyond the Italian peninsula), the Raetii were exposed to this culture early on, and subsequently adopted much if it. So when we talk about Raetho-Roman today, we need to consider that the constant movement of people in this region created a language with heavy Roman influence, yet still with Celtic elements.

Dialect: A Window into the Past

From the original version of the ballad, as it is printed in *Mythos und Kult in den Alpen* (Myth and Cult in the Alps) by anthropologist Hans Haid (2002), you can easily see how close Raetho-Roman is to Italian. My English version is based on a translation from Raetho-Roman into German by the nineteenth-century Catholic priest P. Maurus Carnot. As this translation is rather mechanical, I would like to propose a contest for all those interested in the Bardic arts or on the Bardic path reading this article. Shortly we will see that this song is evidence of pagan culture in the Alps, based on at least partly Celtic origins. It would be a great feat to make it available for generations to come in a form that not only informs but speaks to us poetically as well.

But before we go into the bits and pieces of information contained in "La Canzun," let's explore how much of a mix and match the Raetho-Roman language really is. This will allow us to connect a German dialect as it is spoken in the twenty-first century to this old tongue of some of our Celtic ancestors. Words like *allura* and *ella* clearly show the influence of Italian and Latin. However, there are also words in there that are difficult to trace back to one or another language, including an early form of German. There is one expression in particular that I find of great interest, linguistically: the word *pietigott*. It appears in several verses of the song, such as the following:

> *Allura va Sontga Magriata dabot*
> *E da tut ella prien pietigott:*
> *"Pietigott, ti miu bien signun!*
> *E pietigott, ti mia buna caldera!"*
> *This translates as, "Then, St. Margaret leaves / And says farewell all around. / 'Farewell, my good herder! / And farewell, my good cauldron!'"*

In the eastern Alps, folks speak High German (the southern version of the German language), particularly Austro-Bavarian, as opposed to the Low German spoken in northern Germany. There are linguistic variations between these two types of German,

such as different words for the same object, and intonation of vowels and consonants, not unlike the difference between British and American English. These differences are a result of the second Germanic consonant shift, in which the northern Germans did not participate. The Angles and Saxons didn't either, which is why English and northern German are very close. The English word "ship," for example, would be *Schipp* in northern Low German, but *Schiff* in southern High German. To make things even more complicated, a number of dialects are spoken in both of these German language regions. In the dialects spoken in the eastern Alps (you guessed it, folks in the western Alps speak yet a different kind of German, Alemannic) it is still custom to say *Pfiat-di-gott* or, more casually, *Pfiat-di* for "good-bye"—just as St. Margaret says pietigott to all when she leaves the alp.

This shows beautifully that even though society forces the many variations of Europe's most-spoken language into one format, so-called Standard German, the very old is not forgotten in the common tongues spoken by the locals.

Who is Sontga Magriata Anyway?

We need to consider another important clue to the deeper meaning of the song before actually delving into what the lyrics tell us, which is the identity of the main character. It is St. Margaret—and not any other Christian saint—and this is not arbitrary at all. When we visit remote village churches in the lands where the ancient Celts dwelled, particularly the land of the Raetii, we often find church paintings depicting three saints: St. Catherine, St. Margaret, and St. Barbara. There is even an old adage telling us about them:

> *Marg'ret mit dem Wurm*
> *Barbara mit dem Turm*
> *Katharina mit dem Radl*
> *Des sind uns're drei heiligen Madl.*

While this rhymes perfectly in German dialect (*Madl* is Austro-Bavarian dialect for *Mädchen*, meaning "girl," and *Radl* is *Rad*, meaning "wheel"), the English translation would go like this: "Margaret with the worm / Barbara with the tower / Catherine with the wheel / These are our three holy girls." The significance lies in the fact that the three saints are usually depicted with these three attributes, a "worm" (an old word for snake), a tower, and a wheel, in these old church paintings. And the three women

are typically dressed in white, red, and black dresses, respectively (Kutter, 2003). The colors are not chosen randomly, but are associated with the ancient Goddess trinity: white for the maiden, red for the mother, and black for the crone. The author Ernie Kutter also draws a link to an old, matriarchal way of time keeping that connects the phases of the moon with those of the menstrual cycle. In my book *Mountain Magic* I describe this idea as follows:

> *"The cycle of the year was originally not based on the number four—as in the four stations of the Sun determining the seasons—but on the enchanted number three. Three as a magical number was already part of the Neolithic consciousness. The first section of the Moon's cycle is the white one, where the uterus builds up the white mucous membrane, which corresponds to the waxing Moon. This is followed by the red phase in the centre of which we experience the Full Moon, as well as the high point of fertility, ovulation. After this follows the dark or black episode, finding its end with the New Moon. White, red, black—the same three colours associated with the Goddess Trinity, with Wilbet, Ambet, and Borbet. (Brunner 2015)"*

The wheel held by Catherine (dressed in white) has eight spokes and resembles the sun wheel and the wheel of the year. The tower held by Barbara (dressed in black) is a symbol of the castle keep, the place of protection and the warm hearth.

The worm or snake associated with the central goddess needs specific consideration here, not only because it is Margaret's attribute, but also for its meaning. "Worm" is an old German word for "snake," which, more importantly, also signified a dragon (the snake on a mythical scale). Among the ancient Celts, dragons were believed to be more snake-like creatures, as legs and wings were added later. In fact, the main sightseeing attraction in Klagenfurt, capital of Austria's province of Carinthia, is a statue of a dragon (with legs and wings) called Lindwurm. We not only have the old word for dragon in its name, but also the ancient Celtic term for lake, *lind*. Thus, the creature cast in bronze in this regional capital is a lake snake, or water dragon, really (Resch-Rauter, 1992).

When we look at the church paintings mentioned above, we almost always see a snake winding around St. Margaret's feet, symbolizing a dragon, one of the most powerful creatures of old myths (see the story of Merlin, for example). In statues of Mary (mother of Jesus) we also sometimes see the same snake under her feet or winding

Figure 2:

Carved figurines of Saints Barbara, Catharine, and Margaret in the parish church of Klein Sankt Paul, district Saint Veit on the Glan, Carinthia, Austria. Public domain fcrom Wikimedia Commons, https://commons.wikimedia.org/wiki/File:Klein_Sankt_Paul_Pfarrkirche_Barbara_Katharina_Margarethe_21092007_20.jpg

around the earth ball upon which she stands. So, the "worm" in the old adage above is in reality a snake, with all its pre-Christian symbolism, and with the powers and status of the dragon.

Let's for a moment revisit this symbolism of the snake. It can be best described as a physical manifestation of the magical power of women. When we imagine a snake of dragon-like proportion, we can get a feeling for its immense strength. When we consider how people and snakes have this kind of offish relationship, we get a hunch about how difficult it is to describe this power. Yet it is really ancient, prehistoric almost, reaching back into the realm of the dinosaurs, which explains the fear some people have of this

relentless, hard-to-grip (because it grips you as soon as you touch it), female power that stares you down with nonblinking eyes, hissing at you when you challenge it. It is a strength that is not to be ruled over, especially not by men. And thus it is vilified by them.

Figure 2 shows a later baroque altarpiece with painted and gilded wood carvings of the Three Ladies. Borbet's tower is at her feet here; Wilbet's wheel is broken (which could be interpreted as a Christian pun for having broken Pagan faith); and Ambet's worm is an actual dragon over which she now has control, symbolized by the chain. The garments of each of the figures show all three colors of the Goddess, with dark green for black.

A Pagan Goddess Survives in a Christian Song

This is the Margaret we encounter in the song, and by now we have to ask ourselves, is this woman, who is associated with the dragon or snake, who wears a red dress in sacred paintings, whose companions have the sun wheel and the castle keep and who wear dresses in the other two colors usually associated with the ancient Goddess trinity, really just a saint?

We can delve even deeper into the symbolism of these three figures by considering that in the oldest of these paintings, the names of the three women are not Catherine, Margaret, and Barbara, but Wilbet (remember, she carries a wheel, and there is in fact a linguistic connection there), Ambet, and Borbet, respectively.

The syllable *bet* all three of them share means something like "eternal," and words like "bed" in English (because people lay directly on her when sleeping, or harvested crops from her) or the German *beten*, "praying," are associated with it. Since that syllable is in the names of all three figures, we can conclude that all three were "eternal ones." Wilbet represented the eternal cycle (wheel) of the seasons, and Borbet the eternal warmth and safety of the castle keep.

Ambet is, in a sense, even more eternal. *Am* in her name comes from the ancient term ana, meaning (eternal) mother. The Celtic goddess names *Anu*, Dana, or Danu are derived from this ancient word, as is Danube, that is, the Mother River, believed to be the center of Celtic culture. The Irish people of Dana, the Túatha Dé Danaan, are named after her, as is the Roman goddess Diana, "Diana" meaning Dea Ana or Goddess Mother. In German, the words for ancestors, *Ahnen*, and for midwife, *Amme*, are also rooted in the ancient words *ana* and *am*.

A number of towns and rivers in the wider Alpine region bear witness to her name, too—with and without the syllable *bet*. There is the Austrian town Amstetten, the Italian ski resort Cortina D'Ampezzo, the Hungarian city Syombathely (say "Shambetey"), or Austrian rivers like Ammer, Amper, and Amperbettenbach. When we put together the two syllables *am* (mother) and *bet* (eternal), we get the true meaning of her name, "eternal mother." In some versions of Ambet's name, such as Anabet or Einbet (both meaning "One-Bet"), another aspect shines through, which is the central position she holds not only in many of the paintings but also in the trinity of the "Three Holy Girls" (Resch-Rauter, 1992).

So, although St. Margaret seems to be the one the song is about, her direct link to the ancient goddess is already apparent in her name—and even more so in what the lyrics tell us:

1. *Sontga Margriata ei stada siat stads ad*
alp, Mai quendisch dis meins
   In di eis ella idadal stavel giu,
   Dada giu sin ina nauscha plata,
   Ch'igl ei scurclau siu bi sein alv.
   Paster petschen ha quei ad uguri catau.
   "Quei sto nies signun ir a saver,
   Tgeinina ventireivla puschalla nus
havein."

1. St. Margaret stayed on the mountain
   For seven summers, less fifteen days.
   Once she went down the meadow,
   And slipped on a steep plate so that her naked buttocks were seen.
   And the herder's boy noticed that.
   "The herder needs to know that,
   What a beautiful lady we have here."

2. *"E sche tiu signun sto quei bucc saver,*
   sch'ta ti vi jeu dar treis biallas camischas,
   Che pli to scarvunas e pli alvas, ch'ellas
vegnen."
   "Quei vi jeu buc, quei prend jeu buc!
   Quei sto nies signun ir a saver,
   Tgeinina zezna purschala nus havein."

2. "And if the herder doesn't need to know,
   I will give you three beautiful shirts,
   Which will become whiter
   The more often you wash them."
   "I don't want that, I won't take that,
   The herder needs to know that,
   What a beautiful lady we have here."

3. *"Sche ti vul quei buca dir ora,*
   Sche vi jeu dar a ti treis bialas nuorsas,
   Che ti sas tunder treis gadas igl onn
   E mintgaga ventgaquater crenas launa."

3. "And if the herder doesn't need to know,
   I will give you three beautiful sheep,
   Which you can shear three times a year,
   And each shearing yields 24 clews of

"Quei vi jeu buc, quei prend jeu buc!
Quei sto nies signun ir a saver,
Tgeinina zezna purschala nus havein."

wool." "I don't want that, I won't take that,
    The herder needs to know that,
    What a beautiful lady we have here."

4. *"Sche ti vul quei buca dir ora,*
   Sche vi jeu dar a ti treis bialas vaccas,
   Che ti sas mulscher treis gadas il di,
   Mintgaga siu bi curtè latg."
   "Quei vi jeu buc, quei prend jeu buc!
   Quei sto nies signun ir a saver,
   Tgeinina zezna purschala nus havein."

4. "And if the herder doesn't need to know,
    I will give you three beautiful brown
cows, Which you can milk three times a
day, And a full bucket of milk each time."
    "I don't want that, I won't take that,
    The herder needs to know that,
    What a beautiful lady we have here."

5. *"Sche ti vul quei buca dir ora,*
   Sche vi jeu dar a ti in bi curtgin,
   Che ti sas segar treis gadas igl onn,
   E mintgaga siu bi ladretsch fein."
   "Quei vi jeu buc, quei prend jeu buc!
   Quei sto nies signun ir a saver,
   Tgeinina zezna purschala nus havein."

5. "And if the herder doesn't need to know,
    I will give you a beautiful pasture,
    Which you can mow three times a year,
    And a huge haystack each time."
    "I don't want that, I won't take that,
    The herder needs to know that,
    What a beautiful lady we have here."

6. *"Sche ti vul quei buca dir ora,*
   Sche vi jeu dar a ti in bi mulin,
   Che mola il di segal e la notg salin,
   Senza mai metter si buc in."
   "Quei vi jeu buc, quei prend jeu buc!
   Quei sto nies signun ir a saver,
   Tgeinina zezna purschala nus havein."

6. "And if the herder doesn't need to know,
    I will give you a beautiful mill, That grinds
rye during the day and wheat at night,
    Without you having to fill it."
    "I don't want that, I won't take that,
    The herder needs to know that,
    What a beautiful lady we have here."

7. *"E sche tiu signun sto quei saver,*
   Sche ti sas fundar entochen culiez."
   "O, buna Sontga Margriata,
   Lai po vegnir viado,
   quei sto nies signun buc ir a saver."

7. "And if the herder needs to know,
    Then sink into the ground to your neck!"
    "Oh good St. Margaret,
    Oh help me out of here,
    This the herder doesn't need to know."

Cu la sontga Margriata ha gidau ô il
paster petschen,
Ha quel puspei entschiet a dir:
"Quei sto nies signun ir a saver,
Tgeinina zezna purschala nus havein."

St. Margaret helped the herder boy out,
But the boy decided to say,
"The herder needs to know that,
What a beautiful lady we have here."

8. "Sche ti vul quei dir ora, Sche dueis ti
fundar treis tschuncheismas ault."
Allura va sontga Margriata dabot,
E da tut ella pren pietigot!
"Pietigot, ti miu bien signun,
E pietigot, ti mia buna caldera,
Pietigot mia buna panaglia,
E pietigot ti mia buna fueinetta,
Che jeu durmevel adina cun tei.
Pertgei fas quei miu bien paster?
Pietigot mias bunas vachettas,
Vus vegnis a schigiar dil latg.
Ah, pietigot entuorn, entuorn,
Sappi Dieus cur jeu cheu tuorn!"

8. "And if the herder needs to know,
Then sink into the ground three yards!"
Then, the holy maiden leaves
And says farewell all around.
"Farewell, my good herder,
Farewell, my good cauldron
Farewell my butter keg,
Farewell my little hearth,
Where I had my sleeping quarters.
Why did you do that, good herder?
Farewell my good cows,
Your milk will dry up.
Oh, farewell, farewell everything around!
God knows when I will return again!"

9. Epi mav'ella sul Cunclas ô.
La caldera e las vaccas mavan suenter,
Aschi lunsch sco ellas han viu,
Han ellas buca calau de bargir.
Epi eis ella ida sper ina fontauna ô, a
cantond:
"O ti, o ti fontaunetta,
Sche jeu mond ir naven
Sche vegnas lu schigiar si!"
E la fontauna ei schigiada si.
Epi eis ella ida sper ina plaunca ô, a
cantond:
"O ti, o ti plaunchetta,
Sche jeu mond ir naven,

9. Then she left the valley.
And the milk bucket with her,
And as long as they could see the leaving
maiden,
The cows couldn't stop crying.
Then she passed by a well and sang,
"Oh well, oh little well, when I leave,
You will surely dry out!"
And the well dried out.
Then she left the pasture behind and sang,
"Oh pasture, oh pasture so close to my
heart,
When I leave, you will surely wither."
And wither did the pasture.

Sche vegnas ti guess a seccar!"
E la plaunca ei seccada.
"Ah, mia buna jarva,
Sche jeu mond ir naven,
Ti vegnas lu seccar e mai verdegar."
E la jarva ei seccada e mai verdegada,
E cur ch'ell'ei ida sut il zenn da sogn Gieri
e sogn Gagl,
Tuccavan ei d'ensemen, ch'ei devô il battagl.

"Oh you good herbs, when I leave,
  You will wither and never green again."
  And wither did the herbs, and they never
greened again.
  The maiden passed the bells of the churches
of St. Jörgs and St. Galls,
  And the bells rang so loud,
  That the clapper fell out.

First, the "saint" has already stayed on the alp for a long time, a magically long time: seven summers. But what she does fifteen days before the end of the summer is somewhat surprising and rather unbecoming for a saint. She slides down a rock, and a young boy sees her naked buttocks (there was no underwear back then). Although it may appear that this was an accident, it really refers to something else, something truly pagan. Sliding stones are common in the Alps. They are slanted rocks, often with a groove or two next to each other, and they are very smooth. Some have engravings or cups carved into them, often a set of nine (three times three). The cups are believed to be made to hold gifts, maybe milk and honey, and the boulders themselves are designed for women to slide down. Pagans of old did that as part of fertility rites, whether to induce fertility in a young woman generally or if she had problems becoming pregnant, or as part of a coming-of-age ceremony. And it would seem logical that women did that naked, or at least lifted their skirts to be in direct contact with Mother Earth.

For today's Druids, as healers and helpers, we can extract some ideas from this very first verse of the song and its deeper meaning, if we were called to help someone with fertility. In safely sliding down a rock, the mere contact of the woman's body, particularly of her buttocks—naked skin to ancient stone—could become part of a ritual designed to increase or induce fertility. Obviously, ancient sliding stones with their own ritualistic history, as they exist in the Alps, cannot be found everywhere. But it should not be a problem to locate a boulder anywhere, where a woman could at least sit in direct contact with Mother Earth as part of such a ritual. Offerings typical for Celtic worship and for the spirit of the land can be given to the Goddess by leaving them in natural dents or crevices in the boulder.

<u>Figure 3</u>:
Sliding rock. Photo by author.

Druid celebrants involved in coming-of-age rites for young women could also have girls sit on a boulder during the ritual. Utmost consideration must be given to the girl's particular feelings at that stage of her life, obviously. A dress or skirt would be appropriate to wear.

Figure 3 shows a small sliding rock near the town of St. Wolfgang in the Austrian Salzkammergut area. The stone is about a thirty-minute walk from a major Celtic cult place, the Falkenstein, and was certainly used for fertility rites. The Catholic Church altered the story of the rock, though, and tells that the tenth-century Saint Wolfgang of Regensburg sat on the stone to contemplate where to build a new church. Because place, the Falkenstein, and was certainly used for fertility rites. The Catholic Church altered the story of the rock, though, and tells that the tenth-century Saint Wolfgang of Regensburg sat on the stone to contemplate where to build a new church. Because of his holiness, the stone became soft and adopted the shape of the saint's buttocks. The wayside shrine tells this tale. Figure 3 also shows the author's daughter sliding down the stone to illustrate it's ancient usage. Utmost care was taken, however, not to invoke any fertility magic in this teaching moment.

Gifts of Magic

St. Margaret did not slip and slide down the stone by accident. She held a fertility ritual. And the little herder boy saw her doing that, saw the saint doing something he knew

would not be condoned by his master, the herder. That's why the boy says that the herder needs to know. But why is he so obsessed with having a beautiful lady up there in the remoteness of the high pastures (see Figure 4 on page 83 for an example) in the first place?

Because it was taboo for unmarried women to work there in medieval times, and it was still punishable by law in Tyrol in the 1960s (Haid, 2002). Herding sheep was a male domain, and a woman up there with a lonely man, so far from orderly village life where people pried into each other's affairs left and right, could only mean one thing: sinful, lusty behavior. When the little herder boy sees a woman in this male realm, practicing old, pagan ways of worship, which reveals her naked buttocks—that can only upset him. And so he cries out that he has to tell on her.

But the Goddess sees an opportunity, a glimmer of hope that the child may come back to her and the old ways. For he is a little boy and possibly gullible. So she promises him a gift. And when he shows no interest, but insists on telling the herder, she offers him another gift, and another one. Five in total. But the boy is relentless in his wish to tell the herder, and the gifts are all meaningless to him.

If we look at the gifts more closely, that is surprising, actually. A shirt that gets whiter the more often it is washed? Sheep that can be sheared three times a year? And cows that can be milked three times a day? That is impossible! Why, it is impossible, unless you know magic.

Consider the folk ballad "Scarborough Fair" for a moment. Throughout the song, a person—either a man alone or a man first and a woman later—asks the listener to tell a person to perform some magical act, like sewing a shirt without seams and needlework, to wash it in a dry well, to buy an acre of land between the water and the beach, to plow it with a ram's horn, and so on. At one of the eisteddfods during the 2016 East Coast Gathering of the Order of Bards, Ovates and Druids, David Smith (Damh the Bard), the order's Pendragon, explained one possible meaning of this ballad. It may be about a man of the Fae, the original faeries, who dwells at the Scarborough fairground and who loves a human lady. But he can only be with her if she proves that she knows magic. She has to verify her skills by performing these impossible tasks, which she can do only with magic.

We have a similar concept here. The magic is agricultural and pastoral, in the sense that the gifts offered by the Goddess are quite impossible in the apparent world, but

would be very beneficial and profitable to have. If the herder boy stayed with the Goddess, she lets him know, he would not have to worry about anything ever again. He would be well dressed and rich.

But, obviously, the boy is not interested. Even after the Goddess buries him neck deep in the ground, and he briefly gives in to her wish not to tell his master, he turns against her as soon as he is freed. That's when the Goddess sees no other way than burying him for good.

Why, you may ask, why is the little boy so determined to tell on her, to tell his master of the broken taboo, of the forbidden worship in the old style, and of the naked buttocks? Why does he refuse the gifts, and why doesn't he grant the Goddess's wish even after a threat to his life?

A Historical Perspective

Let's take a break here for a moment from analyzing the song and ask ourselves what the general meaning behind this story could be. Let's explore the history of the ballad for a few moments, which will help us better understand the boy's motives and next section of the song.

Based on the lyrics and the melody, the song was probably composed sometime between 650 and 750 CE (Caminada, 1961). Unlike so many songs and stories from that era, this ballad is not an ancient, pre-Christian song penned on parchment by some medieval monk to preserve it. It was a new song back then, and the main character was just disguised as a saint. That was the proper way to make sure an old song could be sung, and survive, despite Catholic Church dogma. This and the mention of churches and bells in the end—which most probably was a later addition—made the song less dangerous to sing (Haid, 2002).

When we look at the first part of the ballad, it clearly speaks of the Goddess and her magic. But we hear already that this magic is not appreciated anymore by the common folk, represented by the master herder and the boy. That is the first indicator that the song was composed at a time when the old faith had been replaced by the new one. The second part, where we learn what happens when the old faith is lost, can only be interpreted as a lament for the old faith vanishing. This can only mean that the ballad was composed during this time of change, or shortly after, but definitely

<u>Figure 4:</u>
Pasture. Photo by author.

not before. However, while it is therefore not ancient and hence not of Celtic origin, it tells us much about what the people creating this song thought, and how they were still immersed in these old, pagan traditions.

Even though we can establish that the ballad comes from a time when Christianity had already spread throughout the land, we must not think that this new faith was fully accepted everywhere. On the contrary, Christianity was still fighting hard to be accepted or even to survive. As in any society to this day, there must have been gullible people and early adopters who embraced the new religion right away. Some of the intellectual establishment may have been intrigued by early science, and then convinced at least some of the nobility to convert to the new faith. That process took centuries. Recall that the Church felt the need for such a radical scheme as the Inquisition to fortify their position some 500 years after the ballad was written.

And there must have been, then as now, those who were wary of anything new, who held on to the older traditions and saw these teachings from the Near East via Rome as a threat to their lives. It is easy to imagine that these folk were most numerous in rural areas, especially in the remote valleys in the Alps, not only because of the geographic distance to the urban centers, but also because it is farmers we are talking about. Ever since Neolithic times, when farming replaced hunting and gathering, certain ways of worship, especially of the Earth Mother, guaranteed a good harvest and survival during the harsh winter months. Pagan ritual developed over tens of thousands of years to help people endure, year after year. If a cobbler, merchant, or noble in the city converted to the new faith and it turned out that this was a bad choice because it offended "the land," their actions wouldn't have affected their own livelihood or that of others in the city that much. But here we are considering the providers of crops, of food. What if following the liturgy of the new faith didn't yield the same amounts of corn, vegetables, fruit, and meat? Or none at all? If your job were to supply your community with basic food resources, would you be willing to risk giving up what had worked for generations and try something new, without evidence that it would yield any success?

When looking at this time of change, it is not surprising that we still find sacred paintings in remote Alpine churches, with the three saints bearing all their pagan symbols, sometimes even their original names. It shouldn't strike us as odd, either, that the bishop of Brixen in Tyrol had to escort the feared medieval inquisitor Heinrich Institoris out of the area when he visited the diocese, a center of the Goddess cult at that time, and wanted to start the first witch court there in 1485. The bishop seemed to have been very aware of how his flock would feel about some outsider interfering with their traditions and was rightfully afraid that the angry mob would lynch the inquisitor right then and there (Kutter, 2003).

When Goddesses Leave

In the next segment of the song of Sontga Margriata, we can easily see that the composers must have been traditionalists, what their fears were, and how they eternalized the message of doom caused by neglect of the old faith—all that in an innocent ballad sung during work in the fields.

To recap what has happened so far, we learned that there was a woman on the high Alpine pasture, although that was taboo. What's more, that woman, who is really the

Goddess, engages in a pagan ritual, which a young herder boy observes by chance. Indoctrinated by the new faith, the naive boy insists on telling on her, despite being offered magical gifts. He refuses even when she threatens to kill him.

We never learn why the Goddess feels the need to leave, for the herder boy is dead, and the song doesn't say that his master actually learned of her presence or her pagan activities. We can only conclude from her reaction that she must have felt that if neither gifts nor threats to life and limb can bring the people back to her, all she can do is to concede to the new faith and leave the field to its followers.

And leaving is what she does. However, she knows that her absence will cause the land to become barren, for she is the land. Thus, the cows' milk dries up and so does the well. And the pasture and the grass on it withers, as she foresees.

Clearly, these are the fears of a rural population who see changing to the new faith as a risk not worth taking. Not only will the abundance—the magical gifts—given to them by the land be a thing of the past, they are even predicting that the land will waste away. Even thick iron bells, wrought in the heat of the smith's fire, fall apart when she passes by.

There is Always Hope

But there is a light at the end of the tunnel. The Goddess does not leave without sparking a glimmer of hope in her beloved children. Although she concedes to the Christian god insofar as she claims that only he will know when, she does not rule out returning entirely.

This old song from the ancient Celtic lands has made us understand that more than 1,200 years ago, people were already concerned that breaking with tradition could mean doom and decay. Today, as Druids, we have the most delicate challenge, expressed in the triad at the beginning, to uphold these traditions while, at the same time, listening to the voice of tomorrow. It is our duty to progress as much as it is our duty to conserve, and we can do so only by searching for this fine line, no thicker than a hair, and, once found, walking along it. However, learning these rather peripheral pieces of tradition equips Druids with the necessary wisdom and tools to tread this narrow path.

References

Brunner, C. (2015). *Mountain magic: Celtic shamanism in the Austrian Alps*. Raleigh: Lulu.

Caminada, C. (1961). *Die verzauberten Täler: Die urgeschichtlichen Kulte und Bräuche im alten Rätien*. Freiburg: Verlag Olten.

Göttner-Abendroth, H. (2005). *Frau Holle—Das Feenvolk der Dolomiten: Die großen Göttinnenmythen Mitteleuropas und der Alpen, neu erzählt*. Königstein: Ulrike Helmer Verlag.

Haid, H. (2002). *Mythos und Kult in den Alpen. Rosenheim*: Rosenheimer Verlag.

Kutter, E. (2003). *Der Kult der Drei Jungfrauen: Eine Kraftquelle Weiblicher Spiritualität Neu Entdeckt*. Norderstedt: Books on Demand GmbH.

Resch-Rauter, I. (1992). *Unser Keltisches Erbe: Flurnamen, Sagen, Märchen und Brauchtum als Brücken in die Vergangenheit*. Vienna: Eigenverlag.

Wolff, K.-F. (1913). *Dolomitensagen: Sagen und Überlieferungen, Märchen und Erzählungen der ladinischen und deutschen Dolomitenbewohner. Mit zwei Exkursen Berner Klause und Gardasee*. Bozen: Verlagsanstalt Athesia.

Crafting a Wizard's Staff

By Rick Derks

Rick Derks (Skyllaros) holds the second degree in the AODA and the Ovate grade in OBOD. He considers himself a Hedge Druid, whose own Druidry is heavily influenced by the arts of sorcery and hermetics. He is a priest of Cernunnos and Hekate, and the editor of the devotional anthology Hoofprints in the Wildwood. *He writes online at his blog, Feral Druidry (*https://bloodandbone.wordpress.com/*).*

I have always thought of Druidry as a sort of nature wizardry. When you conjure the image of the wizard, of course, one of the first things that comes to mind is the wizard's staff. The notion is not as preposterous as it seems, as the staff can be an indispensable tool for the Druid mage. A staff can serve multiple functions. It is perfect to use on nature walks as a walking staff. Additionally, I find that it can serve as an instrument of one's spiritual authority when dealing with spirits. Traditionally it can be used to help connect yourself to the heavens and the depths and to transmit your prayers and invocations to the denizens of those realms. With time and use it can become your magical counterpart, a living, breathing entity in its own right. The magical tool can take on much of your essence. The process begins when you begin to fashion it, imparting your own energy into its creation. With frequent use, it will absorb more of your essence and the energy of your ritual or working each time, becoming effectively consecrated through use. If you use it long term, you will have a powerful tool and companion. Really, no self-respecting wizard should be without a staff.

The staff can take many forms and be as ornate or nondescript as you wish. You can craft it yourself from scratch or buy a suitable staff and embellish it to your taste. It may take you some time to find the right staff or material to craft one. You will find that your need changes over time, and what works at one time in your life may no longer serve a purpose later. Thus not only may your staff change perhaps many times

over your magical career, but it may take time to find the right one. Once you do, there is a lot of personalization to be done even if you buy a ready-made staff.

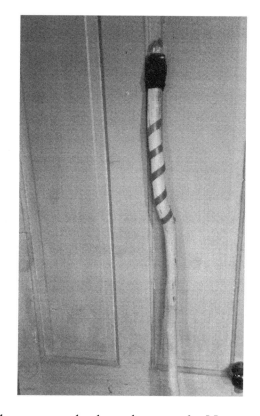

For example, I have two staffs, one I made myself and one I bought and embellished. My first staff (which I still use often) I bought at a renaissance faire, which is an ideal place to find craftsmen who make quality staffs, even though I was not looking for one at the time. While I would have preferred oak, a fine maple staff called out to me, and I knew once I grabbed it that it was coming home with me. I've embellished it by attaching a large quartz crystal that I've had since I was a child to the top with epoxy glue. I then tightly wrapped the rough seam between the rock and the wood with a high-quality black leather strap, which you can find at any craft store, secured with a well-placed screw. I then used my Dremel tool to engrave both an Awen and a Norse Helm of Awe on either side of the top. Any symbols you like can be placed on it. I've heard of some engraving the four directional animals (hawk, stag, salmon, bear), as well as Ogham runes that relate to your work. It can also be adorned with feathers, bones, and rocks to further personalize it and tie it to your familiar and guardian spirits.

My second staff I created myself, though I looked for about three years for the materials before I finally found them. I happened to find just the right branch on display in the local antique shop, which lent it a rustic ambiance. I negotiated for and purchased the display branch, much to the owner's curiosity. Ideally you would find a branch in the wild, choosing one that called out to you. If you do so, however, be careful that it is not weathered or rotten. Often what looks suitable on the outside may turn out to be rotten once you begin working on it. At home I began to whittle away the bark to reveal the natural wood underneath. The shape of the tines lent themselves naturally to making a forked staff, taking inspiration from the stang of Traditional Witchcraft. Then I began to sand it, using sandpaper, until the rough-hewn wood gave way to

a smooth and symmetrical stave. Again, you could choose to decorate it and woodburn it at that point, but I chose not to, leaving it unadorned. I placed a nail in the crook of the fork, which can be used to hang talismans or materials (bones, feathers, etc.) that are in agreement with my work and can be changed as necessary. It can even hold a lantern in a pinch. To seal it I used linseed oil, which is a natural and traditional oil. It seals the wood against water and the oils in your own hands, while allowing the wood to breathe and giving it a nice rich stain. Multiple coats may be necessary, and it takes several days to dry completely.

Both of my staffs hold different significance for me. My crystal-topped staff I tend to use for most of my daily workings, and in particular it seems oriented to the solar current. My forked staff is more suited to telluric and chthonic workings, and I use it whenever dealing with the Horned God, doing ancestral work, or working with telluric powers.

Following the crafting, you may wish to imbue your staff with a spirit to work with. To do this, take it to a sacred place. Most druidically inclined folk know of such a place. Even your own yard may suffice. I would begin by quietly entering the area and stating your intentions to the local spirits and asking permission to work there. If you feel you have received an affirmative, create sacred space by doing the Sphere of Protection. This will not only create a safe working area but act as a filter to invite spirits who are agreeable and in harmony with Druidic work. If you wish to work with a particular type of spirit (elemental, solar, telluric), you can state that during the calling portion of the rite that works with that direction.

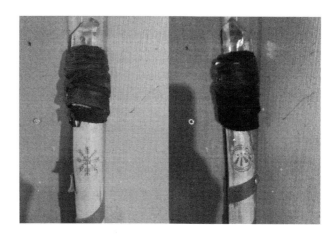

Then leave offerings of grain, incense, and pure water while reciting your wish that a suitable spirit who wishes to work with you enter the staff. This can either be a partner who acts as a familiar in your work or a tutelary spirit to guide you. Leave the staff there overnight and retrieve it the next day. It should have a numinous quality. Those adept at divination (a pendulum is ideal for this) can use their arts to divine the presence and nature of the spirit. Over time it will make itself known to you as you work with it. I often leave my own staff out on full moons to absorb the lunar energy and feed it. Don't be surprised if someday the spirit leaves the wood when its work with you is finished. A staff may end up having several occupants in its lifetime. Again, however, this step is optional for those uncomfortable with this type of work.

When used in your rites, the staff will become an extension of you, as natural as your own limbs. For instance, I often hold my crystal-tipped staff when I call the six directions while doing the SOP. During the invoking stage, I see the color of the element filling myself and the crystal glowing with it. While I personally use a knife or wand in my other hand to draw the symbols for the elements, for spirit above and below I find the staff is most useful to draw the symbols and connect to them. It serves as its own axis that lends itself well to this work (another symbol the staff can represent is the tree of life).

An important caveat here, though, is that the staff should always be a supplement to your work, not a crutch. Don't let yourself fall into the trap of not being able to work

without it. A little tip, however—if you work with it often and have truly integrated its use into your work, you will find it is always present, even if not physically, and you can call on its otherworldly counterpart to be with you. Thus you will never truly be without it.

If approached with sincerity, the work of finding, crafting, and magically attuning yourself to a staff will change you as much as you change the material composition of the tool.

Stones, Circles, and Spirals: Seeking, Developing, and Tending Sacred Sites in North America

By Dana O'Driscoll

Dana O'Driscoll is the Chief Editor of Trilithon: The Journal of the Ancient Order of America, *a Druid Adept in the AODA, and serves as the Archdruid of Water. She also is Druid grade graduate in the Order of Bards, Ovates, and Druids, a member of the Druidical Order of Golden Dawn, and a traditional western herbalist. Her AODA Druid Adept project explored the connection between druidry and sustainability and how to use permaculture design principles and community building to engage in druidic practice. By day, she is a writing professor and learning researcher; by night, an organic gardener, natural builder, mushroom forager, and whimsical artist. Dana is typically covered with paint, dirt, or both, and loves to sneak into the forest to play her panflute when other people aren't looking. Dana's writings can be found on the web at druidgarden.wordpress.com.*

One of the most quintessential images of druidry is a group of white-robed druids performing ritual in an ancient stone circle—a sacred site—as the sun rises over the hills. Of course, this image was constructed, in part, from Revival druidry's roots in the United Kingdom with its abundant ancient sacred sites and white-robed druids. Regardless, this image has shaped modern ideas of what druids do, what they look like, and where they seek spiritual connection. In the UK, where stones circles and other sacred sites are plentiful, visiting such sites is woven into the tradition of Druidry. But in an American context, the idea of what a sacred site is and what can be done at sacred sites is much more complex. The idea of a sacred site raises a number of questions: What is a sacred site here in the USA? How can we work with the idea of a sacred site, while avoiding much of the cultural appropriation and other complications? Where can we

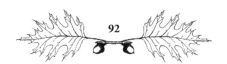

seek these sites? How might we create them? In this article, I'll explore the concept of a sacred site in the American Druid context. I'll provide suggestions that anyone, regardless of their living circumstances, can enact to create sacred spaces upon our great mother earth. So come with me as we begin this journey into sacred spaces and places.

Defining "Sacred"

The term "sacred" implies a connection to the divine, something set apart from the everyday experience where one can find communion and spiritual connection. A sacred site, then, is some kind of consecrated or holy space, a place set aside for spiritual contemplation or religious observance. When most think about the classic definition of a "sacred site," especially in the context of modern Druidry, we often think about ancient sites. These ancient sites might be natural wonders, or possibly built or adapted by humans, that have been sites of ceremony and reverence for years. These locations fill us with wonder and awe, encouraging stillness and providing one with a spiritual or magical experience. This isn't the only kind of sacred site, as we'll explore in this article, but I think it's currently the most prevalent in our minds. Some Druids would say that all spaces are sacred, and I'll not disagree. However, at the same time, there's quite a difference between a busy parking lot and a secluded stone circle set upon a hillside overlooking a river.

Challenges with Sacred Sites in North America

When we think about the "ancient site" definition of sacred sites applied to the North American context, we immediately encounter several serious challenges:

Native American Sacred Sites, Desecration, and Cultural Appropriation. Most ancient sacred sites in the Americas are Native American in origin. Because most of us do not carry the blood of the native peoples, nor live within their communities, the issue of cultural appropriation is a serious one. Even for those of us who carry a small amount of Native American blood, but have grown up divorced from native culture (like myself), the idea of working with Native American sacred sites is extraordinarily uncomfortable. Given with the long history of abuse, eradication, and genocide between the United States and Canadian governments and the native peoples, appropriating any other culture's site for spiritual use is, in nearly all cases, unethical.

The longstanding destruction of native sacred sites is also a noted concern. For example, in the Great Lakes region in the USA, I've visited several Native American

"sacred sites" that have suffered substantial abuses--White Rock, located about 30 miles north of Port Huron, MI on the coast of Lake Huron, Inscription Rock, located on Kelly's Island in Lake Erie, and the Petroglyphs, located in the "thumb" region of South East Michigan. White Rock in particular is worth noting, because it was an extremely sacred rock—set out into Lake Huron by a few hundred yards. Despite how sacred it was to the native peoples, it was desecrated repeatedly through the centuries, the most recent being that it was used as a bombing target by the US government during WWII. Likewise, Inscription Rock, which once featured various pictures inscribed into limestone, was "re-inscribed" by tourists for over a century and a half and continues to be to this day. In both cases, what was once a sacred site of the native peoples of these lands has been degraded by those who came after.

Given this long history of abuse and appropriation, the energies of these sites is generally not conducive to spiritual work--what I've done at both of these sites, when visiting, is to offer apology and ask if there is any work I can do to offer healing and recompense. If I receive an affirmative to healing work while at the site, a seasonal AODA ritual (from the *AODA Grove Handbook*) or a simple Sphere of Protection working is very appropriate. For these kinds of sites, healing or apology is likely the only appropriate work you can do.

Sacred Sites and Tourist Attractions. Many of the most amazing sites of natural wonder and beauty in the Americas have their own kind of sacredness. Unfortunately, these kinds of sacred sites also hold something else—truckloads of tourists. I'll note the difference here between secular tourism to that of a pilgrimage or sacred journey, such as the one discussed in Chaucer's *Canterbury Tales*, where pilgrims are traveling and visiting for a spiritual purpose. Tourist energy is not conducive to the sacred, and little meaningful spiritual work can usually be done in such places. Tourists are often visiting to photograph selfies, to tromp about, and to experience a canned and predigested experience on the most superficial level. Tourism makes these major sites of natural beauty inaccessible for any kind of spiritual or magical work. (The one exception is to go to these sites when tourists *aren't* milling about—in bad weather, storms, etc.)

Land and Site "Management" practices. The other issue at most well-known "sacred sites" in the USA is that the land management practices that govern potential sacred sites are not conducive to spiritual work of any kind, nor can an individual or small group typically gain privacy at any site. A few years ago in California, a group of Native

Americans encountered just such a problem. They had been lighting a sacred fire on a sacred mountain for as long as their history went back. The chief of this group was arrested because they refused to follow US Park Service law, which reflected a recent ruling disallowing fires in that spot regardless of the circumstances. The National Park Service had no sympathy or religious tolerance for the Native Americans; this kind of thing happens all the time, most of it less public than this particular story. Because earth-based spiritual traditions of all kinds are not given equal treatment and respect, and most of us are still in the closet, so to speak, it becomes even more difficult to have access to a public sacred site for the purposes of a private ritual.

This leaves those of us in the US interested in working with sacred sites in a bit of a conundrum—how do we meaningfully and respectfully work with sacred sites, if at all? How can we avoid cultural appropriation, tourist traps, and find some privacy in which to work? For this, I'd like to propose two ideas that we'll explore through the rest of this article: seeking unmarked and hidden sacred sites and creating new sacred sites over time.

Seeking Secluded Sacred Sites

Are there sacred sites that don't involve direct human interaction or human tending that we can also work with? Are there secret places of wonder and magic worked by other beings? Would they welcome us there even if we were able to find them? Sometimes, the answer is yes. I have found that if you go out into the world with an open mind, you'll be surprised by how many amazing, sacred places you can find. When you come across a naturally occurring sacred site or a site that someone has created some time before, one that isn't on the maps, I've found it's best to let your intuition lead the way. You can spend time reading the messages of the plant, animal, and stone kingdoms to know if you are welcome. It might be that you have to establish a relationship over time with a site before the spirits of that site will give you access--listen and be mindful of what you hear.

Intentional Sacred Sites

Perhaps someone else created a sacred site some time ago, and you happen upon it and have a magical experience. Such an experience has happened to me numerous times, each an unexpected delight. A few summers ago while I was still living in Michigan, a small group of friends and I—all Druids—went into a state park that had been largely closed down and was no longer maintained. The pathways were

covered in branches and trees, the roads were washed out, and it was quite a challenge to even to get to where we were going. And it was one of the most sacred places I had visited in Michigan, precisely because it had been left alone. Toward the end of our 5-hour hike, we came across a small stone circle just to the left of the path we were walking, with larger stones for the north and south, and covered with moss. Several small trees, at least 15-25 years old, were growing up through the center of the circle. We felt welcome, having been lead by the forest and the winding paths to this place. Entering the circle in reverence and respect, we sat there for some time, feeling the sacred energies of that place. Nobody had been by for a long time, and it was only because we asked to enter that we were able to experience this sacred place and honor it. In this example, the sacred site was created by someone else, a long time ago, and left for us to find and enjoy.

Natural Sacred Sites

A second kind of sacred site—naturally occurring places of power—may be tucked away in many forests, fields, streams, and other natural areas. One such place of sacred power that I visit often is a six-acre old growth Eastern Hemlock grove in South-Western Pennsylvania, in a state park called Laurel Hill. Old growth groves of any kind are extraordinarily rare in a state with such a longstanding timber industry, so this is a real gem. According to the story of this site, the loggers were approaching it about 100 years ago, and for reasons nobody knows, they turned back, and that particular tiny piece of land was spared. The path takes about 15 minutes to walk from the road, and as soon as you enter the grove, you know. The hemlocks literally tower above you (the tallest trees on this side of the USA), and there is a stillness and peacefulness not present in any other forest I have ever visited. I've taken others to this place, and it's always been interesting to watch people first enter—as soon as they walk up to the first large hemlock everyone goes quiet, and feels the presence and majesty of those trees. Even those who aren't attuned call it a "sanctuary of trees." This is a welcoming and incredible place to be, and I have returned to it many times. And so, these naturally occurring sacred places are those that we find—often when we least expect it!

Sacred Sites Where You Are Unwelcome

Not all natural places of power are welcoming to visitors, however. When I visited Kelly's Island in Lake Erie for a family vacation a few years ago, I saw that now all naturally sacred sites welcome visitors. You can use your intuitive senses to quickly sense whether you are welcome to visit a natural place—as well as your eyes. In this

particular forest, I was amazed by how unwelcome humans were. I had never seen so much poison ivy in such a small area—all of the forests were protected by the beautiful poison ivy vine, covering the trees, matting the ground, going right up to the edge of any path. I could sense the tranquility and sacredness of those forests behind the ivy line: the old-growth cottonwoods and maples, the mayflies darting about. However, the poison ivy sent a very clear message to anyone able to read the language of the plants—these forests are to be left alone. Knowing a bit about the history of that island helps understand the protectiveness of the ivy and spirits there. This beautiful island had a long history of industrialization and abuse, where glacial grooves were destroyed by stone quarries and pristine forests destroyed through logging...and now, the ritzy houses and expensive yachts have mostly moved in (yet we did find a nice state campground and hiking trails!) No wonder what remains of this unique ecosystem is so fiercely guarded by poison ivy!

Revered Sites and Springs

One final kind of sacred site exists—these are sites frequently visited or revered, but not viewed as overly sacred in a religious sense. I recently discovered this fourth kind of sacred site by accident—I had moved back to my beloved Appalachian mountains in Pennsylvania and noticed a small roadside spring along a heavily-forested and mountainous area. I stopped at the spring, called "Heffley Spring," and met a few travelers there, all of whom spoke quite highly of the spring and its ability to never run dry, the purity of the water, and the high quality and taste. These visitors had been coming to the spring for years, and using this spring as their sole source of drinking water. I filled my bottle and drank with delight. Afterward, I did some research on the spring and discovered a number of different key things: my family, including grandparents, had been visiting the spring for generations. Once, I even saw a woman quietly dip her rosary in the spring flow and then put it back into her pocket. I realized that this spring was a sacred site—one that people travel to often, one that is respected and revered, one that is maintained, but without any overt spiritual connection. I have since made visiting this spring and working with its water a regular part of my own spiritual work.

Setting up Sacred Sites for the Druid Tradition

I think one of the challenges that we face in the Americas is that we assume a sacred site should already be there, set up by others, and ready for our use. Revival Druidry is a few centuries old, and while the British druids have done an amazing job in reclaiming sites connected with the ancient sites like Tara, Glastonbury, and Stonehenge, we have

few to no such sites in the Americas that are overtly "Druid" in nature. This brings me to another key point: that we gain much by establishing our own sacred sites.

Why is a site sacred to begin with? To go back to my earlier definition, it's sacred because someone—or a group of someones—recognized its significance, energetically and/or naturally, and made it a point to visit it, tend it, and work various kinds of ceremony there. Over a period of time and with appropriate practices, we can establish these same sacred spaces for our own tradition.

One of the key reasons for doing so, in this time, is that we can set up spaces that honor the land and that work to energetically counter much of the environmental desecration and destruction locally. The disruption of the telluric pathways from the relentless pursuit of fossil fuels, the harm to the planet from industrialized farming and pesticide use, and the continued logging and pillaging of earth's resources are just a few reasons that the work of building sacred sites, especially today, is so critical. The more of us who spend time intentionally honoring the land with dedicated spaces and work, the more healing we can bring to our lands and the more we are able to promote a counter-narrative to the destruction—that of cultivating a sacred relationship with the land.

I know we can work to establish sacred spaces of our own because I've done this myself through the work on my own land as well as in the wild places and desecrated places I frequently visit. When I arrived at my homestead in Michigan years ago, the land was energetically drained, the spirits were angry from the mistreatment of the previous owners (pollution, garbage, careless cutting of trees, spraying, etc.). It took me a long time to shift those energies. But, slowly, a group of us worked to heal the land, to create a sacred space there. We set up a stone circle and began doing regular ceremonies. Over the period of five years, the energies of the land dramatically shifted in a positive direction—I had multiple people tell me that they didn't even feel they were still in Michigan when they crossed onto that sacred land. Like many such sites, the site is in the process of shifting, and that shift will take much more time to complete. So with this story in mind, let's look at some specific practices you can do to establish sacred spaces both on the inner and outer planes of existence.

Finding the Right Spot

Part of the challenge in establishing a sacred site is letting the universe/gods/spirits (however you conceive of them) lead you to where you are to work. This might be a

piece of land that you own (like my above example), a place you've found, or a place that you've been drawn to. Much of this work is intuitive, at work in the mind's eye and in the heart. Trust your feelings to lead you to the right place and open yourself to what unfolds.

One way to establish sacred sites is by directly countering recent desecration of the land. This is work that I've been doing for many years, even intuitively before I officially took up the Druid path. Western Pennsylvania is an area with so many environmental challenges: fracking, strip mining and mountaintop removal, extensive logging, acid mine runoff, boney dumps (sites for mine refuse), and more. I've taken to using many of the techniques explored in this article to help energetically heal those sites. It's pretty amazing what a single standing stone, stone cairn, or small shrine that you visit regularly can do. The logged land more quickly rebounds, the polluted stream feels more at peace, even the energies around the fracking well improve. I will say that this can be difficult work, and you should only take it on if you feel strongly led to do so. Regular working of the Sphere of Protection and making sure you aren't draining yourself is an important part.

Spiritual and Energetic Practices in Establishing Sacred Sites

My experience has taught me that the most important work you do to establish a sacred site comes long before you set the first stone or plant the first seed. This is the work of healing on many dimensions beyond the material plane. It is, then, to these practices that we first turn—and the greatest blessing is that many of the core practices in AODA are the tools that help us begin our work.

Listen and observe openly before you act. In the AODA, all of our members are asked to go out and directly observe nature, spending time in stillness and focus. This is extremely useful for the establishment and working of any sacred site. This practice, combined with the quietude and deep listening skills that one gains through discursive meditation, are the first two tools to help you listen and observe openly before action.

Thus, if you want to establish any kind of sacred site, you should first ask the spirits of the land about the nature of the potential site and heed their responses. Combine this listening with your own observation and interaction of the site over a period of time. This listening and observation process can take quite a bit of time, so be patient and understand that it's all part of the process. It might be that the spirits of the land

are testing you—and your patience—so keep at it until you are firm in your answer. You'll be glad you've done this work—the spirits of the land will guide you in the work of establishing your site and can give you vision about how to go about creating it. This listening, then, can help you create a space for use beyond just the human realm. Divination tools can be particularly useful here to help confirm what you are sensing or to open up other avenues of communication with the spirits of that land.

For example, in establishing my stone circle at my homestead in Michigan, I had several potential locations. I spent a period of weeks in meditation at each of the potential sites, visualizing the circle I had hoped to create, listening, sending questions, and the spirits of the land led me firmly in one direction over another—years later, I would realize how suitable this spot was for a number of reasons that were not revealed to me immediately. Further, that experience helped establish a collaborative, positive relationship with the spirits there so the work of building a sacred site could continue.

Use Small, Slow Actions. To borrow a principle from permaculture design, you can't establish a sacred space overnight. The sites in the UK of relevance to Druids are thousands of years old. Recognize that sacred spaces and shifting energies take a lot of time. I have found that daily work, such as the AODA's Sphere of Protection ritual (SOP), helps maintain and build energies slowly over time (see next section). It is with this regular ritual work, and regular observation, that you can establish energetic connections and frameworks. This principle also suggests that physically building a site itself—like a stone circle—may also take a good deal of time.

Shifting Energies and Regular rituals. An extensive amount of energetic work may be required when establishing a new sacred site. Just like people, spaces over time can build up various kinds of astral and etheric crud. We can help clear that through energetic and ritual work—and the AODA's practices are extremely well suited to such work. Energetic work can obviously take many different forms, although AODA gives us a number of core practices that do this work exceedingly well. Doing a Sphere of Protection ritual in a sacred site can really address any lingering problematic energies and bring in positive energies. If this spot is easily accessible, go out there as often as you can and do the SOP—the SOP's summoning and banishing of the elemental energies can cut through a lot of energetic grim, and the connecting to the three currents can help bless and consecrate the spot over time. You might think about

this like a small drip in a glass—each day, the drip accumulates, and pretty soon, the glass is full!

In addition, regular group rituals and/or solo rituals during Druid holidays or other fortuitous times can help with the energetics of the space. Because the four core AODA seasonal celebrations found in the *Druid Grove Handbook* strongly incorporate elements of healing and blessing, they are extremely appropriate for this kind of work. Specifically, our core rituals draw the solar current down into unity with the telluric currents, bringing healing and light. These rituals draw upon much more ancient understandings of the relationships between the currents of the heavens and those of the earth—and these rituals are extremely effective for this work. Other kinds of rituals honoring the spirits of the land and recognizing the sacredness of the place over time are also appropriate.

An added benefit one gets from performing regular ritual or spiritual activities in a single space is what hermetic magicians know as "tracts in space" (as described in the *Cosmic Doctrine* by Dion Fortune (2000.)). Regular work leads to an easier time summoning and working energies in that particular spot. This is part of why certain sacred sites pack so much of a punch, so to speak—a particular set of energies has been being worked there for a very long time, and the energetics are already established. This makes any regular working there go smoothly. If enough time passes, this principle explains why certain places, when you enter, just feel holy.

Watch it evolve. The other thing that I've found is that once you've set your intentions, established the initial space, and begun doing the regular energetic work, the space will evolve—both physically and energetically. Physically, you might see new plants growing, trees appear that weren't there before (or that you couldn't see), and other kinds of magical occurrences take place. After I had established my homestead land as a sacred space, I began finding trees that I could swear hadn't been there when I moved in. These included several hawthorns on the tree line behind the sacred grove, a spiral willow on small island in the middle of the pond, and a foxglove flower growing behind the sacred circle. Keep a record of what is happening—you will be amazed by the changes over time. Energetically, you may also sense, or see, changes (depending on your own personal gifts that go beyond the five senses). As I was working to establish my homestead as sacred land, I worked to first create the rainbow sphere of light around the land. Imagine my surprise when, about three years after doing the

SOP daily around myself and the land, the sphere grew vines, then bees and butterflies came, and then great big thorns emerged from the vines—all on the energetic realms, but also clear in my mind's eye.

Healing and energetics. A sacred site has tremendous potential to heal the land, not only in the immediate vicinity but in the surrounding landscape. Doing energetic work with this principle in mind, and designing a sacred space with this principle in mind, can be a useful activity. This principle is reflected in the old Wassail traditions—in a Wassail, a single tree is chosen to represent the whole orchard, and all wassail blessing activities are done with that one tree (see Maxine Rogers' article in this issue for more on wassail traditions). A similar event occurred with the ancient Incan temples - the temple was the site of ceremony, and physical lines on the landscape radiated that energy outward (see *Lines Upon the Landscape* by Pennick and Deverux for more information on this and other such ancient practices). This is all to say that when you are thinking about what long-term energetic effect your sacred site can have, keep this in mind. This particular idea is very useful if you are living in a region that has many sites under duress (like I am at present). Working to turn one such site under duress (or in the process of recovery) into a sacred site and doing long-term healing and ritual work there can radiate that work out to many others. Again, this requires advanced understanding of our AODA rituals and methods, but it certainly can be done successfully.

Developing Outdoor Sacred Spaces on the Physical Realm

Now that we have some sense of the energetics of setting up a sacred space and the magic that we can work there, let's talk about some physical actions in the world. Many sacred sites have physical markers that distinguish them from the surrounding landscape—this might be a circle of stones, a beautiful natural feature, a special garden, a sacred old tree, or so on. I have found that its useful to work energetically as well as on the material plane—and later in this article, we'll cover a number of specific kinds of sacred sites you can create. For now, start thinking about how you want to physically manifest your space.

Design from the patterns in nature. In permaculture design, one of the key principles is to mimic patterns found in nature in designing garden and outdoor spaces. I believe this principle is critical to creating outdoor sacred spaces—look around you, and when you are designing a sacred space, think about what inspires you. Is it the circle of the

sun or the moon? Is it the branching pattern on the veins in leaves or on the trees? The spiral pattern of a snail shell? The curve of a tulip or the flight path of a bird? These patterns found in nature can be your inspiration and your guide.

Source materials very carefully. I would suggest that you should try to acquire as many of your materials for your sacred space from the land around you. If you have buy materials, please source any materials you need that are not already present on the land very carefully. If you are creating a sacred space, it's really critical that you mindfully and substantially limit your purchasing (or better yet, keep it all free/found/reused, etc). Everything that is purchased, especially new, carries its own energy with it—the energy of the process of extracting natural resources, the energy of the factories where it was produced, the energy of the waste that was generated in its creation, the energy of the people who suffered to make it, and so on. Given the extremely high environmental and human cost of most items created in an industrialized system, you want to keep in mind where you source material. For the stone circle I created on my Michigan Homestead, I received a number of free trees to surround the circle from the Arbor Day Foundation and from a friend who had extra seedlings. The wood altars were already on the land as stumps lying in the brush, as were nearly all the stones for the circle itself—and the rest were gifts from neighbors and friends who would bring a stone to me when they visited. I did purchase some handmade plaster castings of the four druid animals for each quarter (hawk, stag, salmon, and bear) from an artist, and I felt good about that purchase as I was supporting someone in their bardic arts!

See your site as evolving. Your outdoor sacred space doesn't have to be "complete" at any one time—like our own druidic paths, the circle can grow and change. Recognize that some projects, especially those involving living things, work on their own time schedule and nothing can be done but let time pass while your trees grow, or your flowers take root, or the perfect standing stone finally comes into your life. These sites can grow organically in their own time, and in many cases, need to do so. And sometimes, materials you need for the site will come as the time is right.

Invite Others. A sacred space is all the more powerful if it's created with friends and fellow travelers on the path. In a number of specific projects I'll detail below, while I was often the primary initiator of the project, I have frequently invited others to plan and build. These spaces become a group effort, and I think the energies of the places reflect that positive interaction.

Let the Awen Flow. Creating sacred outdoor spaces is not just a physical or intellectual pursuit--you must also approach it intuitively and creatively. Figure out what you want to build, where you want to build it, and how you want to build it with both careful planning but also your spiritual senses and creative core. Listen to the land, to the wind in the trees, and you will know what you are to build and where.

Recognize sacred activity and energetically protect the space. Protect the sacredness of the space you are creating—if you are working on your own land, or if you are taking others to a sacred site on some other land, make sure they understand the rules for the sacred space (e.g. no consumption of alcohol in the space for non-ritual purposes, remaining quiet in the space, leaving an offering after use, no cigarette smoking, don't bring your cell phone into the sacred space, and so on. Since I hosted regular rituals and gatherings at my sacred site, both for Druids and for sustainability/permaculture-themed events, this particular issue was a critical one (and may not be as critical to you if your space is fully private/hidden/etc.).

You'll find that some well-placed signage also helps visitors and/or family respect the space. It doesn't have to be overly dramatic, but a small sign saying "Quiet Contemplation Garden" or some other low-key thing can help set the tone. On my sacred land in Michigan, I had all kinds of signs that helped set the mood, "Be mindful of the lessons of the bees" near my beehives, "Listen to the voices of the trees" along the path to the grove, "Dig deeply and discover the secrets of the soil" in the garden, and "The land speaks" when you first came onto the property. It may also be that there are certain kinds of people you simply don't want in that space, and that's ok too.

Creating Sacred Sites and Sacred Spaces

Now that we've covered some basic principles, let's look at a number of possibilities for creating large and small sacred sites: standing stones, stone circles, sacred gardens, and more!

Setting a Standing Stone

Perhaps the most quintessential thing you can do to help establish a sacred space is to set a standing stone. Standing stones are an ancient tradition; in the AODA's framework, it gives us a landscape feature that allows you to work with the three currents. The standing stone, placed 1/3 in the ground and 2/3rds out of it, is a welcome addition to a garden, sacred circle, or other landscape feature in need of a blessing or

energizing effect. What this stone does, essentially, is channel the light of heaven (the solar current) into the light of earth (the telluric). The telluric is in deep need of our help these days—all sorts of things are disrupting the flows of the telluric (fracking, oil pipelines, and mountaintop removal being the most recent of a long line of offenders). A simple standing stone does so much in the same way the ancient sun kings did for the lands they ruled: a well-placed standing stone can energetically help the healing process along. The standing stone should be a single solid piece of stone, preferably some derivative of quartz or sandstone. Something that will have a good chance of moving the energy flows through it.

Standing stones and other stone structures set by ancient peoples are more and more threatened with the modern era's flurry of activity. Watkins, in his classic *The Old Straight Track*, discusses a farmer who got the nickname "Rockbreaker" for taking the ancient stones set in the landscape, heating them up, and shattering them because he didn't like them in his fields. There are a lot less standing stones than there used to be, and I think it's a good practice to begin to set some more to aid in the disruption of the telluric current in today's age and bring the sacred energies back into the landscape.

The thing is—you will have to *find* this stone. It may take you a long time to find—but the search, and the patience, is worth it. Whatever you do, please don't go to the typical store and buy a standing stone—that's missing the whole point, and that stone is likely corrupted with the energies of industrialization, strip mining, or however else the stone was procured. You do not want to set that stone, coming out of a quarry and transported by fossil fuels, or gods know where else, into the ground. Finding the stone might mean that you can source this stone ethically from local source—and that is great! I have found that, often, it is the stone that finds you! Let the land know you are looking (it really helps to just ask, aloud, and set your intentions), and then when you're out and about, keep an eye out for the right stone. I've been in such a search for a few standing stones for about two years, and recently after doing some important energetic and initiatory work, all of the necessary stones came into my life! I don't think those stones wanted to be found until recently; I had actually walked past that exact spot where I found the stones several times since I began my search but saw them the last time I walked past. But for whatever reason known to the gods and spirits of the land, the time became right for placing the stones, so now they were found. This is to say that the timing of when you find your stone matters, and it may not always be on your own personal timeline!

The size of the stone is important only as it should be tall enough to be able to easily sink 1/3 in the ground and have the rest rising into the heavens. A few feet high is ideal, but the problem of whether or not the stone can be lifted and moved is also an important consideration. Most of my standing stones are much smaller. If you are working alone, as so many of us are, the lifting and moving of a large stone is no easy task. It so happens that one of the key stones that I found recently isn't movable just by me, but I've got a druid friend who wouldn't mind helping me carry a 100 lb stone 1/2 mile up the mountain for fun.

A Ritual for Blessing Your Standing Stone. You can use a number of frameworks for blessing and setting your standing stone. One of the methods that I've used is with a modification of the AODA Solitary Grove Opening. I begin the standard solitary opening and do the first part of the opening, purifying and consecrating the stone and the hole for the stone with the first part of the ritual. I then set the stone right before the Sphere of Protection (SOP). After the stone is set, then I perform the SOP calling in the elements around the stone, and connecting it firmly with the solar, telluric, and awakening the lunar within the stone. I do not close the ritual space, instead just circulating the sphere only on the inside of the stone, so that the stone is always in ceremony, doing its healing work. Other ideas for setting standing stones using druid magical practice can be found in *The Druid Magic Handbook* by John Michael Greer, our Grand Archdruid Emeritus.

Stone Circles

Perhaps the most iconic druidic symbol is the stone circle. Ancient peoples on the British Isles built massive stone structures; we also see other kinds of stone circles in the Americas. While these stone circles had various meanings and purposes, nearly all of them were ritualistic or sacred in origin. Although the ability to make a massive stone circle may be out of our reach, a single druid or a few druids still have many possibilities at their fingertips!

Small, portable circles. The most simple way to create a circle of stones, and a useful technique if you don't have the space for a permanent outdoor circle, is to have a set of small, portable stones—gathered from a nearby stream, ocean, lake, or other waterway. Keep the stones in a bag, and when you need them, set them up indoors or outdoors where you have need of such a circle. This was my very first circle, and it was portable and highly effective. I went with 16 stones in this

circle—eight for the quarters and cross quarters, and then eight to fill the spaces in between. I set them up anytime I wanted to do inner journeying, meditation, or other ritual work. The circle could be as large or as small as I needed it to be. It was more like a "transportable" sacred space, but worked exceedingly well (even for hotel rooms!)

The Permanent Stone Circle. Permanent stone circles can take on a variety of forms— they can be large or small. Do only what is in your physical capability to do. I have constructed several stone circles over the years—one on my Michigan property as described earlier and two in wild areas where I was led to create them. There are lots of methods—but the most simple is simply placing stones in a circle (if you want the circle perfectly circular, drive a stake into the center and use a rope like a compass to mark the edge).

More elaborate methods include setting standing stones at the four quarters (or stone cairns, see below), making sure they align with the solstice and equinox sunrises, and setting them at the appropriate time each year (see, again, John Michael Greer's *The Druid Magic Handbook* for more information on appropriate timing and setting of stones). What I mean by this is that you might take a year to set your stones, setting each of the major stones at the cardinal direction where it is indicated—the spring equinox in the east, Beltane in the south-east, the Summer Solstice in the south, and so on). Each circle has its own evolution process!

I'll share the story of one of these circles I built—this was the 25' stone circle at my land in Michigan. After meditation and selecting the site, as I described above, the site began as an area that I mowed into a circle with a small electric mower every few weeks. At my first Fall Equinox, I added four elemental altars on the four quarters using large wooden, round altars made from a dead tree stump. After that, I slowly added stones—first around each of the quarter altars, and, slowly, filling up the whole circle. Since I was hosting regular druid events, I would ask people to bring a stones, and the circle would grow. I also brought stones back from visiting various places and the circle grew even more. At Beltane, we planted young seedling trees the whole way around the circle in the areas that were still fairly open. Then I planted herbs appropriate to each quarter. I also added two stone cairns as gateways for the major entrance to the circle. The circle continued to grow and evolve as the years passed.

Stone and Plant Spirals

Another thing you can build is a stone or plant spiral. You can do this in many different ways—I like my labyrinths or spirals to be edible or medicinal, working with plant allies as well as the stones. One of the spirals I built more recently was a strawberry spiral—it had a spiral stone path, winding inwards, with three kinds of strawberries (so that harvest times are different) and a simple stone spiral pathway. It was delightful to walk the spiral in any point of the year, but walking it in June and July when the strawberries were in season was particularly delightful! The small strawberry spiral, no more than 15' across, yielded 20-40 lbs. of strawberries each year!

Now you may say, "oh, this sounds more like a garden than a true sacred space." I think that these are one in the same. Each time I go to pick the strawberries, I will walk a spiral, and be reminded of all that spirals represent. When I pick the strawberries I grow, I exert less demand on an already stressed global ecosystem—I am not contributing to the burning of fossil fuels to ship the strawberries to me, the exploitation of farm workers to pick the berries, the addition of chemical fertilizers and pesticides that can harm waterways and wildlife, the purchasing of products in non-recyclable packaging that is filling up our landfills, nor supporting a broken big agricultural system. If growing my own strawberries along a sacred spiral path has that much impact, how can it be anything but a serious spiritual act? If I invite children or friends over to pick the strawberries, they, too, walk the spiraling path. It truly becomes a sacred, welcoming space for all to enjoy.

Labyrinths

Another sacred space is a classic labyrinth. These can be permanent or temporary. Labyrinths come in many designs, and what I really like about them is that they are fairly intuitive for people to use—you simply walk, slow down, and be mindful of your path. I have helped in the construction of several labyrinths and have walked countless others on various sacred lands, at churches, and even one in the woods behind a local hospital! As you walk, the pattern of the labyrinth weaves its way into the energies of the landscape and into your inner landscape. Different labyrinth patterns, obviously, can weave different designs, and selecting an appropriate design is a key step. I have helped plant a smaller herbal labyrinth at a friend's house that used a number of low growing, easy to control herbs like lavender, sage, rosemary, and thyme—we planted these in a Baltic spiral design, and she trims the labyrinth by cutting the herbs (which is brilliant and awesome). Building the labyrinth can be done with very simple tools like stakes and rope.

For a less permanent, but not less sacred, activity, you might also consider the snow labyrinth. I liked to do this as one of my sacred practices around Imbolc each year. I would go walk a simpler pattern in the sacred stone circle, each day returning to walk it again. Each new snowfall, I again walked it. For more elaborate patterns, I would go out on my ½ acre pond years when there was a lot of snow and make a spiral pattern there, returning to walk it many times. These would be done in the dead of winter but had a profound energizing effect. Even in the summer, the resonances of those winter labyrinths were present on the landscape!

Sacred Gardens and Garden Shrines

Gardens are yet another wonderful way to create a sacred space. Placing a small shrine, some stones in a pattern, a small statue of a deity, or even some signage can help shift your garden's energy to sacred energy (which is like icing on the cake, given how sacred most gardens are to begin with!) I have found that everything about a garden can be sacred—from planting and designing your garden itself, to spending time in awareness and deep connection with nature, to placing key features in the garden (a standing stone with water pool, representing the three druid elements of nwyfre, calas, and gywar, for example). You can consider how to incorporate other sacred elements here (spirals, stone circles, standing stones, stone cairns) in your garden designs.

Stone Cairns, Stone Balancing, Stone Stacking

The art of balancing stones has origins in many cultures. In many parts of Asia, stones are balanced and stacked as a sign of prayer and meditation. In North America, native Americans used stone cairns to watch over animals and forests while humans were not present, and to this day, wandering sages are found stacking stones in remote forest locations. As Druids, we often meet among stacked stones or in stone circles. I see stone balancing as a kind of natural poetry—an aesthetic that is difficult to put into words. When we balance stones, we connect the depths of our souls to the depths of the earth and create something of beauty and harmony. What do the stacked stones convey? Ask them, and you may find out.

Stone balancing and stacking is a very simple, yet profound activity. You can do it anywhere that stones exist, and you can leave your stacked and balanced stones for others to find. Stone balancing allows you, at your core, to connect with the ancient energies of the earth. As you stack stones, you can enter a deep communion with the land, a movement meditation. You might begin stone balancing by simply seeing how

stone A stacks upon stone B and stone B stacks upon stone C. Try these kinds of stacks for a while, and once you get the hang of simple stacking, you might want to try more complex stone stacking, where stone C depends upon both A and B, or where B and C need each other to sit atop A. When I started stone balancing, I made stone stacks very simply with the larger, round stones found so commonly in Michigan. I maintained several active stone stacks—these simple stacks of rounded stones would fall over each time the weather changed by more than 20 or 30 degrees. But over time, I started adding complexity to my stone stacks—when small pebbles were added between the larger stones, I created a more solid structure that could withstand the changing seasons, wind and rain. I also began balancing stones in more interesting patterns— these stacks are more ephemeral but not less powerful. You'll find that your stacks of stones depend heavily on what raw materials you have to work with. In Western PA, I found that the rocks there were much more conducive to stone building—nice, flat rocks allowed me to stack in many different patterns. I could create more permanent stone structures and could do interesting things with trilithons and other designs not possible with Michigan's round stones. One such stack I created almost eight years ago, and it is still standing in exactly the same place I left it!

To stack stones, its important to pick out a good site. Something that firm should be used for a base (a stump, a stone in the ground, a bit of flat earth with the leaves cleared away). You should also start with an ample supply of good stones in the area (for this reason, building stone cairns nearby or in rivers/streams is an excellent activity). As you are working, let the shape of the stones determine how you work with them—they will speak to you and the stone building will just flow.

I have found stone balancing to be a wonderful activity for both my own property and for visiting natural areas and leaving a tribute, to add a bit of a human touch to an already sacred landscape. I frequently build stone cairns on public land where I am visiting: state parks, local township parks, along city walking paths, and so forth. Make sure you aren't disrupting local wildlife with your stone building, of course! I have some stone cairns that I return to often or once a year, and some that I build and never come back to again. Sometimes, I have found that if you build an impressive enough and visible enough cairn, others may add to your stone cairn or build others around it, creating a kind of shared poetry. I also purposefully build stone cairns that I know will be temporary—building them along quiet summer riverbeds means that the spring will sweep them away—but to me, this is yet another blessing to

the land—the energy in the stones then going into the waterways to bless everything downstream!

Again, here, AODA rituals can be extremely useful. You can use a solitary grove opening to open a space in which to build. You can infuse energy into the stones with one of our seasonal rituals or an SOP working, connecting the energies of the earth to those of the sun, awakening the lunar current in the stack itself. There are so many possibilities here for stone work in this way.

Stones as Shared Poetry

The photo to the right was a small stone cairn I built while exploring the forest with a group of three other

women, all of whom were spiritually aware and respectful of the land. When I finished building the cairn, I asked each of them how the stone cairn spoke to them; if they had happened upon it in the forest, what would it say to them? Here are their responses:

If I had come upon this stone cairn without knowing it was built by human hands, I would have thought that it rose up from the earth on its own. The earth had built it just to communicate with me.

I go hiking often, and many trails have these cairns as markers. So I see this cairn as something that helps guide you along your way.

I see it as a place for the energies of the forest to converge. A focus point. I also see it where the water and the earth meet.

My own intention was that the cairn was built to revere and respect the land. But the beauty of the stone cairn is that it allows for many kinds of interpretation and communion with the natural world.

Maypoles

Another very traditional land blessing and sacred space activity is the Maypole. While I owned my land, I made sure to do a maypole every year—it was a wonderful way to have fun, see friends, engage young ones, and give a strong blessing to the land that would stand throughout the year. The wound maypole serves as another physical representation of our relationship to the living earth. Our particular maypole was a fallen ash tree, destroyed by the Emerald Ash Borer (an invasive beetle, threatening ash species all over the Eastern and Midwest USA). We selected this pole very carefully and used the pole to help bless the remaining ash trees and recognize their struggle while also sending a land blessing out to all. We kept our maypole up year round, taking it down a few weeks before we would celebrate Beltane for the coming season. It was a firm reminder of the bounty and sacred relationship that we were forging with the land.

Small Nature Shrines

You can build small natural shrines out of feathers, stones, shells, sticks, bark, leaves, dried flowers, seed pods, reeds, nuts, and other natural things. Some shrines may only be meant to look nice for a few hours, while others are more permanent. In my designs, I sometimes incorporate "reclaimed" junk that has been there a long time—for example, taking the rusted barbed wire I pulled from an ancient tree and sticking daises in every twist. When paying homage to the land and her spirits, its really important that you stick with used/re-purposed items and natural materials that you can find readily and easily. I think it defeats the whole purpose of building a natural shrine if you go buy a bunch of stuff for it brand new at a department store.

Fairy houses and other natural assemblages provide one way that you can build using natural materials—these are especially appropriate for children and children's magic. These small spirit houses are meant to attract, appease, or otherwise encourage the fey folk from the spirit world to take up residence and stay a while. At Beltane a few years ago, one of our grove members brought his three daughters, and they spent the

afternoon building fairy houses and shrines out of reclaimed material, leaving them all over the property! Around the same time, I found a wooden carved man's face someone had put out by the curb for trash pickup and I thought he reminded me a bit of the green man. So now, he inhabits the tree where the fairy shrine sits. The spirit of the maple tree was happy with his new face!

I should also mention that *timing* and *regular maintenance* is an important part of creating any nature shrine. I like to build things when the earth's energies are aligning with such a process—at Beltane we put up our maypole and build fairy shrines, at the equinoxes I build shrines and circles to bring balance and healing, and so forth. You should also plan on regularly maintaining and visiting your permanent shrines if they are to become part of your spiritual practice.

Signage, Hanging Mirrors, Ribbons, and More

One of the absolute simplest things you can do is just hang little things around; things that have meaning, that convey a message or help hold a sacred space. I have four elemental ornaments that I created and hung in a tree in each of the quarters of my property. These helped remind me that the entire property is sacred land, and I am always mindful of how I interact with it. Another time, a friend had owned an antique shop that had closed, and she had all of these lovely glass sun catchers—we hung them in an apple tree and that tree always held such magic. It immediately created a shift in the space!

Reconnecting to the Land

Energetically, as you do this work with these sacred spaces on the land, you will feel your own connection to the land growing. Right now, so many people are so disconnected—and the quiet work of building and maintaining these spaces does much to help us shift our own energies and connection. There is nothing like coming into a space that someone else has worked on and feeling the healing energies flowing around. None of us know what the long-term impact of such work may be—but it's work worth doing in the present moment!

I hope that this article has opened up new avenues for you to enact and practice your Druidry. I encourage you to be creative; to create simple yet profound sacred spaces that allow you to respect, revere, and commune with the natural world around you. The key is to create things that are of the natural world or that have no negative impact: these

kinds of sacred building activities will deepen your connection to the land. A sacred space doesn't have to be elaborate or showy—sometimes the most simple creations can yield powerful results. The AODA equips us with many tools to begin this journey and to empower these spaces with creativity, light, and life!

References

Fortune, D. (2000). *The Cosmic Doctrine*. York Beach, ME: Weiser Books, p. 34-5.

Greer, J. M. (2007). *The Druid magic handbook*. San Francisco: Weiser Books.

Greer, J. M. (2011). *The Druid Grove Handbook*. Traverse City, Lorian Press.

Devereux, P. and Pennick, N. (1981). *Lines on the Landscape: Ley Lines and Other Linear Enigmas*. London, Robert Hale.

Watkins, A. (1973). *The Old Straight Track*. New York: Ballatine Books.

Mabinogi Skies:
Astronomy of the Third Branch

By Tracy Glomski

Tracy Glomski's passion for star lore was first ignited by her work as a presenter, from 1989 to 1994, at the J. M. McDonald Planetarium in Hastings, Nebraska. She has remained active in the field as a volunteer, assisting with programming at the Sachtleben Observatory of Hastings College since 1994 and serving as the treasurer of a regional club, the Platte Valley Astronomical Observers, since 2002. A past Grand Pendragon of the Ancient Order of Druids in America, Tracy is also a member of the Order of Bards, Ovates and Druids. She welcomes comments at tracyglomski@gmail.com.

Introduction
A Curious Venture Continues

In last year's issue of *Trilithon*, I outlined a framework of astronomical allegory within the First and Second Branches of the *Mabinogi*, a four-part work of twelfth-century legends that continues to fascinate students of contemporary Druidry and scholars of Celtic medieval literature (Glomski, 2015). Originally composed in Middle Welsh by an unknown author, the *Mabinogi* is extremely rich in multiple meanings. Some of these meanings arise from an extensive and structurally significant matrix of celestial symbols that impart an extra layer of liveliness to the tales wherever they are heard. In the "*Mabinogi* Skies" series of articles, which will conclude in *Trilithon* 2017, I examine the role of astronomical allegory in the composition of the *Mabinogi*, identify numerous correspondences between key features of the narrative and the heavens above, and demonstrate the continued functionality of this literature as an aid to learning the constellations and the motions of the celestial sphere. When these aspects of the *Mabinogi*

are fully discerned, they help to facilitate a stronger awareness of the cycles of nature as they are expressed in the skies overhead. The process of contemplating and assimilating these symbols can also catalyze a more vibrant experience of the spiritual teachings within the narrative of the *Mabinogi*—at least, that is how it has worked for me.

The previous article began the task of tracing the astronomical symbolism from the ground up. The opening correspondences of the First Branch linked the character of Arawn to the constellation of Orion the Hunter, and the character of Pwyll to the constellation of Hercules the Strongman. These two similarly shaped constellations swap positions seasonally, above and below the horizon, in a manner that resembles the characters' travels to and from the otherworld. In the cultures of ancient and medieval peoples, the knowledge of such celestial motions was vitally important, because the risings and settings of the stars provided necessary calendrical cues for planting crops and honoring holy days. So the First Branch supplied a basic orientation to those motions, and also established certain symbolic connections between the territory described in the narrative and various features of interest in the skies overhead. Many of the First Branch metaphors remain important in the Third Branch, and these are revisited in greater detail in this year's article.

Last year's article then continued to an analysis of the Second Branch, which mainly concerned a noble family of five siblings: the visible planets. If the character Branwen and her four brothers are viewed from this astronomical angle, certain puzzling and sometimes disturbing plot points become much easier to fathom. Efnisien's violent mutilation of the lips, ears, and tails of the horses, for example, is manifested in the sky as the motion of Mars traveling along its orbital path beneath the constellation of Pegasus the Winged Horse. This path normally carries the warlike planet from the head to the hindquarters of the horse, except when Mars goes retrograde, which sometimes enables him to reach back and attack the eyes, too. More generally, the actions of all of the main Second Branch characters appear to match, play-by-play, with sequences of historical planetary alignments that were concentrated in the early 1140s. The positions of the planets on March 1, 1142, for instance, would perfectly emulate the seating arrangement of the characters at the wedding feast of Branwen (Venus) and Matholwch (the Moon). The same would be true for the feast immediately preceding the battle with the Irish, on April 10, 1143. These alignments occurred during the daytime when the planets could not be physically observed, which opens up the intriguing possibility that the author of the *Mabinogi* was familiar with the construction

of horoscopes. Ten horoscopes from England, created in the years 1123 to 1160, have survived to our day (North, 1986). It is not unreasonable to ponder whether the author of the *Mabinogi* may have encountered similar charts. In the Middle Ages, astrology was commonly regarded as a practical application of astronomy. Several allusions to astrological knowledge also appear in the Third Branch, described below.

The general trajectory from the First Branch through the Second appears to represent an upward exploration through the solar system as it was understood by medieval thinkers. In their models, the Earth rested at the center of a set of nested spherical shells, with each of the shells bearing a planet, the Sun, or the Moon. The planet farthest from the Earth was Saturn, and beyond Saturn, there was an additional shell bearing the stars. So the next sensible step, within the astronomical allegory of the *Mabinogi*, would be a fuller examination of this stellar realm. If my interpretation of the Third and Fourth branches is correct, that is indeed what happens. The celestial symbolism of the Third and Fourth Branches essentially divides the sky into quarters. These quadrants are then paired into two hemispheres, and the Third Branch addresses the group of constellations lying in one of these hemispheres, while the Fourth Branch addresses the other. This technique of grouping various items into compartments was a favorite mnemonic strategy during both ancient and medieval times (Carruthers, 2008). One of the main purposes of this article is to reveal the specific arrangement of constellations that is referenced within the narrative of the Third Branch. In the course of providing this information, I also describe key sources that may have been important to the author, share additional tidbits about the construction of medieval star maps, uncover parallels in the astronomical symbolism of a related tale known as the *Hanes Taliesin*, and examine differences between my model and one previously published model.

Several of the astronomical symbols that I named in last year's article retain considerable momentum into the Third Branch. The most important of these include Pryderi's associations with the constellation Aquarius and also with the Sun; Rhiannon as the constellation Andromeda; Manawyddan as the planet Mercury; the mound Gorsedd Arberth as the Tropic of Cancer, which functions as an "elevation" (the correct astronomical term is *declination*) that mysteriously transmits currents of inspiration and initiation along its path; a wide pool of watery constellations that was envisaged by the ancient Greeks and also by the *Mabinogi* author as a celestial sea, and which may be found in the area of sky between Capricornus the Sea Goat and Eridanus the River; and a new otherworldly forest, unique to the *Mabinogi* as far as I know, that is

situated between the two riverine constellations of Eridanus and Hydra, and which is primarily occupied by the constellations of Orion the Hunter, Taurus the Bull, and the dogs Canis Major and Canis Minor.

Nearly all of the constellations relevant to the Third Branch are situated in a region of the sky that stretches from Pisces the Fish to Cancer the Crab. The rationale for this arrangement was not entirely clear to me when I began to intensively examine the astronomy of the Third Branch in January 2013. I have since concluded that the tip-off lies in the name of the character whose misfortunes constitute much of the heart of the Third Branch: Manawyddan fab Llŷr. Scholars believe that Manawyddan's Welsh name shares the same toponymic derivation as an Irish god of the sea, Manannán mac Lir (Bromwich, 2014). The *Commentary on the Dream of Scipio by Macrobius*, a fifth-century Neoplatonic work that served as an important philosophical teaching text in the Middle Ages, also provides a description of the solar system that classifies Mercury as a water planet (Stahl, 1990). Astrologers consider Pisces and Cancer to be two of the three signs, along with Scorpio, that correspond with water. While the narrative is coy about these associations, it does make sense that a story about a character associated with a sea god and with a water planet would unfold between two water signs. But why these particular signs? Why would the Third Branch not focus instead on the area of sky between Cancer and Scorpio, say, or between Scorpio and Pisces? This is a nontrivial question that sheds considerable light on the internal construction of both the Third and Fourth Branches. A three-part answer is provided in this article.

Sorting Out the Sources

Before going into further detail concerning narrative structure, I would like to over-view a few of the sources that have been most critical to my analysis. When I first began researching the topic of astronomy in the *Mabinogi*, I was already personally familiar with the night sky and with the star lore of antiquity, but I had never before studied medieval literature, Celtic myth, or the Welsh language. One of my greatest challenges has been simply figuring out which texts and ideas may have plausibly influenced this author, ultimately shaping the body of symbolism that he employed and developed. This has involved a process of digging into increasingly academic literature, paying close attention to the sources that scholars cite most frequently and reliably in their own work, and following each of those leads like a strand of yarn in a labyrinth. Along the way, I have occasionally come across new ideas that integrate well into my own

interpretations, or that necessitate a reassessment of my earlier impressions. I continue to make refinements and small modifications in my model accordingly.

I have included a more extensive list of sources at the end of this article, but over the next few pages, I highlight two types of references that I regard as especially useful starting points for self-guiding students who would like to build their own understanding in a similar fashion. The first type of reference consists of annotated English translations of the *Mabinogi*, and the second type consists of resources pertinent to the study of astronomy as it was understood in medieval Europe. Readers who are already knowledgeable about one or both of these topics may wish to proceed directly to the following section, which explores the significance of a celestial feature called the *colures*. The section after that examines similarities in astronomical symbolism between the *Mabinogi* and another medieval Welsh work, the *Hanes Taliesin*. The analysis of the Third Branch proper then begins in earnest on page 131.

Familiarity with the text of the *Mabinogi* is essential for getting a handle on the upcoming analysis. For English-speaking readers with Internet access, good annotated translations may be read for free at Mabinogi.net (Parker, 2003) and at the Internet Sacred Text Archive (Guest, 1877). Among the several in-print, annotated English translations currently available in paperback format, I most strongly recommend *The Mabinogi* by Sioned Davies (2007) as a foolproof place to begin. Davies's compact, affordable, and highly readable work has been widely praised for scholarly accuracy. In addition to the three sources above, the other translations that I have regularly consulted for my analysis include Patrick K. Ford's (1977) deservedly respected classic, *The Mabinogi and Other Medieval Welsh Tales*, which is particularly useful in the literalness of its translation; the Dolmen Arch lesson packets, taught by John Michael Greer, which first brought the *Mabinogi* to my attention and which offer thought-provoking introductory material and footnotes (Greer & Guest, 2009); and OBOD's delightful audiobook, *The Mabinogion: The Four Branches*, a lightly adapted retelling of Lady Charlotte Guest's historic translation (Hadley & Hutton, 1996). As much as I like the OBOD version, I generally advise that it be enjoyed as a supplemental resource rather than as a primary translation. The OBOD script incorporates small alterations and explanatory remarks into the narrative, and although these edits are undoubtedly helpful to the newcomer, they are presented in a manner that draws no distinctions between translation and interpretation. For further information about the strengths and weaknesses of other editions of the *Mabinogi* released during the past couple of

centuries, an excellent little practical guide can be consulted online at the University of Rochester's Camelot Project (Rider-Bezerra, 2011).

The astronomical references that have been important to my analysis run the gamut from scans and translations of texts that were popular in the Middle Ages to a recently published textbook on the history of Irish and Welsh astrology. An ancient star catalog, modern planetarium software, and a specific type of star atlas are also among the resources that may be helpful to students of this topic. Here is a brief look at each of these in turn.

In an introductory paragraph above, I already cited Stahl's (1990) translation of the *Commentary on the Dream of Scipio by Macrobius*. Macrobius's commentary is an encyclopedic discourse on the nature of the cosmos, originally in Latin, that was definitely familiar to scholars in medieval Wales (Williams, 2010). A twelfth-century copy of it, cataloged as MS Cotton Faustina C.1, has survived from Llanbadarn Fawr. I cite the *Commentary on the Dream of Scipio* several times in this article because I think it did in fact influence the allegory that the *Mabinogi* author employed in both the Third and Fourth Branches.

As mentioned in my first article last year, all Four Branches also appear to be generously sprinkled with allusions to Aratus's *Phaenomena* (Mair & Mair, 1921). Written in the third century BCE, the *Phaenomena* is a lengthy and popular poem, originally composed in Greek, that describes constellations, celestial mythology, and weather lore. It received multiple translations into Latin in antiquity. During the Middle Ages, the *Phaenomena* was fairly ubiquitous as an elementary teaching text in monasteries, where it was commonly stocked in the libraries (Carruthers, 1998). *Phaenomena* manuscripts were frequently supplemented with star maps that were originally drawn from celestial globes. Independent scholar Elly Dekker (2013) has compiled a fabulous catalog, *Illustrating the Phaenomena*, that reproduces and investigates every known surviving example from the ninth century to the fifteenth century, a total of thirty-three maps in all. The maps shown in Dekker's book have been an invaluable resource to me, as an aid to imagining the skies in the same way that the author of the *Mabinogi* may have pictured them.

In this article, I refer several times to the celestial maps that accompanied one particular *Phaenomena* manuscript, NLW MS 735C (c. 1000–1150). The copy of the

Phaenomena that appears in NLW MS 735C was executed around the beginning of the eleventh century. It was later appended with an incomplete, twelfth-century copy of Macrobius's *Commentary on the Dream of Scipio*. The two portions of the manuscript both originated in the Limoges area of France, and aside from this provenance, nothing is known about their early history. The manuscript as a whole had unquestionably landed in northeast Wales by 1816, and its binding and one handwritten entry provide further evidence that the manuscript was in Britain by at least the early seventeenth century. Due to established connections between Limoges and England in the eleventh century, it is possible, albeit extremely speculative, that the first portion of the manuscript may have arrived on the island not long after it was copied, with the second portion following later (McGurk, 1973). Unfortunately, there is absolutely no way of knowing whether the author of the *Mabinogi* would have encountered this exact manuscript. NLW MS 735C is nonetheless a great manuscript for illustrating the manner in which medieval European astronomers visualized the sky, and I have chosen to highlight it for this reason. The star maps of NLW MS 735C are in many ways quite typical of their era, and yet they also feature some fascinating quirks that I discuss later in this article. Direct scans of these maps may be viewed in the digital gallery of the National Library of Wales at the medieval astronomy webpage (NLW MS 735C, c. 1000–1150). For those who prefer a printed reference, images and detailed descriptions of every map except the solar system diagram may also be found in Dekker's (2013) *Illustrating the Phaenomena*.

The *Phaenomena* was part of the Greco-Roman tradition of descriptive astronomy that endured in Europe even after the fall of the Roman Empire. There was also a tradition of mathematical astronomy that was largely lost to the West until a Latin translation of the *Almagest* began to circulate in the last quarter of the twelfth century. Written by the astronomer Claudius Ptolemy in the second century, the *Almagest* was a monumental treatise that aroused considerable excitement wherever it was later read and understood. The odds that the *Almagest* reached the *Mabinogi* author are slim. Many scholars believe that the *Mabinogi* was completed in about 1060–1120, and that would be at least a couple of generations before the *Almagest* went into translation (Davies, 2007). I tend to prefer Parker's (2002) arguments that the *Mabinogi* was not completed until the late twelfth century, but that is still cutting it very close. Regardless of whether the *Mabinogi* author had his own copy of the *Almagest*, I would still recommend its star catalog as an essential reference. The ancient Greek constellations that are presented in the *Almagest*, which are also called the Ptolemaic constellations,

are the same or very close to the ones that medieval European astronomers would have recognized—if not through the *Almagest* itself, then somewhat less precisely through the *Phaenomena* and other nontechnical texts. To avoid anachronisms, it is important to grasp the differences between the historical system of forty-eight Ptolemaic constellations and the modern system of eighty-eight. For this information, I personally rely on Toomer's (1998) translation of the *Almagest*, a paperback edition that includes the full work plus an introduction and notes. Spreadsheets of the star catalog are also hosted online by physicists John P. Pratt (2015) and Dennis Duke (n.d.)—while these are more difficult to read than Toomer's version, they are downloadable for free.

Charts and catalogs are static representations, whereas celestial objects are constantly in motion. From the observer's perspective, the locations of stars and planets are affected by several factors, including the latitude of the observer, the time of night, the season of the year, and the historical era. Stellar motions become relatively easy to understand with practice, but planetary motions are considerably more complicated, even for experts. To really see what was happening in the skies over medieval Wales, it is best to run simulations with a planetarium program like Stellarium. Stellarium generates accurate views of the sky for virtually any location, date, and time you care to enter. My seven-year-old computer prefers an older version (Chéreau et al., 2009), but Stellarium continues to be regularly updated and supported. Free downloads are currently available at stellarium.org for Windows, OS X, Linux, and Ubuntu.

For the type of research and interpretation I describe in this article, it is best to go easy on Stellarium's zoom function, since the program allows the user to effortlessly magnify the sky well beyond the limits of the unaided eye. Maps showing dim stars and deep sky objects are great if you have a telescope, but I am pretty sure the author of the *Mabinogi* was not so lucky, since telescopes were not even invented until the seventeenth century. So to stay properly oriented in Stellarium, it is occasionally handy to also refer to a companion atlas that excludes faint stars. I prefer my trusty, old-school copy of *Norton's 2000.0* (Ridpath, 1989), an edition that is now difficult to find. My astronomy club provides each new member with a complimentary copy of Wil Tirion and Brian Skiff's (1990) *Bright Star Atlas 2000.0*, an affordable and serviceable alternative. Several other options, generally more deluxe, are also in print. The main criterion is that the atlas should not plot stars with magnitudes larger than 6.5. Bigger numbers indicate dimmer stars, and smaller numbers indicate brighter stars. That is admittedly rather counterintuitive, and to top it off, the scale is logarithmic. Don't

blame me—blame the Greeks. They were thinking of it this way: Stars of the first magnitude are the shiniest, stars of the second magnitude get second prize, and so on. The *Almagest* categorizes each star with a brightness from 1 to 6, and anything much fainter than 6 was of no interest because those stars were only infrequently visible, if at all. The same story held true in medieval times. And it is the same story today, for naked-eye observers who are away from the direct glare of city lights and under good atmospheric conditions that are clear, steady, and dark.

In addition to astronomical symbolism, the Third Branch contains some astrological content. The book that I would recommend as most relevant to this topic is Mark Williams's (2010) *Fiery Shapes: Celestial Portents and Astrology in Ireland and Wales, 700–1700*. This scholarly text, which is based upon an earlier doctoral dissertation by Williams, contains only a few tidbits specific to the *Mabinogi*. *Fiery Shapes* nonetheless excels at providing a solid, general sense of the present limits of knowledge concerning medieval Welsh astrology. While we do have the twelfth-century set of English horoscopes mentioned earlier, no horoscopes specifically from medieval Wales have survived to modern times. Does this lack of physical evidence imply that no such horoscopes ever existed, or has this situation arisen from the confidential nature of the business, which would typically prevent charts from being bound and preserved in codices? At present, there is too little information to reach a conclusion. Some evidence does exist, however, that scholars in nearby Hereford were attempting to practice mathematical astrology as early as the mid-twelfth century. That is interesting in light of the fact that Hereford is the first town in England that Manawyddan and Pryderi visit in the Third Branch of the *Mabinogi*, when they try to reverse their fortunes. And it is certainly true that quite a few nontechnical allusions to astrology appear elsewhere in medieval Welsh literature—Williams devotes an entire chapter of analysis to Geoffrey of Monmouth's *Prophetiae Merlini*, c. 1135, and *Vita Merlini*, 1148–1151, and also to NLW Peniarth MS 2 (c. 1300–1350), the Welsh manuscript compiling the *Book of Taliesin*.

I first came across *Fiery Shapes* in the bibliography of *The Mabinogi Decoded*, a monograph by another professor, Edward Arfon Rees (2012). There appears to be little, if any, overlap between Rees's and Williams's research, however. For example, the Welsh term *Caer Gwydion*, meaning "fort of Gwydion," has long been employed as a metaphor for the Milky Way, yet the earliest source that Rees cites for it is the work of Sir John Rhŷs (1901). Williams reports with much greater precision that this

figure of speech has been documented from the sixteenth century, with indications that the poet Gruffudd Grug used it as early as the fourteenth century. This would suggest that the term was in existence by the time the oldest surviving manuscripts of the *Mabinogi* were copied (Peniarth MS 4, c. 1350; Jesus College MS 111, 1382–c. 1410). While this admittedly does not constitute proof that the author of the *Mabinogi* had this exact idea in mind, an association between Gwydion and the Milky Way does fit seamlessly into my model of the Fourth Branch. Rees simply discounts any special connection between the two.

I examine several other differences between my model and Rees's toward the end of this article. Before I go into that, I must first describe a special feature from the art of celestial mapping: the colures.

Coming to Terms with Colures

In the previous section, I described a few modern tools, such as planetarium software and bright star atlases, that may be helpful for visualizing the night sky as it would have been seen by observers in medieval Europe. These present-day star charts do have a somewhat different appearance than those in the medieval manuscripts, however. So in this section, I would like to draw attention to one particular item that is more conspicuous on the old maps than on the new: the colures.

The colures may be defined as a pair of great circles that meet at right angles at the north celestial pole and at the south celestial pole, and that also pass through either the equinoctial or solstitial points (figure 1). The equinoctial colure intersects the celestial equator at the points where the Sun crosses the equator during the spring and autumn equinoxes. The solstitial colure, as the name implies, intersects the points on the ecliptic where the Sun stands at the summer and winter solstices. Sometimes the two colures are treated as four semicircular colures that meet at the poles: the spring equinoctial colure, the summer solstitial colure, the autumn equinoctial colure, and the winter solstitial colure. This allows for clearer discussion of the specific arcs of the colures that pass through various seasonal constellations. The colures are an integral component of every extant seasonal sky map that accompanied medieval copies of Aratus's *Phaenomena*. They are always present within the construction of these maps, and they are normally explicitly shown.

Eleven examples of *Phaenomena* seasonal charts, described as either summer or winter hemispheres depending on the solstitial colure that runs through the center of each

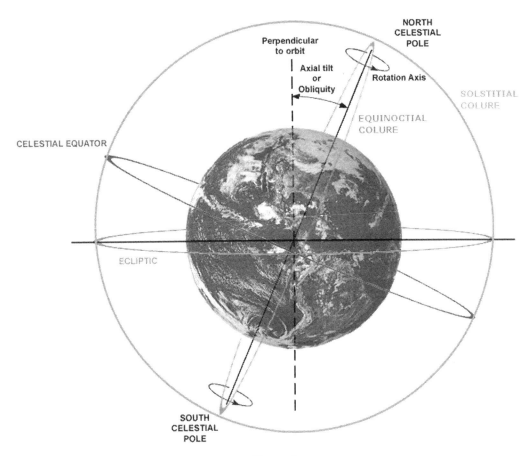

<u>Figure 1:</u>

The equinoctial colure, illustrated nearly edge-on in this diagram, intersects the celestial equator at right angles. These points of intersection represent the location of the Sun at the March equinox (center of diagram) and the September equinox (behind the Earth). The solstitial colure, illustrated face-on, intersects both the equator and the ecliptic at right angles. These are the places where the Sun may be found on the ecliptic at the December solstice (far left) and June solstice (far right) (Basilicofresco, 2009).

map, have survived to this day. In every case, the equinoctial colure defines the circular boundary of each map. Also for every set of hemispheres except those attached to the *Phaenomena* manuscript of NLW MS 735C, the edge-on solstitial colure is represented as a bisecting line passing through each chart from top to bottom. It is possible that the omission of the solstitial colure from NLW MS 735C is a corruption that arose in

the copying process. These hemispheres are otherwise among the more accurate ones that have survived from medieval times, however, so I am inclined to agree with Dekker's (2013) suggestion that the suppression of the conventional grid may have been a conscious artistic decision. This edit would have allowed the illustrator to circumvent certain technical difficulties in the plotting of these maps, while improving the aesthetic quality. The NLW MS 735C illustrations also contain at least one flourish—a picture within a picture—that does not appear in any of the other *Phaenomena* manuscripts. Because this added detail meshes especially well with the astronomical symbolism of the Third Branch of the *Mabinogi*, I discuss it below.

Parallel Universes of Transformation

Starting in the Third Branch and continuing into the Fourth, the character Pryderi undergoes a series of transformations that appear to function as an extended reference to seasonal divisions of the celestial sphere. These divisions closely resemble those that are traced out by the arcs of the colures. Because this allegory is subtle yet structurally significant in the *Mabinogi*, it is helpful to first examine a more obvious example. For this, we turn to the *Hanes Taliesin*, a tale that also goes by the alternate title *Ystoria Taliesin*. This particular story is worth examining in part because Taliesin also turns up in the *Mabinogi*, as one of the characters who survives the battle in the Second Branch.

The *Hanes Taliesin* is generally regarded as a legendary account of the origins of a historical bard, Taliesin, who is believed to have sung in the courts of Brythonic kings in the latter parts of the sixth century. Somewhat varying versions of this tale have come down to us. The earliest surviving manuscript was compiled by Elis Gruffydd during the first half of the sixteenth century (Ford, 1977). Gruffydd's opinionated remarks leave little doubt, however, that he was recording and commenting upon older material from the Welsh tradition.

My own favorite version of the story is the one by John Jones of Gellilyfdy, as recorded in Peniarth MS 111 (Hughes, 2012). In this account, the boy who will transform into Taliesin, and whose original name is Gwion Bach, passes through a series of four distinct forms while fleeing an enraged enchantress, Ceridwen. He initially changes into a hare, only to find she is hot on his heels as a greyhound. He jumps into a river and tries to swim away as a fish, and she becomes a fearsome otter. He next flies up into the air as a bird, and she pursues him as a hawk. He finally spots some wheat on the

Figure 2:

The positions of the seasonal colures for the year 536 are indicated by a vertical line through each pair of constellations. *Upper left:* the summer colure at the dog and hare, with the hare enjoying a slight lead. Both animals are facing in the direction of the river Eridanus. *Upper right:* the spring colure at the fish and "otter."

Lower left: the winter colure at the bird and "hawk." *Lower right:* the autumn colure at the wheat (the bright star Spica) and "hen." Illustration by the author, incorporating images from Stellarium (Chéreau et al., 2009).

floor of a barn, and in desperation, dives in as a single grain. Ceridwen, now a tufted black hen, plucks him out and swallows him.

In my opinion, each of these transformations is plainly visible in the sky as adjacent pairs of Ptolemaic constellations (figure 2). The first duo requires hardly any imagination at all: Lepus the Hare and Canis Major the Big Dog. The next step is a little trickier, and it consists of Pisces (or more specifically, the easternmost of the two fish in that constellation, the one who jumps up straight out of the water) and Cetus the Sea Monster. On medieval star charts, Cetus is styled as a creature with an elongated body, not unlike an otter. The bird and hawk are Cygnus the Swan and Aquila the Eagle, who are two of the three avian constellations. The wheat is found at the star Spica, known since ancient times as an ear of grain in the hand of Virgo, and the hen is Corvus the Crow, the third avian constellation and the only black one.

Precession, a slow wobble in the orientation of the Earth's rotational axis that completes one cycle every 26,000 years, causes gradual shifting in the positions of the constellations with respect to the grid of celestial coordinates (and also with respect to the astrological signs) as seen from different historical eras. In the sixth century, the colures intersected one or both constellations in all four of these pairings (figure 2). By the latter half of the ninth century, the colure at Cygnus and Aquila had slipped off the side of the eagle's tail, and it began to drift measurably away from these constellations. If a modern storyteller wished to adapt the setting of the *Hanes Taliesin* to the present century, it would be necessary to employ a pair of constellations like Lyra and Hercules for the winter colure instead of Cygnus and Aquila.

One of the most interesting aspects of the transformations in the *Hanes Taliesin* is that they are provided in reverse seasonal order. In the sixth century, Lepus and Canis Major were at the summer colure, Pisces and Cetus were at the spring colure, Cygnus and Aquila were at the winter colure, and Spica and Corvus were at the autumn colure. Clearly this is not the normal progression of the Sun's annual eastward trek along the ecliptic. It indicates instead a retrograde motion. As with the movements of Gwern, the boy in the Second Branch of the *Mabinogi* who greets his four planetary uncles in an east-to-west direction along the ecliptic, the most obvious explanation for this backward movement is that it represents the regression of lunar nodes (Glomski, 2015). The lunar nodes, which shift westward along the ecliptic during a cycle lasting 18.6 years, are the only points at which a solar eclipse can occur. In the chase scene

of the *Hanes Taliesin*, one character leans toward solar symbolism (the name Taliesin means "radiant brow"), and the other leans toward lunar symbolism (Ceridwen keeps a cauldron, not unlike the lunar character Matholwch in the Second Branch of the *Mabinogi*). The Moon runs at a faster pace than the Sun, completing a full circuit around the sky in only a month instead of a year. It is thus a certainty that the lunar body will eventually catch and descend upon the solar body and eat him. Although they lacked the precise predictive models that scientists use today, scholars living in the Middle Ages were hardly ignorant of this fact. Hundreds of records of medieval European eclipses have survived to the modern era (Stephenson, 2010). These have been transmitted to our times by later compilers and copyists (Gorodetsky, n.d.). The records include multiple notations for total solar eclipses that occurred in the years 447 (which may be found, among other places, in the *Annals of Wales*), 512 (one source is the *Annals of Ulster*), and 538 and 540 (both are in Bede's *Ecclesiastical History of the English People* and also in the *Anglo-Saxon Chronicle*). The solar eclipse that best fits the narrative, however, occurred on September 1, 536 (Espenak, 2015a). The path tracked directly over Wales, and the Sun and Moon were in Virgo, the sign that rules the belly in astrological medicine. According to the story, Ceridwen carried Gwion Bach within her womb for nine months after eating him, and she cast him into the sea on April 29 when he was reborn as Taliesin. On April 29, 537, the Sun was positioned above the constellation of Eridanus the River at the liminal eastern shore of the celestial sea. And this birth date would fall within the ninth lunar month (although not yet the ninth calendrical month) following the September 1, 536, eclipse.

Unlike the constellations in the *Hanes Taliesin*, the seasonal markers embedded in the *Mabinogi* would correspond to colure positions that considerably predate the story's setting. The analogous quartet in the *Mabinogi* consists of four single constellations along the zodiac: Aquarius the Water Carrier, Taurus the Bull, Leo the Lion, and Scorpius the Scorpion. The colures were last positioned at these star patterns around 2500 BCE. It is very improbable that the author would have been thinking that far into the past. It is more likely that these constellations would have been of special interest due to their later association with the four fixed signs of Western astrology. Of the four, Taurus is by far the most difficult to see in the narrative of the *Mabinogi*. In the words of a famous advertising campaign from my youth: "Where's the beef?" The bull temporarily vanishes in the Third Branch along with the rest of the cattle in the narrative, but I have faith that we will find him again, if we first hunt down the pork. We will proceed to sniff out that particular celestial trail in the next section.

<u>Figure 3:</u>

The tetramorph of man (upper left), ox (lower left), lion (upper right), and eagle (lower right) is present in the biblical verses Ezekiel 1:10 and Revelation 4:7, in the writings of St. Jerome, in the traditions of Western astrology, and arguably also in the structure of the *Mabinogi*. Public domain image of f. 27v from the *Book of Kells* (c. 800 CE).

Scorpius is also not immediately obvious, since the author has employed an alternate astrological symbol for the scorpion: the eagle. Further discussion about the eagle will come in next year's article, since the constellation of Aquila the Eagle and the sign of Scorpio become factors of interest in the Fourth Branch.

Why would the author of the *Mabinogi* emphasize this particular fourfold structure, as opposed to any other in the heavens? The motif of man-ox-lion-eagle was actually fairly common in the author's day (figure 3). A number of examples have survived in medieval art, particularly in illustrations accompanying the four Gospels, which were often bound together in codex form, separate from other parts of the Bible. It would be somewhat surprising, in fact, if the author of the *Mabinogi* had somehow not heard of this tetramorph, and it is plausible that he would have considered it important enough to put to good use. To more fully illuminate the Aquarius-Taurus-Leo-Scorpius allegorical sequence, I provide a couple of spoilers for Fourth Branch symbolism in this year's article. The primary focus of the Third Branch, though, does fall heavily upon the first two figures: the man with a water jar and the steer. Let us now take a closer look at these and see if we can discover a possible location for the Sun at the time Pryderi gets colured, er, collared.

Astronomical Analysis of the Third Branch

The Tale of Manawyddan Son of Llŷr

"After the seven men we spoke of above . . ." the Third Branch begins. The phrasing of this opening line differs from the formula of the First, Second, and Fourth Branches (Davies, 2007). These other branches start with a sentence introducing a key character—Pwyll, Bran, and Math, respectively—and then launch forth with a "once upon a time" or "one afternoon" or "at that time." The wording of the Third Branch emphasizes more strongly the continuity with the preceding branch. This continuity is present in the astronomical layer of meaning as well as in the narrative more generally.

The seven aforementioned men are the only warriors who have survived the ghastly battle in the Second Branch. The Third Branch transmits a tale of further woe and eventual triumph for two of these men: Manawyddan and Pryderi. These two characters are sufficiently complex that each of them can be identified not only with a planetary body, but also with one or more constellations. By the conclusion of the

Third Branch, several other celestial beings are introduced, each placed within a group of constellations that spans nearly half the sky. We will encounter an unusual tusked beast, as well, who is about to draw our heroes into a deeper series of tribulations.

The Boar, the Bees, and the Bull

If you ever find yourself chatting with a stargazer at a social gathering, this might be a fun riddle to pose: "What type of creature materializes into visibility not far from the Sun, gleams a brilliant white, runs very fast, always manages to slip past the Hunter's dogs, and possesses a pair of tusks, the crescents of which appear at either side of his face?"

If "a supernatural boar" is the response, you must be at a wild party indeed. More likely your quick-witted companion will reply, with a wink and a smile, "Why, surely you must mean the Moon.
"

This troublesome beast makes his appearance more than three years into the narrative of the Third Branch. To learn how Manawyddan and Pryderi cross paths with the lunar boar during a hunting excursion, we first need to backtrack to a planetary conjunction described in last year's analysis of the Second Branch (Glomski, 2015).

At the conclusion of the third and final feast in the Second Branch, the door at Gwales had been opened and the last of the entertainments came to an end. Manawyddan, accompanied by Pryderi and five other survivors of the battle with the Irish, had been carousing for eighty-seven years in the company of his brother's decapitated but otherwise surprisingly lively head. At last, the awareness dawned that Bran's head was no longer alive in the ordinary sense, and that it required immediate burial.

If Manawyddan, Bran, their sister Branwen, and their two half-brothers Nysien and Efnisien are reconceptualized as the five visible planets—Mercury, Saturn, Venus, Jupiter, and Mars, respectively—it becomes possible to trace the historical motions of these planets in the skies over twelfth-century Wales, and to do so in a manner that is highly congruent with the narrative. This approach certainly makes sense for the character of Bran, since it was not uncommon for medieval manuscripts to depict planets as heads. On folio 4v of NLW MS 735C, for example, the visages of the planets bear a charming family resemblance, and the head of Saturn gazes steadily at the reader from his position at Capricornus the Sea Goat. This placement undoubtedly

suits him, since in astrology, Capricorn is one of two signs (or houses) that Saturn rules, along with the adjacent sign of Aquarius. I like to imagine that Bran—a giant in the sense that his orbit was the tallest of all the medieval planets—feels relatively comfortable each time he strolls through this duplex, despite the fact that not even two houses put together can fully contain him. Perhaps the author held a similarly sympathetic attitude toward Bran. In astrological symbolism, Saturn is an agricultural god associated with sorrow, ill luck, and disastrous events, and thus he is called the planet of greater misfortune. Yet the formal name for Bran in the *Mabinogi* is Bendigeidfran, meaning "blessed crow." That is more suggestive of good fortune than bad. To my mind, this suggests a spiritual lesson, and the moral of the lesson concerns our ability to reframe the various traumas that befall us, and to successfully transmute liabilities into assets.

In my astronomical model of the *Mabinogi*, Bran's head is a long way from his home in Capricornus at the end of the Second Branch. After Saturn has made three circuits of the sky during the eighty-seven-year period, Manawyddan inters the head on the Gwynfryn in London. The Gwynfryn is a white mound that is usually interpreted as the hill beneath the Tower of London. Towers and mounts direct our attention upward, which opens the possibility that this landmark signifies not only a burial site, but also a pointer toward the sky. What is it pointing at? As I reflect upon the mythological resonances between this passage and traditional Western star lore, I keep coming back to Regulus, the star at the heart of the constellation of Leo the Lion. If the burial is connected to this star, the best historical match that I have found so far for this event would be the conjunction of Mercury, Saturn, and Regulus on August 23, 1182 (Glomski, 2015). As we shall see in a bit, a burial date in the early 1180s would make sense as a lead-in to the most important celestial event of the Third Branch, a historical alignment that will symbolize Pryderi's disappearance and initiatory experience.

Despite his ties to greater misfortune, Saturn is also the planet of *logistikon* (reason) and *theoretikon* (understanding). In Macrobius's *Commentary on the Dream of Scipio*, the human soul acquires these two admirable qualities in Saturn's sphere (Stahl, 1990). So at the conclusion of the Second Branch, Bran's noggin can be visualized as a seed of higher thinking planted in the heart of a future adept, Leo. At least one further incarnation will be required before conditions are right for that seed to grow toward fruition for Pryderi. In the Fourth Branch, and in a new form, he will transition away from Aquarius and become more closely connected with Y Llew, the Welsh term for

Leo and also the nickname that Pryderi will receive as Lleu Llaw Gyffes. His story carries him from a sign that puts the Sun in astrological detriment (Aquarius) to the sign that he himself rules (Leo). These signs are 180 degrees apart, immediately suggesting a direct reading for the otherwise enigmatic phrase "nine-score attributes" in the upcoming poetry of the Fourth Branch.

"The road was long," the *Mabinogi* reports, in the description of the journey between Bran's temporary grave and the territory that Pryderi has promised to the dispossessed Manawyddan, along with his mother Rhiannon's hand in marriage. I am inclined to think that this trip required seven months. That would be enough time for the Sun and Mercury to travel from Regulus to the vernal equinoctial point. In the Second Branch, the vernal point—the location of the Sun at the March equinox—served as the "table" for two different feasts, with the seating arrangements of the characters signifying historical positions for their corresponding planets. The vernal point is the place where the head and tail ends of the zodiac join, and the author seems to have also made it a place of union for the characters in the *Mabinogi*. This metaphor appears to be in use again for the opening wedding feast of the Third Branch. On March 14, 1183, the date of the first spring equinox following the funeral on August 23, 1182, Mercury and the Sun arrived at the vernal point literally side-by-side, at a minuscule separation of only four arc seconds along the ecliptic. Astrologically speaking, they were also conjunct with Alpheratz, the star that marks the head of Rhiannon's constellation, Andromeda. It is not exactly rare for Mercury and the Sun to reach the vernal point together, but neither does it happen every year. The next closest occurrences to either side of the 1183 date were in 1174 and 1187, with the Sun and Mercury separated by a little over a degree in ecliptic longitude in each case.

At his marriage to Rhiannon, Manawyddan picks up a constellation identification that is reinforced multiple times throughout the narrative of the Third Branch. Manawyddan's constellation, Perseus the Hero, is immediately adjacent to Andromeda the Princess. Although Perseus's accessories are not described in the *Almagest*, the Greek myths make it clear that he wore fancy shoes and carried a shiny shield. Toward the end of the Middle Ages, Perseus was also coming to be seen as a rider of the winged horse Pegasus, which is easy to connect with the idea of a saddle. These three items—saddle, shield, and shoes—are the same ones that Manawyddan will later craft in England. In the Greek stories, Perseus rescues Andromeda and then marries her. In the *Mabinogi*, Manawyddan marries Rhiannon and then rescues her. Perseus holds in his left hand

a severed head, marked by several stars that are listed in the *Almagest*. This imagery is of course reminiscent of the Second Branch, in which Manawyddan carries Bran's head around with him. The head that Perseus carries is much less pleasant, that of the snake-haired woman Medusa. He pops it into a bag, for safekeeping and for later use to defeat an enemy. Manawyddan instead tucks a thieving mouse into a glove, for safekeeping and for later use to defeat an enemy.

From this point in the narrative and for the remainder of the Third Branch, discerning the celestial meanings requires deep and careful listening. In the story of Manawyddan, the author is transitioning from the planet-dense allegory of the Second Branch toward a broader exploration of the celestial sphere that begins in the Third Branch and continues into the Fourth Branch. As he shades from one set of legends to the next, a thickly interwoven mass of concepts is coming together: astronomical constellations; astrological signs; motions of the "errant planets" that are nowadays known simply as planets; motions of the "luminous planets" that are the Sun and Moon; and various motions of the celestial sphere that are sometimes diurnal, sometimes annual, and sometimes precessional. An additional complication is the author's love for mystical numbers—he seems especially enamored of the numbers three and seven. If the author rounded the narrative's timings to incorporate number symbolism into historical sequences of celestial events, this would unavoidably introduce uncertainties into any model that aims to synchronize plot developments with the actual motions of the sky. The fact that such inexactitudes are present in my own model has cost me more than one night of sleep. Next year's article will include a somewhat fuller discussion of this issue, along with a more general assessment of the strengths and weaknesses of the model as a whole.

Meanwhile, the best and really the only hope for hearing the celestial melodies of meaning among all the chords that have been struck is to intently train the ears toward the context. A particularly clear example of this occurs near the beginning of the Third Branch, immediately after the wedding has taken place. The royal family of Manawyddan, Rhiannon, Pryderi, and Pryderi's wife Cigfa made "a circuit" together, and "during that time a friendship developed between the four of them, so that not one wished to be without the other, either day or night" (Davies, 2007). In the astronomical layer of meaning, this lyrical phrasing is all about diurnal motion. A togetherness that is cemented through both day and night is a pitch-perfect analogy for the manner in which the constellations rotate as a single unit, always maintaining

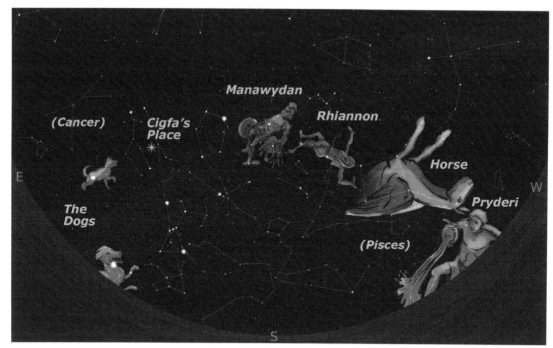

<u>Figure 4:</u>

Manawyddan, as the constellation of Perseus, is positioned among his family one hour before sunrise in mid-August during the late twelfth century. This timing would have coincided with the wheat harvest in medieval Wales, in years when the weather was sufficiently agreeable (Staples, 2011). Farmers rising at the first glimmer of morning twilight to check their ripened crops, just as Manawyddan does in the Third Branch, would have seen the stars in this orientation. Illustration by the author, incorporating images from Stellarium (Chéreau et al., 2009).

fixed positions with respect to one another, while the Earth turns on its axis through a full twenty-four-hour day. To remind the reader to also keep paying attention to planetary motions, the author then quickly retunes the narrative to note that the characters are wandering through the land. The word "planet" means "wanderer," a reference to the fact that planets move in odd ways as seen against the stellar background. When the author is next ready to introduce the lunar boar, which happens after the foursome has returned from the first expedition to England, he drops in an extra little beat about Pryderi and Manawyddan going hunting for a month. The idea of "hunting for a month" can be read at least two ways: as an outing that lasts for a specific period of *time*, but also as a quest for a more conceptual *thing* (a

"moon-th," so to speak, which cues the readers to begin thinking in terms of lunar motions). The author then immediately refers to the passage of an additional year. In terms of celestial mechanics, this represents annual motion, the same motion that causes the seasons and that governs the positions of the seasonal constellations. In my opinion, it is not unreasonable to regard this phrasing as a subtle form of signaling that the author has a particular season or seasons in mind. As discussed in last year's article, identical signaling appears to be employed in the First Branch (Glomski, 2015).

Among the constellations that represent Manawyddan's new family, we have already found three of the four (figure 4). Pryderi is in the lead as Aquarius, followed by his mother Rhiannon as Andromeda with her horse Pegasus, next accompanied closely by Manawyddan as Perseus, and . . . where is Cigfa?

Cigfa is more of a cipher. In the Dolmen Arch notes, which transmit certain Druid Revival teachings about the *Mabinogi*, the name Cigfa is translated as "house of flesh" (Greer & Guest, 2009). Taken at face value, that would provide an easy celestial solution for Cigfa's identity. There are many instances in the *Mabinogi* in which the word "house" appears to be used as an indicator for zodiacal signs. The sign that would make sense for Cigfa is Cancer. Macrobius's *Commentary on the Dream of Scipio* specifies this particular sign, Cancer, as the portal through which human souls depart the company of the gods and sink down to become embodied in the world of flesh (Stahl, 1990). As they descend into incarnation, human beings are unable to retain their full memory of the divine order, with some individuals slipping into deeper states of forgetfulness than others.

I have so far failed in my efforts, however, to find any evidence that *cigfa* is attested as a term meaning "house of flesh" prior to the sixteenth century. The earliest known usage of this word dates to 1567 (University of Wales, 2016). In Middle Welsh, the character's name was actually Kigua or Kicua. There is relatively little discussion of the origin of this name in the academic literature. One scholar (Rhŷs, 1901) has written that it is not Brythonic and may have stemmed from the Irish character Ciochba, while another (Parker, 2003) has linked Cigfa with Gloucester and the Cotswold region.

Over its long history during the past three centuries, the Druid Revival has incorporated a variety of unusual inspirations that do not always, upon closer inspection,

accord well with meticulous scholarship. But I feel it is important to avoid dismissing such interpretations out of hand, because they can and often do contain insights of value. Whether or not her name means "house of flesh," Cigfa is a character who is strongly attuned to the material world, not to spiritual concerns. She frets over mundane matters of social convention, urging Manawyddan to avoid work that is unsuited to his rank and fussing over his handling of a mouse even when there is little reason to think anyone will see. Additionally, because they are such close companions, it seems reasonable to assume that Cigfa's astrological house, if she has one, would be close to Manawyddan's. Cancer is immediately next door to Gemini, the sign that Mercury rules in this area of sky. Due to precession, the point of connection between the signs of Cancer and Gemini actually rested within the constellation of Gemini in the twelfth century. This identification is more abstract and more tentative than the others. It is nonetheless a better fit than any other idea that I have considered, so I have provisionally designated this point in the sky as "Cigfa's place" (figure 4).

So this is the family of constellations—Aquarius, Andromeda, Perseus, and possibly the sign of Cancer in the care of Gemini—who travel together. In the heavens over twelfth-century Wales, the full curve of these characters would become visible in the gray dawn skies shortly before sunrise in mid-August, when the wheat was fully ripe. Aquarius would be in the west, Cancer in the east, and Andromeda and Perseus between. The star marking the head of Perseus, τ Persei, would be directly overhead, within three degrees of the zenith. That is Manawyddan, appropriately positioned uppermost among his family in a generous territory that stretches from horizon to horizon. This arrangement constitutes the first answer to the question posed in the introduction to this article: Why would the author focus on the sky between Pisces and Cancer for the narrative of the Third Branch? It is because Manawyddan, when he takes an upright stance in the south, is centered atop a memorable arc of constellations between Pisces (just to the east of Aquarius) and Cancer.

The territory that Pryderi bestows upon Manawyddan teems with wild game, fish, and honeybee swarms. The narrative emphasizes this point twice, clarifying that it remains true even after an evil spell denudes the land of its human subjects and livestock. What might this indicate astronomically?

There is more than one star pattern that could conceivably represent the fish, and likewise with the game. The bees, on the other hand, are a toughie. One seemingly

obvious choice, the Beehive Cluster, is not likely to be a valid candidate, since it did not yet go by that name in the medieval era. In astronomical terminology, a cluster is a group of stars in close association. The cluster that we now call the Beehive had a different name in antiquity that would have been more relevant to the author of the *Mabinogi*, as I explain later. But perhaps the bees are part of a more elaborate literary-visual pun of the type that medieval authors loved.

I cannot read about the bees, fish, and game without also thinking of the *Life of Saint David*, a late eleventh-century hagiography that was originally written in Latin and later translated into Welsh (Wade-Evans, [1923] 2013). The author of this work, Rhygyfarch ap Sulien, was a well-educated poet and clerk who may have briefly succeeded his father as bishop of St. David's. Several scholars have suggested that Rhygyfarch himself wrote parts or all of the *Mabinogi*—Proinsias MacCana's (1958) study of Branwen is the source I have seen cited most often in that regard. In any case, the *Life of Saint David* opens with a description of St. David's father dreaming that he will encounter a stag, a fish, and wild honey. St. David's father is instructed to send portions of these gifts to the Monastery of the Deposit for the benefit of his future son. Although this account is rather fanciful, Rhygyfarch did not invent the idea of these gifts. They were previously referenced in the Laws of Hywel Dda, a codification of Welsh law named after a tenth-century king. According to one of the earliest extant manuscripts of these laws, Peniarth MS 28 (c. 1250), the first royal occupants of a wilderness area "ought to guard the king's waste, and they shall have the honey, and the fish, and the small sylvan animals . . . until the king shall do his will concerning it, and until men shall come to inhabit it" (Wade-Evans, [1923] 2013). This context would tend to suggest that although Manawyddan and his family are benefiting from the resources of the land, they are somehow no longer fully in charge—there is another king to whom they may have to answer.

Still, the author could have driven home that point in a variety of ways. It seems unlikely to me that the set of symbols appearing in the *Life of St. David* just happened to show up in the *Mabinogi* accidentally. Dozens of manuscripts of Rhygyfarch's *Life* have been preserved and cataloged, and it clearly was circulating in the twelfth century (Sharpe, 2007). For our immediate purposes, the aspect of the text that matters the most is Rhygyfarch's explanation of the gift of the fish, which he interpreted as presaging St. David's nickname of Dewi the Aquatic (in Latin) or Dewi the Waterman (in Welsh). St. David and his followers became known as Watermen because they drank only water and abstained from wine and other intoxicants.

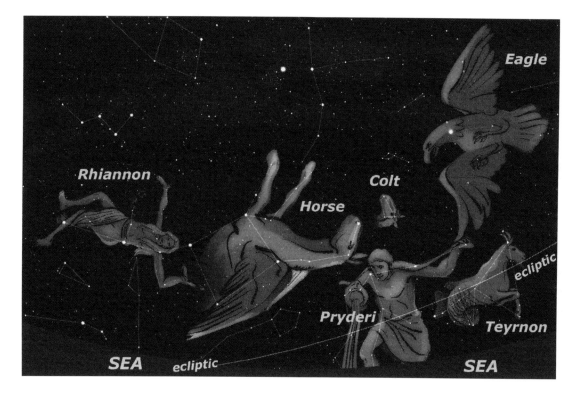

Figure 5:

The constellation representing the young Pryderi would have looked like this each time he rose over the eastern horizon in twelfth-century Wales. His official astronomical name is Aquarius. The official names of the other constellations, from left to right, are Andromeda, Pegasus, Equuleus, Aquila, and Capricornus. Illustration by the author, incorporating images from Stellarium (Chéreau et al., 2009).

There is exactly one constellation that conspicuously depicts a man with a container of water—Aquarius. This celestial Waterman shows up early in the *Mabinogi*, in the First Branch passage describing Pryderi's youth. By the age of four, Pryderi has grown big enough to bribe his foster father's grooms for the opportunity to water the horses. An unambiguous portrayal of this scene appears in the night sky: Aquarius is situated just below the heads of the winged horse Pegasus and the little horse Equuleus, and he is pouring out a stream of water (figure 5). To date, I have found no other astronomical interpretation of the *Mabinogi* that makes this connection, however. In Rees's (2012) model, Pryderi is represented directly by Pegasus, with an imagined figure of Pegasus's

original rider, Bellerophon, rolled into the mental picture. This idea starts with Rees's proposition that Pryderi's actions exhibit prudence and fortitude. He designates Pryderi as one of two characters in the *Mabinogi* who, along with Branwen, are "representatives of unalloyed virtue." Rees draws a parallel between Pryderi and the titular character of Euripides's play *Bellerophontes*, additionally citing Homer's *Iliad* and its description of Bellerophon as "the blameless" one "whose will was virtuous." This is a radically different reading than I would give to the character of Pryderi, although I would agree that the narrative of Third Branch is concerned with the issue of virtue.

If I am correct that the author wanted the audience to associate Pryderi with St. David, I suspect he was employing a degree of irony. The life of Pryderi and the impulsive choices he makes are perhaps not very much like the ascetic habits of Dewi the Waterman. Medieval thinkers frequently used contrasts such as this one to collate ideas into memorative webs. These webs worked just as well whether the elements they contained were similar, dissimilar, or a complex blend of the two (Carruthers, 1998). To my mind, this particular contrast between Pryderi and Dewi also extends an implicit invitation to the reader, to reflect upon a matter of moral edification. This is done with a light and skillful hand. The author has supplied outcomes for Pryderi's behavior, but he does not explicitly spell out rules concerning how one must live. The manner of living that is most appropriate is something that each reader must individually determine, and the options are not limited to the examples of Pryderi and Dewi.

At least one additional literary association is worth considering here. Among readers in the Middle Ages, one of the most popular Roman poets was Virgil. Virgil lived in the first century BCE. His works were held in such esteem that by the mid-twelfth century, he had picked up a legendary status as a prophet and a mage. Virgil wrote about beekeeping in the book *Georgic IV*, explaining that the seasons for honey collection can be determined by observing the rising and setting of the star Taygeta, one of the seven sisters in the Pleiades star cluster. Virgil also described at length the ritual of bugonia, a technique that reputedly restored lost hives of bees by regenerating them from the carcass of a steer. When viewed in this context, the royal family's dependence upon wild swarms instead of domestic colonies suggests a subtle form of foreshadowing. In astronomical symbolism, it hints that the Pleiades and the constellation of Taurus the Bull might become factors in their shifting fortunes. The instructions in Virgil's account are to "search out a bullock, just jutting his horns out of a two year olds forehead" (Kline, 2001). Since all of the cattle on the ground have vanished, it is the bull in the sky that will matter.

The stars that form the V-shaped pattern of the bull's face are called the Hyades (figure 6). In the Roman era, these stars also picked up the nickname Suculae, meaning "little pigs." The orator Cicero expressed disdain for this etymological corruption in his work of 45 BCE, *De Natura Deorum*. "The Greeks were wont to call them Hyades," he wrote, "from their bringing rain, the Greek for which is *hyein*, while our nation stupidly names them the Suckling-pigs, as though the name Hyades were derived from the word for 'pig' [*hus*] and not from 'rain'" (Rackham, 1967). This injection of pigs into the bull's face was sufficiently clumsy that the concept eventually did fall out of favor, and it is no longer widely known today. During the medieval era, however, the Suculae were still referenced in popular books such as Pliny's *Natural History* (Bostock & Riley, 1893). Cicero's *De Natura Deorum* was not itself often read in the twelfth century, but there is evidence that the scholar Adelard of Bath, at least, was familiar with the work (Silverstein, 1952). The

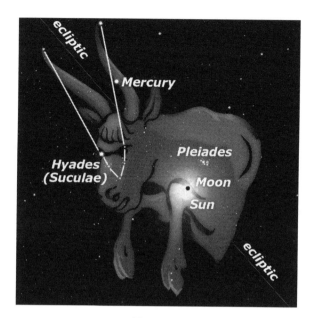

Figure 6:

Taurus the Bull is among the most ancient of all constellations. Thanks to its distinctive star clusters, it is also among the easiest to find. The Hyades are the widely spaced, V-shaped cluster at the bull's face. The Pleiades are a more compact and very pretty cluster to the west. The positions of Mercury, the Moon, and the Sun have also been plotted for May 1, 1185, the date of a solar eclipse over Wales. Illustration by the author, incorporating images from Stellarium (Chéreau et al., 2009).

author of the *Mabinogi* may have formed his own conclusions about the matter. In the Fourth Branch, when Math, the king of Gwynedd, is persuaded under false pretenses that pork is superior to beef, mayhem ensues and swine start popping up in place names everywhere. There are many ways to interpret that upcoming passage—the triad notes by the Welsh language and literature scholar Rachel Bromwich (2014) concerning the "Three Powerful Swineherds of the Island of Britain" give an excellent taste of the complexity of porcine symbolism in Celtic mythology. But from a strictly astronomical perspective, this incident reads like a satirical comment on the dubious quality of Roman contributions

to the Greek tradition. I will revisit this point again briefly next year while discussing Boötes the Ox-Driver. Boötes's feet are at the lap of Virgo the Virgin, and he cannot go the circuit of the land, since the star marking his head is too far north to set upon the horizon. In antiquity, Boötes carried a staff. On f. 5r of NLW MS 735C, the object in his hand looks just like a wand. These qualities of Boötes, and more, will all fall into place during the Fourth Branch analysis of Math.

Meanwhile, back in the Third Branch, Pryderi and Manawyddan have been hunting in the *Mabinogi* forest, in the vicinity of Taurus, when they encounter the Moon in the form of a gleaming white boar. As this lunar boar flees the hunters, he runs along the ecliptic above the constellations of the dogs. The Moon's path in this area of sky takes him right toward the Suculae, exactly as if the boar is seeking safety and reinforcements among the company of his own kind. Astrologically speaking, he succeeds in gaining strength as he enters this "fort." In Taurus, the Moon is in triplicity—a mild form of rulership—and is also exalted.

The porcine and bovine imagery in this passage are admittedly an awkward jumble, but take heart. The correspondences do become more distinct in the Fourth Branch. In traditional Western natural magic (Greer, 2005), cattle are associated with the Moon in Taurus, and this symbolism is fully congruent with the narrative of the Third Branch. Pigs, on the other hand, are chthonic animals associated with Saturn in Scorpio. The pigs will finally go all the way home in the Fourth Branch. That part of the story describes Lleu Llaw Gyffes as a wounded eagle whose decaying flesh falls to the ground and feeds a sow until he is rescued by his uncle Gwydion. In the sky, this scene is depicted at the constellation of Ophiuchus, the figure who braces his feet against Scorpius. Ophiuchus's well-defined lap, which is unambiguously depicted on the planisphere of f. 10v of NLW MS 735c, is positioned beneath Aquila the Eagle after the eagle has culminated and begun his descent toward the western horizon. This arrangement constitutes the second answer to the question posed in the introduction to this article: Why did the author bookend Manawyddan's story with the water signs of Pisces and Cancer, and not Scorpio? It is because he has secreted up his sleeve the powerful symbolism of Scorpio, as a card to be played later in the Fourth Branch.

Pig-related problems will bedevil Pryderi for the remainder of his life, and into the next one, too. But by the time he enters the fort himself, he sees neither the boar nor the Suculae. There is only a golden bowl, hanging from four chains that extend upward

farther than the eye can see, situated at the edge of a fountain. The conditions are set for a period of confinement in which Pryderi might become initiated into knowledge of his true self, if he has done enough preparation. As with the transformational tale of *Hanes Taliesin*, there is a historical celestial event that matches this passage well enough to be worthy of consideration: a solar eclipse.

On May 1, 1185, a deep partial solar eclipse occurred in the early afternoon over Wales (figure 6). At Narberth, the fraction of the Sun's diameter that was obscured by the Moon was 0.853 (Espenak, 2015b). This was definitely dark enough to be noticed. The *Brut y Tywysogion*, the Welsh *Chronicle of the Princes*, contains a record for it: "In that year [of 1185], on the calends of May, the sun changed its colour, and some said there was an eclipse of it" (Williams, 1860). Although this alignment would not have been directly visible in the sky, the Sun and Moon were conjunct with the Pleiades (figure 6). Mercury (Manawyddan) was positioned next to one of Taurus's horns and also at his high seat in the astrological sign of Gemini. Starting on May 1 and continuing over the next few days, the celestial story unfolded in the following fashion. During the eclipse itself, the Moon (the otherworldly boar) rushed across the path of the Sun (Pryderi), heading in the direction of the Hyades (the fort of the Suculae). The Sun then lagged behind while deliberating whether to rescue Canis Major and Canis Minor (Pryderi's dogs). By the time the Sun finally pulled up alongside the fort, the Moon had already reached the constellation of Cancer. Upon reaching that spot, the Moon was not only well past the hunters, but also at the backside of the dogs, whose noses would now pointed be away from him.

Pryderi both is and is not ready for what happens next. Upon grabbing the bowl, he is stunned. The moment his hands touch it, he becomes immobilized and unable to speak. Taurus is the sign the rules the throat in astrological medicine, so it is no surprise that a character in trouble here would be thus affected. This outcome suggests that Pryderi's impatient and rather greedy approach might not be the ideal way to reach for inspiration, poetic or otherwise. There has been much feasting in Pryderi's life, and relatively little rumination. So he is now obliged to stand still for while, digesting and chewing his cud, as it were.

Pryderi is very fortunate, though, to have an ally in Mercury. In Macrobius's *Commentary on the Dream of Scipio*, the human soul acquires the quality of *hermeneutikon*, the ability to interpret and to speak that interpretation, in Mercury's sphere (Stahl,

1990). It thus falls to Manawyddan to help restore Pryderi's voice in this world. The Irish warriors who lost the power of speech in the Second Branch were not so lucky, for the author placed the god of eloquence on the side of the Britons, the forefathers of the Welsh. In the process of assisting Pryderi, Manawyddan also negotiates a deal that restores cultivation and culture to the land. It is ultimately Pryderi's responsibility, however, to restore his own memory of his essential self. Although he receives friendly aid along the way, no one else can do this task for him. A case could be made that the same applies to all of us who are seeking to know ourselves as individuals, and who desire to know our proper course in the universe.

Back in the mundane world, the eclipse has the effect of further deepening the curse on Manawyddan's land. While the specific astrological sources that the author may have consulted are unknown, the following reading would at least be congruent with the general material of that era: "It would predict trouble caused by a foreign king, or involving one—the Sun is eclipsed in the ninth house, which is the house of long journeys and faraway lands. The trouble wouldn't be fatal, since the eclipse isn't complete, but Saturn is rising, which is a baleful sign" (J. M. Greer, personal communication, April 19, 2015). We will eventually meet this mysterious foreign king in the next section. His name is Llwyd son of Cil Coed, "gray, son of the corner of the forest" (Greer & Guest, 2009).

The date of May 1, which in Wales is also called Calan Mai and traditionally regarded as the first day of summer, has appeared once before in the *Mabinogi*. In the First Branch, the infant Pryderi was abducted and dropped at the door of Teyrnon Twryf Vliant on the eve of this date. When I first began reflecting upon that passage, I thought, "How odd. Surely the baby Sun, whose true self is briefly revealed when he is originally named after his golden hair, should have been born at the winter solstice. Was there a scribal error, perhaps, or have I misunderstood this allegory?" If the eclipse of May 1, 1185, is behind Pryderi's adult disappearance, however, the First Branch date looks less like a mistake and more like a motif. Pryderi is snatched twice: once as a newborn during the night before Calan Mai, and once as a grown man during a daytime darkening of the Sun on Calan Mai itself. In Celtic culture and mythology, May 1 is also considered to be a date of liminality—that is, a time of more fluid contact between the otherworld and the ordinary apparent world. But there is also at least one other traditional date of liminality, November 1, that the author could have chosen if this aspect was his sole concern. I think he selected Calan Mai for the First Branch

Figure 7:

At top: this photograph shows a working replica of the twelfth-century Durham Cathedral door knocker (Beckwith, 2011). At bottom: this star chart, generated by Stellarium, plots the circlet of the western fish in Pisces (Chéreau et al., 2009).

kidnapping specifically to prefigure the events of the Third Branch. The *Mabinogi* as a whole is masterfully interwoven with such recurring symbolic elements, which are incorporated at varying levels of subtlety throughout the work.

In this section, we have journeyed deeply through the wilderness symbolism of the first half of the Third Branch, discovered important links between the characters and the star patterns in the sky around the constellation of Perseus, found two possible justifications for the author's decision to highlight this particular celestial region for his tale of Manawyddan, and determined the date of a solar eclipse that appears to be subtly referenced in the Third Branch narrative. It is now time to leave the pigs and cows behind and to leap ahead to the denouement at the end of the Third Branch, which introduces us instead to a couple of donkeys.

The Hammer, the Harness, and the Hay

After their spouses have been taken hostage, Manawyddan and Cigfa travel to England for a year to try to earn a living there. Upon returning home, Manawyddan plants three fields of wheat. The ripened crops are systematically stripped bare overnight. Manawyddan finally manages to catch one of the culprits: a pregnant mouse. He is then able to use the mouse as a powerful bargaining chip in the confrontation that ensues with Llwyd son of Cil Coed. Llwyd is the mastermind behind Pryderi and Rhiannon's abduction, and Manawyddan not only forces him to return the missing family members, but also extracts an explanation of their whereabouts during their absence. "Pryderi had the gate-hammers of my court around his neck," Llwyd confesses, "while around hers Rhiannon had the collars of the asses after they had been hauling hay. And that was their imprisonment" (Davies, 2007). These two bonds are termed Mynord, the hammer, and Mynweir, the

collar. We are about to locate all of these things in the sky, and with even greater speed than the god of quicksilver himself.

To discover Mynord and Mynweir, we simply need to look at the patterns beside the upper bodies of Aquarius and Andromeda. The star patterns in those positions become the bonds of Pryderi and Rhiannon in the *Mabinogi*, but they are more commonly known as the two fish in the constellation of Pisces.

The fish that represents Mynord, the hammer, has a rounded shape like the ring in an old-fashioned door knocker. Door knockers in medieval Europe commonly featured lions as the anchoring design element. The example pictured in figure 7 is among the more famous—it is a painstaking replica of the original twelfth-century design that graced Durham Cathedral. The ring that visitors would use for hammering hangs from the lion's mouth toward his neck. This imagery is significant in more ways than one. Before exploring those ideas further, the first step is to recognize that the circlet of stars at the western fish also resembles a special type of hammer. In keeping with the theme of bondage, a long tether of stars connects the circlet to a knot below.

Draft collars, which conform to the animal's chest and shoulders, have more of an ovoid shape, as is shown from above and from the side in figure 8. In the *Almagest*, the stars cataloged for the east-

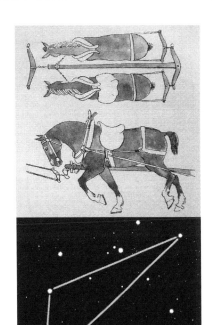

Figure 8:

At top: this public domain illustration from *Medieval Costume, Armour and Weapons* shows the teardrop shape of horse collars (Wagner, Drobná, & Durdík, [1956] 2000). At bottom: this star chart, generated by Stellarium, plots a similar shape for the eastern fish in Pisces (Chéreau et al., 2009).

ern fish of Pisces trace out a similar teardrop shape. Stellarium plots a simplified triangle for this fish, omitting some of the fainter stars from the pattern. But in either case, the shape is approximately correct for the collar, Mynweir. This collar is connected by its own tether of stars to the same knot that secures the hammer.

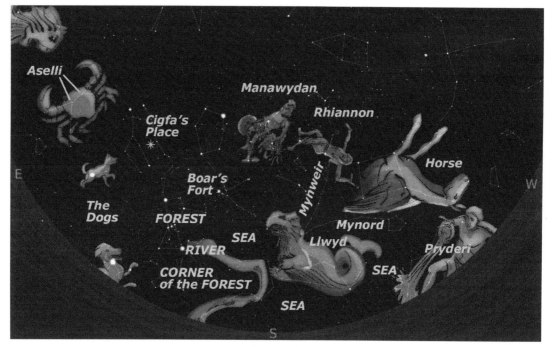

Figure 9:

Here again is the chart previously shown in figure 4, but with further details revealed. The constellation representing Llwyd has been sneakily present in the depths all along. True to his name, Llwyd is positioned adjacent to a corner of the otherworldly forest, a threshold represented by a hairpin turn of Eridanus the River. The astronomical symbolism of the Third Branch plays this entire group of constellations like the strings of a harp, the frame of which extends from horizon to horizon. Illustration by the author, incorporating images from Stellarium (Chéreau et al., 2009).

And who holds the knot? According to the *Phaenomena*, the tethers "end in a single star of Cetus, set where meet his spine and head" (Mair & Mair, 1921). We have already encountered this monster in the story of the enchantress Ceridwen, who took the form of an otter, an animal shaped much like Cetus. In the *Mabinogi*, the transformed character is instead a sorcerer named Llwyd, who comes disguised as a man of the cloth. And ultimately in the heavens, Llwyd is also a celestial sea monster at odds with a god of the sea, Manawyddan (figure 9). There is a deeper mystery in this, perhaps, about the ebb and flow of power between that which draws distinctions (symbolized by Mercury, who interprets) and that which can potentially dissolve distinctions (symbolized by the sea itself, which might or might not be as monstrous as we fear).

The abduction of Rhiannon and Pryderi by Llwyd resonates well with both Greek and Roman star lore. In the Greek myth referenced in the *Phaenomena*, the princess has been chained in place as a sacrifice to Cetus: "Andromeda, though she cowers a good way off, is pressed by the rush of the mighty Monster of the Sea" (Mair & Mair, 1921). As hinted in last year's article (Glomski, 2015), there is also a Roman story that dovetails well, especially since it incorporates a mother-and-son pair. This later myth can be read in the fragment of *De Astronomica* by pseudo-Hyginus that appears on f. 3v of Harley MS 647 (c. 820–850), and it is also included in Book II of Ovid's *Fasti*, a Latin calendrical poem published in 8 CE that was still studied in the medieval era. In the Roman version, Dione (whose name here is an epithet for Venus) and her son Cupid are attacked by the monster Typhon. They are rescued by the two fish who now appear in the night sky as Pisces (Kline, 2004). The *Mabinogi* puts a different and intriguing twist on this, instead emphasizing the representation of restraint that is present in the constellation of Pisces.

Cetus is next to Taurus, so he is well positioned to catch Pryderi and Rhiannon at the fort of the Suculae. The place of their capture is possibly not the same place where Pryderi and Rhiannon are penned up, though. The fort disappears with them in it, implying that the author wants the audience to look for their prison elsewhere in the sky. To understand where they went, we need to return our attention to the lunar boar.

The constellation that the Moon reached after the May 1 eclipse, just as the Sun was coming up alongside the Hyades, was Cancer. There is something strange about the Cancer in the star maps of NLW MS 735C. Two little animal heads appear inside the crab's body on the summer hemisphere of f. 3v, and also on the full planisphere of f. 10v, and again at the top of the solar system model on f. 4v. No other surviving celestial map from the medieval era includes this flourish (McGurk, 1973). The two animals are the stars γ Cancri and δ Cancri, also known as the Aselli, the asses.

Between the Aselli is a manger. In the real sky, this object is a soft little smudge of light that dims when atmospheric conditions deterirate. The smudge is actually a cluster of stars, though nobody knew that prior to the invention of the telescope. At magnitudes of 6.3 and fainter, the stars are too dim to be individually distinct to the unaided eye, whereas the gentle glow of their combined light can often be easily perceived. Nowadays the cluster is named Praesepe. This Latin term means both "manger" and "hive"—a

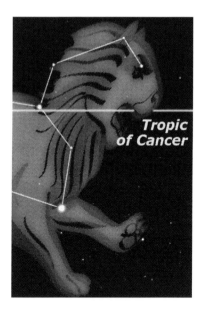

Figure 10:

A small segment of the Tropic of Cancer is shown here at Leo for the year 1185. Due to precession, the tropic's position has shifted slowly through the centuries. If a modern author were to set the tale of Mynord and Mynweir in the year 2016, the current of inspiration would enter the lion through his eye, instead of passing through his mouth. Illustration by the author, incorporating images from Stellarium (Chéreau et al., 2009).

perfect moniker, since the cluster has also picked up the nickname "the Beehive" in modern times.

Aratus's *Phaenomena* predicted that rain would soon fall if the manger dimmed while the Aselli remained bright. A sudden and total disappearance of the manger, though, signaled potentially serious trouble: "not slight then is the storm with which the fields are deluged" (Mair & Mair, 1921). In the *Mabinogi*, a moist and turbulent atmosphere also arises at Gorsedd Arberth, both during the initial disappearance of the land's inhabitants and their livestock and also during the later disappearance of Pryderi and Rhiannon: "Then, as soon as it was night, there was a tumultuous noise above them, and a blanket of mist, and then the fort disappeared and so did they" (Davies, 2007).

The author seems to have developed a theme around the idea of challenges for the Sun between the dates of Calan Mai, the Welsh summer holiday on May 1, and the summer solstice, which in 1185 occurred on June 14. Moving from west to east, the same direction that the Sun travels on the ecliptic, the Tropic of Cancer during that era went through the horns of Taurus, was touched by the Sun at the solstitial point of standstill in the constellation of Gemini, and then passed through the manger in Cancer. Here, then, is a celestial snapshot of the mysterious journey of Pryderi, who entered the fort of the Suculae shortly after an eclipse, proceeded to get stuck in the vicinity of the "high seat," and found himself carried along to a stable where he and his mother were collared. Pryderi was then made to wear a gate-hammer that could well have been an oversized ring from a lion door knocker. I think it is entirely possible that the author had this in mind, because a lion emblem would appropriately herald the next constellation in this zodiacal sequence, Leo. There was in fact a big ring in the sky that ran through Leo's mouth during the twelfth century. This circle was the Tropic of Cancer itself (figure 10).

Once the passage concerning Pryderi's ordeal is seen from this angle, the Tropic of Cancer functions extremely well as a symbolic marker for the transmission of prophetic spirit. Among other things, it foreshadows Pryderi's ability to predict, in his next incarnation as Llew, the exact conditions that will precede his death. The trope of the prophetic spirit entering through the mouth appears also in the *Hanes Taliesin*. In that tale, Gwion Bach swallows three drops of inspiration and ends up confined in Ceridwen's womb. The theme of eating one's source of inspiration is not exclusive to Celtic mythology. In the Bible, the prophet Ezekiel is commanded to eat a scroll of dirges and laments that becomes sweet as honey in his mouth (Ezekiel 3:3). The ensuing vision leaves him dumbfounded for seven days (Ezekiel 3:15), and then the Lord reveals to him that he will be confined in a house, bound in place, and deprived of the faculty of speech (Ezekiel 3:24–26), a situation that resonates oddly well with Pryderi's experiences with the bowl in the Third Branch. Ezekiel was more influential in the Middle Ages than most people realize nowadays. Jerome's commentary on this book, in particular, was one of the best-known and most frequently adapted of the Old Testament commentaries (Carruthers, 2008).

As was true earlier with Dewi, such correspondences do not automatically imply that Pryderi is somehow just like Ezekiel. Rather, I believe the author selectively chose shared elements from the stories to build a memorative web, presumably with the aim of provoking deeper thought in the minds of the audience. The Tropic of Cancer is an invisible circle in the sky, and it is not easy to look at the stars and to intuitively discern exactly where it lies. Aratus handled this issue by simply presenting a list of the constellation parts crossed by the tropic. In the ancient era of astronomy addressed by the *Phaenomena*, the tropic cut "the Lion beneath the breast and belly and lengthwise to the loins" (Mair & Mair, 1921). The author of the *Mabinogi* appears to have been aware of the effects of precession, effectively updating the position of the tropic to his own era, with a new visual of a gate-hammer that draws the audience's attention upward to the protagonist's neck and ultimately to the mouth. If so, this is fantastically clever imagery. Once the tropic is perceived as the ring in the lion's mouth, it is nearly impossible to ever forget where it was positioned in the Middle Ages.

This reference to Leo would also suggest a third reason for the emphasis upon the constellations between Pisces and Cancer within the Third Branch narrative. It is because the constellations in Manawyddan's story fit hand-in-glove inside the larger arc of Pryderi's story, in which Pryderi is moving from his past and present correspondence with Aquarius

(the constellation immediately to the west of Pisces) toward his future incarnation as Leo (immediately to the east of Cancer). When the night sky is oriented in the correct position to manifest the tale of Manawyddan, Aquarius is setting, or preparing to exit the stage (figure 9). And Leo, the Fourth Branch incarnation corresponding to Llew, is rising.

In the astronomical allegory of the Fourth Branch, the author will rotate the celestial sphere 180 degrees, so that he can address the equivalent range of constellations within the opposite hemisphere of the sky. When the visible sky is turned so that it centers upon Ophiuchus (the character of Gwydion) instead of Perseus (the character of Manawyddan), the story arc that nests within the Leo-to-Aquarius framework then runs from Virgo to Capricornus. This suggests the audience will next hear a lot more about virgins and goats. This is indeed what happens. Note that in astrology, these are both earth signs. That underlying elemental symbolism will give the Fourth Branch an earthier feel, as opposed to the dreamlike, oceanic quality of the Third Branch narrative.

To sum up, the primary area of sky referenced in the Third Branch can be determined in the following three ways: (1) by centering Perseus (Manawyddan) at his highest point in the south and then looking at the constellations around him, (2) by peeking ahead at the Fourth Branch and correctly guessing that the Third Branch must cover the area of sky that is opposite to Ophiuchus (Gwydion), and (3) by realizing that Pryderi's story in the Third Branch essentially arcs from Aquarius toward Leo, and that Manawyddan's story has been tucked inside Pryderi's. Figure 9 supplies new *Mabinogi* labels for nearly every Ptolemaic constellation to either side of Manawyddan and also below him, as would be seen from Wales at the season of the year when the wheat was ripe and when Manawyddan triumphed over Llwyd. I have left just one or two items unidentified. Using Stellarium or a star chart similar to the one in figure 9, see if you can find a big, plump, rodent-like constellation that is fleeing toward Cetus, and you will have discovered a good representation of the mouse that is Llwyd's pregnant wife. In next year's article, after I have discussed the astronomical symbolism that remains in the Fourth Branch, I will provide the full list of my model's constellation identifications. For ease of comparison, that table will also summarize the identifications made within two previously published models of astronomical interpretation. Let us take an initial look at one of those models now.

You Like To-may-toes, and I Like To-mah-toes

When I first encountered the *Mabinogi* in 2011, I was keen on reaching my own conclusions about this work. For the next two years, I read, digested, reread, and

meditated extensively on the text, especially the first three branches. To eliminate noise while sorting out my own ideas, I resisted the temptation to seek out other thinkers' work on the *Mabinogi*.

By the summer of 2013, I was nonetheless becoming gradually and inevitably aware that other students and scholars have indeed already explored the astronomical aspects of this great piece of literature. I initially came across three brief but interesting articles on the Internet, each suggesting ideas worth considering (Freer, 2004; Griffiths, 2008; Nichols, 2009). In August, a new blog launched and began to more fully address this topic (Davies, 2013). It was from this blog, *Mabinogion Astronomy*, that I learned an entire book had recently been published on the matter (Rees, 2012). I immediately suffered one of those moments of chagrin that sometimes plague students, when they learn that their seemingly brilliant ideas are perhaps not so novel after all. I have experienced this phenomenon often enough that I now semihumorously refer to it as the Ecclesiastes 1:9 Effect. Alas, as it says in the Bible, there is nothing new under the Sun.

As soon as I read Rees's book, however, I realized that my model does in fact differ significantly from the one presented in *The Mabinogi Decoded*. Among the Ptolemaic constellations alone, with partial credit awarded for partial agreements, the overall agreement between the two models is roughly only 30 percent. For the seven planets of the medieval era (including the Sun and Moon), just one interpretation is shared: Manawyddan as Mercury. My model also disagrees with all twelve of the additional, non-Ptolemaic constellations that Rees suggests are important. Rees lists fourteen examples of these, but he appears to have accidentally counted two items that Ptolemy actually did include in the *Almagest*: the Pleiades star cluster and the constellation of Lyra (Toomer, 1998).

The two models start from similar premises, and yet their conclusions conflict. To understand how this has happened, some scrutiny of their points of divergence is in order here.

First, I found that before I could evaluate the core merits of Rees's reasoning, I needed to disregard a number of factual errors. As I thumbed through the various figures in the book, one issue that immediately caught my eye was that Polaris, also known as the North Star, was misidentified on the relevant star chart. The star that should have been labeled Polaris is present in its proper place in Ursa Minor the Little Bear, but its name has been applied to another star that has been added to the chart some distance

away. This mislabeled star would approximately coincide with the position of HIP 4283, a nondescript star that is listed in modern catalogs but which understandably received no mention in ancient and medieval works. *The Mabinogi Decoded* interprets the seven main stars of Ursa Minor as the seven knights who succumbed in Caswallawn's ambush in the Second Branch. My best guess is that a random star meant to represent Pendaran Dyfed, the young page who escaped this sneak attack, was placed in the vicinity of Ursa Minor to underscore the point, and that this star mistakenly received the label of Polaris. But I cannot say for sure, since Rees's discussion does not specify a stellar identity for Pendaran Dyfed. An identical problem occurs on another chart. The labels for the Aselli have been incorrectly applied, and Rees's text erroneously describes the two stars as "clusters." It is unfortunate that this occurred, since it detracts from ideas in *The Mabinogi Decoded* that otherwise could have been stronger. The description of Ursa Minor in the *Almagest* already includes one "nearby star outside the constellation" (Toomer, 1998). This eighth star, nowadays designated 5 UMi, shines three times brighter in the sky than HIP 4283. The star 5 UMi would have been a more rational choice for Pendaran Dyfed, if I have correctly surmised Rees's line of thought, but that is not the argument that he advances.

Some additional issues in the text include: attribution of color symbolism to stars that are too dim to see with the unaided eye, statements that widely separated constellations are adjacent, and descriptions of celestial motions and alignments that fail to take precession into account. *The Mabinogi Decoded* also features quite a few claims for which more straightforward solutions exist. Rees suggests, for example, that Canis Minor the Little Dog standing on the back of Monoceros the Unicorn "would provide a precise rendering of the image of Rhiannon in the *Mabinogi*." Monoceros is not depicted on any star map or globe prior to 1612, when the Dutch cartographer Petrus Plancius introduced it (Ridpath, 1988). Rees additionally selects four dim stars from Officina Typographica the Printing Office—a defunct nineteenth-century constellation near Monoceros—and nominates this quartet as Rhiannon's horse-mounting block. Rees is aware of the dating issue. He addresses this concern by asserting that the resemblance between this set of constellations and the First Branch punishment of Rhiannon is so strong that it constitutes evidence that these star patterns were already recognized during the medieval era, but unrecorded on charts until several centuries later.

One difficulty with this contention is that an equivalent block shape can just as well be created next to Pegasus, the constellation that corresponds to Rhiannon's horse in

my model. With extra effort, it is even possible to draw a pattern that includes steps, just as the real blocks historically did. One night, I became curious concerning whether I could locate additional four-sided blocks near other animal figures in the sky. Within five minutes, I had built three more, all made from otherwise unused stars in the gaps alongside ordinary Ptolemaic constellations. I recommend this exercise, in all serious-ness, to seasoned observers. At your next opportunity under clear, dark skies, see how many mounting blocks you can craft. The results quickly demonstrate just how easily our pattern-seeking minds can slip into confirmation bias.

I know of one way to militate against this, although it must be said that this tech-nique, at least in my experience, is brutal on the ego. It involves asking oneself, over and over: "Is there some way this idea of mine could be wrong?" And if the idea is not a matter of right or wrong, but a matter of interpretation, I like to ask, "Is there some way this idea could be more elegant?"

Ultimately, my disagreement with Rees's model is not so much about errors as it is about aesthetics. When I gaze at the heavens above, I feel enchanted by the imagery of Rhiannon as a chained princess conjoined to a horse that flies like the wind. This picture has changed my relationship with the night sky, to the point that I can no longer look at Andromeda and Pegasus without seeing the medieval Welsh figures first, and the ancient Greek figures only secondarily. These two constellations sing to me of a dynamic balance between restraint and freedom. They sing of the virtue of spiritedness whenever there is an opportunity to take positive action, and the virtues of acceptance and accommodation if there is not. This is Rhiannon's story, as I hear it. The imagery of Rhiannon as a little dog on the back of a unicorn simply does not grab me in the same way. My reaction is somewhat a matter of personal values and individual taste, however. Rees's model does incorporate its own, different set of mythological correspondences for its pairing of Canis Major and Monoceros. And regardless of whether the *Mabinogi* author himself had that idea in mind, it does potentially work as a mnemonic for recalling the position of the unicorn, which is one of the most difficult of all the modern star patterns to learn.

That said, I do believe that Rees's model is missing something crucial in its assess-ment of Pryderi's astronomical identity. As I mentioned earlier, Rees links Pryderi solely with Pegasus, not with Aquarius, and I think this has arisen from a misreading of *Fasti*. In the entry for March 7, Ovid wrote of Pegasus, "Now he enjoys the sky, that his wings once sought, / And glitters there brightly with his fifteen stars" (Kline,

2004). The star count implies that the poet correctly understood that the winged horse has fully risen into the predawn sky around that date. Rees, however, interprets it this way: "According to Ovid, the neck of Pegasus make [*sic*] its appearance above the horizon on March 7, but in the *Mabinogi* it is only on 1 May that the foal is born and thus becomes fully visible." That statement would position both horses, especially the foal Equuleus, significantly lower in the sky than they would have been seen from Europe during either ancient or medieval times. The little horse rises *before* the neck of the big horse, not two months afterward. Rees is picturing Equuleus as not fully risen prior to May 1, and since Aquarius is below Equuleus, Aquarius is not yet visible in his model on that date. But as can be seen in figure 5, most of Aquarius would in fact have been visible to the author of the *Mabinogi* on Calan Mai.

Because Pryderi is the character that links all Four Branches, this one fiddly constellation identification has cascading impacts upon any further interpretation of astronomical symbolism in the *Mabinogi*. As hinted earlier, it lends a specific meaning to at least one line in the englynion, or traditional Welsh verses, that are sung to the mortally wounded Llew. In the Fourth Branch analysis forthcoming in 2017, I will explain more about that and will also reveal one astronomical solution that would tidily explain each and every aspect of the seemingly strange conditions surrounding Llew's death.

Discussion: Arduus ad Solem/Striving Toward the Sun
In this year's article, I have examined astronomical symbolism in the Third Branch of the *Mabinogi*. The findings of this analysis have coalesced neatly into an extensive, self-consistent model of Ptolemaic constellations that includes depictions of the characters of Manawyddan, Pryderi, Rhiannon, and Llwyd; locations for the boar's fort and the asses of Llwyd's court; and illustrations of additional narrative features such as the collar and hammer. The model has also uncovered a number of correspondences between Pryderi and the Sun, between Manawyddan and Mercury, and between the boar and the Moon. This interpretation allows the reader to retrace Pryderi's journey in the sky, as expressed by the Sun's journey from Aquarius to Taurus and beyond. When understood from this angle, it is possible to correctly anticipate that Pryderi's story will continue along the same path in the Fourth Branch, next incorporating the symbolism of Leo and Scorpio. The model proposes a specific date of May 1, 1185, for Pryderi's kidnapping, a date that not only fits the Third Branch narrative but which would also resonate with a similar episode in the First Branch. Additionally, some intriguing parallels have been seen in the usage of astronomical symbolism in the *Mabinogi* and the *Hanes Taliesin*.

In the interest of keeping all that in perspective, I think it is worth emphasizing again that astronomical allegory, as much as it excites me personally, does not represent the only layer of meaning in the *Mabinogi*. As an informal educator in the field of astronomy, I am delighted by the word-and-picture puzzles in this work and am deeply grateful for their potential as teaching tools. At the same time, my perception of these symbols is that they themselves point to deeper meanings, meanings that seem to me to be of a spiritual nature. My personal understanding of the *Mabinogi* is that it addresses both the nature of the universe and the nature of the self, and it does so with profound eloquence, for those who thoughtfully pause to listen. But I also suspect this type of multilayered approach to literature came a little easier to medieval thinkers than to modern readers, largely because writers in that era tended to be very practiced at finding different senses of meaning within scripture—the literal, the historical, the moral, the allegorical, the anagogical, and so forth (van Liere, 2014).

As I continue to study this material with each passing year, I frequently experience a humbling and exhilarating awareness that there will always be more to learn. I have come to appreciate that there is even a sense in which it is good not to have all the answers. And once in a while, I discover I have been flat-out wrong.

In last year's article, I remarked with admiration that "in an era when the classics were often treated as authoritative, these [rewrites of ancient star lore] were ballsy acts of creativity" (Glomski, 2015). What I have since learned is that the approach taken by the author of the *Mabinogi* was not atypical of his times. It was not iconoclastic, but expected, that thinkers reprocess the great literature of antiquity in their own ways. And this is very much what he appears to have done.

My misconception arose from a book on medieval literature that turned out to be not terribly clear on this matter. Mary Carruthers is the writer whose work has subsequently straightened me out. I have found *The Book of Memory* (Carruthers, 2008) and *The Craft of Thought* (Carruthers, 1998) to be of tremendous aid in my efforts to reach a better understanding of the medieval mind.

In the Middle Ages, the relationship between the author and the reader was regarded as a conversation between two sets of memories. The details of the conversation were thus unique to each member of the audience, although shaped by shared familiarity with the texts available at that time. As Carruthers (2008) drolly clarifies, "the *memoria*

of the composer and the *memoria* of the audience are thus bound in a dialogue of textual allusions and transformations, and not to engage in it is the mark of a dolt."

Let us strive not to be dolts, since there is still much material ahead to engage us. In this series of articles about *Mabinogi* astronomy, you and I have been working both independently and together, as readers and as thinkers, on a venture that is now leading into the Fourth Branch. In the last article, we will pursue the continued destiny of Pryderi. Reborn as Lleu Llaw Gyffes, he will entrust too much of his memory to a florilegium, also known as a "book of flowers," and then be obliged to recompose himself with the aid of a powerful poet-mage of the Milky Way. It is a story that, even today, can still be read and enjoyed in the heavens.

References

Basilicofresco. (2009). Colure [Illustration]. Retrieved September 2, 2015, from Wikimedia Commons: https://commons.wikimedia.org/wiki/File:Colure.png

Beckwith, M. (2011). Durham Cathedral door knocker [Photograph]. Retrieved December 24, 2015, from Wikimedia Commons: https://commons.wikimedia.org/wiki/File:Durham_Cathedral_Door_Knocker_%287166926460%29.jpg

Bostock, J. (Trans.), & Riley, H. T. (1893). *The natural history of Pliny* (Vol. 1). London: George Bell and Sons. Retrieved from https://books.google.com/books?id=aVMMAAAAIAAJ

Bromwich, R. (Ed.) (2014). *Trioedd Ynys Prydein: The triads of the Island of Britain* (4th ed.). Cardiff, UK: University of Wales Press.

Carruthers, M. (1998). *The craft of thought: Meditation, rhetoric, and the making of images, 400–1200.* Cambridge, UK: Cambridge University Press.

Carruthers, M. (2008). *The book of memory: A study of memory in medieval culture* (2nd ed.). Cambridge, UK: Cambridge University Press.

Chéreau, F., Gates, M., Meuris, J., Gajdosik, J., Spearman, R., Kerr, N., . . . Storm, M. (2009). Stellarium (Version OS X 0.10.2) [Software]. Available from http://stellarium.org

Davies, J. N. (2013). *Mabinogion astronomy* [Blog]. Retrieved from http://mabinogionastronomy.blogspot.com

Davies, S. (2007). *The Mabinogion.* Oxford, UK: Oxford University Press.

Dekker, E. (2013). *Illustrating the Phaenomena: Celestial cartography in antiquity and the Middle Ages*. Oxford, UK: Oxford University Press.

Duke, D. (n.d.). Data as found in the *Almagest* [Spreadsheet]. Retrieved from http://people.sc.fsu.edu/~dduke/datafiles.htm

Espenak, F. (2015a). Annular solar eclipse of 536 September 01 [Map]. Eclipse predictions by Fred Espenak, NASA's GSFC. Retrieved from http://eclipse.gsfc.nasa.gov/SEsearch/SEsearchmap.php?Ecl=05360901

Espenak, F. (2015b). Total solar eclipse of 1185 May 01 [Map]. Eclipse predictions by Fred Espenak, NASA's GSFC. Retrieved from http://eclipse.gsfc.nasa.gov/SEsearch/SEsearchmap.php?Ecl=11850501

Ford, P. K. (1977). *The Mabinogi and other medieval Welsh tales*. Berkeley: University of California Press.

Freer, I. (2004). Ancient mysteries: *Mabinogion*. Retrieved from http://www.word-works-uk.com/AncientMysteries.html

Glomski, T. (2015). *Mabinogi* Skies: Astronomy of the first and second branches. *Trilithon: The Journal of the Ancient Order of Druids in America, 2*, 12–39.

Gorodetsky, M. L. (n.d.). Ancient and early medieval eclipses in European sources. Retrieved from http://hbar.phys.msu.su/gorm/atext/ginzele.htm

Greer, J. M. (2005). *Encyclopedia of natural magic*. Woodbury, MN: Llewellyn.

Greer, J. M. (Ed.), & Guest, C. (Trans.) (2009). *The dolmen arch: A study course in the Druid mysteries*. Available from http://aoda.org/publications.html#correspondence

Griffiths, M. (2008, January 13). Under a Celtic sky. Retrieved from http://www.lablit.com/article/341

Guest, C. (Trans.) (1877). *The Mabinogion*. Retrieved from http://www.sacred-texts.com/neu/celt/mab/

Hadley, M. (Producer), & Hutton, R. (Narrator) (1996). *The Mabinogion: The four branches*. Lewes, UK: Talking Myth. Available from http://www.cdbaby.com/cd/talkingmyth

Harley MS 647. (c. 820–850). *Aratea, with extracts from Hyginus' Astronomica*. Retrieved from http://www.bl.uk/catalogues/illuminatedmanuscripts/record.asp?MSID=6561&CollID=8&NStart=647

Hughes, K. (Trans.) (2012). *Hanes Taliesin in English* [Video]. Retrieved from https://www.youtube.com/watch?v=6B4pfPWsvxc

Jesus College MS 111. (1382–c. 1410). *Llyfr coch Hergest*. Retrieved from http://image.ox.ac.uk/show?collection=jesus&manuscript=ms111

Kline, A. S. (Trans.) (2001). *Georgics: Book IV*. Retrieved from http://www.poetryin-translation.com/PITBR/Latin/VirgilGeorgicsIV.htm

Kline, A. S. (Trans.) (2004). *Fasti: On the Roman calendar*. Retrieved from http://www.poetryintranslation.com/PITBR/Latin/Fastihome.htm

MacCana, P. (1958). *Branwen daughter of Llŷr: A study of the Irish affinities and of the composition of the Second Branch of the Mabinogi*. Cardiff, UK: University of Wales Press.

Mair, A. W. (Trans.), & Mair, G. R. (Trans.) (1921). *Callimachus: Hymns and epigrams, Lycophron and Aratus*. London: William Heinemann. Retrieved from http://www.theoi.com/Text/AratusPhaenomena.html

McGurk, P. (1973). Germanici Cesaris Aratea cum scholiis: A new illustrated witness from Wales. *National Library of Wales Journal, 18*(2), 197–216. Retrieved from http://welshjournals.llgc.org.uk/browse/viewobject/llgc-id:1284625/article/000038144

Nichols, M. (2009). The death of Llew: A seasonal interpretation. Retrieved from http://www.witchessabbats.com/index.php?option=com_content&view=article&id=11&Itemid=20

NLW MS 735C. (c. 1000–1150). *Medieval astronomy*. Retrieved from http://www.llgc.org.uk/collections/digital-gallery/digitalmirror-manuscripts/the-middle-ages/medievalastronomy/

North, J. D. (1986). *Horoscopes and history*. London: Warburg Institute.

Parker, W. (2002). Gwynedd, Ceredigion and the political geography of the *Mabinogi*. *National Library of Wales Journal, 32*(4), 365–396. Retrieved from http://welshjournals.llgc.org.uk/browse/viewobject/llgc-id:1291701/article/000037654

Parker, W. (Trans.) (2003). *The four branches of the Mabinogi*. Retrieved from http://www.mabinogi.net/translations.htm

Peniarth MS 2. (c. 1300–1350). *Llyfr Taliesin*. Retrieved from https://www.llgc.org.uk/discover/digital-gallery/digitalmirror-manuscripts/the-middle-ages/bookoftaliesinpeniarthms2/

Peniarth MS 4. (c. 1350). *Llyfr gwyn Rhydderch*. Retrieved from http://www.llgc.org.uk/index.php?id=whitebookofrhydderchpeniart

Peniarth MS 28. (c. 1250). Laws of Hywel Dda. Retrieved from https://www.llgc.org.uk/index.php?id=lawsofhyweldda

Pratt, J. P. (2015, December 14). The Ptolemy star catalog [Spreadsheet]. Retrieved from http://www.johnpratt.com/items/astronomy/ptolemy_stars.html

Rackham, H. (Trans.) (1967). *De natura deorum academica.* Cambridge, MA: Harvard University Press. Retrieved from: https://archive.org/details/denaturadeorumac00ciceuoft

Rees, E. A. (2012). *The Mabinogi decoded.* Birmingham, UK: University of Birmingham.

Rhŷs, J. (1901). *Celtic folklore: Welsh and Manx* (Vol. 2). Oxford, UK: Clarendon. Retrieved from https://books.google.com/books?id=ASXaAAAAMAAJ

Rider-Bezerra, S. (2011). The *Mabinogion* project: A brief history of the *Mabinogion.* Retrieved from http://d.lib.rochester.edu/camelot/text/rider-bezerra-mabinogion-project

Ridpath, I. (1988). *Star tales.* Retrieved from http://www.ianridpath.com/startales/contents.htm

Ridpath, I. (Ed.) (1989). *Norton's 2000.0.* Essex, UK: Longman Scientific and Technical.

Sharpe, R. (2007). Which text is Rhygyfarch's *Life of St. David?* In J. W. Evans & J. M. Wooding (Eds.), *St. David of Wales: Cult, church and nation* (pp. 90–105). Woodbridge, UK: Boydell.

Silverstein, T. (1952). Adelard, Aristotle, and the *De Natura Deorum. Classical philology, 47*(2). 82–86. Retrieved from http://www.jstor.org/stable/267376

Stahl, W. H. (Trans.) (1990). *Commentary on the Dream of Scipio by Macrobius.* New York: Columbia University Press.

Staples, A. (2011). The medieval farming year. In *The penultimate Hârnpage.* Retrieved from http://www.penultimateharn.com/history/medievalfarmingyear.html

Stephenson, F. R. (2010). Investigation of medieval European records of solar eclipses. *Journal for the History of Astronomy, 41*(1), 95–104. Retrieved from http://adsabs.harvard.edu/abs/2010JHA....41...95S

Tirion, W., & Skiff, B. (1990). *Bright star atlas 2000.00.* Richmond, VA: Willmann-Bell. Available from http://www.willbell.com/atlas/atlas1.htm

Toomer, G. J. (1998). *Ptolemy's Almagest.* Princeton, NJ: Princeton University Press.

University of Wales. (2016). *Geiriadur prfysgol Cymru: A dictionary of the Welsh language.* Retrieved from: http://welsh-dictionary.ac.uk/gpc/gpc.html

van Liere, F. (2014). *An introduction to the medieval Bible.* Cambridge, UK: Cambridge University Press.

Wade-Evans, W. A. (2013). *Life of Saint David.* Lexington, KY: CreateSpace by Brother Hermengild TOSF. (Original work published 1923)

Wagner, E., Drobná, Z., & Durdík, J. (2000). *Medieval costume, armour and weapons.* (J. Layton, Trans.). New York: Dover. (Original work published 1956)

Williams, J. (Ed.). (1860). *Brut y tywysogion: Or, the chronicle of the princes.* London: Longman, Green, Longman, and Roberts. Retrieved from: https://books.google.com/books?id=kCYJAAAAIAAJ

Williams, M. (2010). *Fiery shapes: Celestial portents and astrology in Ireland and Wales, 700–1700.* Oxford, UK: Oxford University Press.

Saving Our History: How to Create Pagan Archives

Daniel Cureton

Daniel Cureton is a Druid Apprentice living in Salt Lake City, Utah. He holds a master of library science degree from Emporia State University concentrated in archival science. He is currently a student at Weber State University pursuing a master of arts in English degree, studying world literature. He enjoys gaming, nature walks, Netflix, and dinner with friends.

Do you love history? Well, some may find it a tad dusty and boring, but generally most folks love an old piece of Star Wars memorabilia or would love to see the papers of Ernest Hemingway. Programs on television and interesting books also allow people to fill their minds with facts from history. But who keeps all that history? Who safeguards it? Archives and archivists do, that is who! People trained in the field, who may have studied the science of archiving as I have, through a graduate library science program. The following sections will familiarize you with archives and how to create a pagan collection to be donated to an archive or for home use.

Why Should I Archive?

A problem in pagan communities broadly today, especially in the Druid community, is the lack of history, historical documents, and evidence a group of people existed and were doing something significant. Many ancient traditions were oral in nature, which over time caused them to be lost. Only written accounts of the Roman historians give us a sliver of details of the ancient Druids, which are filtered through the lens of the Romans. Even documents from the early period of revival Druidry (eighteenth and

nineteenth centuries) are scarce, and that was only 200 years ago. Many today fail to see the connection—that we are repeating history.

As a minority community, it is important that the historical record is voiced from the community, not about the community, whether by biased outside observers such as the ancient Roman historians or by an objective contemporary archivist. When we allow others to speak for us in the record, we become systematically disenfranchised and dispossessed from history, because those others are speaking for us (Shilton & Srinivasan, 2007). This dispossession leaves out the various cultural ontologies and identities that are unique to our community and history (Cureton, 2015). Often, as reflected in writings from the twentieth century and earlier, pagans have been described in a biased and negative way, as "devil worshipers" and "godless heathens." We as a community do not want to perpetuate this bias by leaving out documents that prove otherwise, that show what we did, our beautiful traditions, and how we shaped history.

I have talked with many in my local Druid and pagan community about archiving their records, and they all decline. A few even fear their identity may be stolen if they share their archives. Most archives can place restrictions on items, such as a ban on photocopying, or can seal records until a certain date if people identified in those records are still alive. The other response I often hear is, "I'll just burn everything; it has my energy." This is even worse. You can take the energy out, salt it, anoint it, or whatever. If you burn your records, you will perpetuate the misrepresentation and restriction of the minority faith community you belong to in the historical record. Burning may be your tradition's way of departing this life. What burning or skipping the donation to the archive on the way out of this life does is to deny the honest and accurate voice of the community in the historical record. It does not allow for the creation or acknowledgment and awareness of the importance of contemporary Druid and pagan history. Burning our records does not allow history to accurately capture what a group, person, community, or culture did in a certain historical period.

Keeping our history, donating materials to archives where materials safe, collected, and contained (not dispersed among your grove or family), validates our standpoint in history and our existence accurately. There exists a body of work from a movement and community of people with a unique worldview. When we donate our history to an archive, suddenly we have vibrant records, properly preserved, about

the lives of pagan peoples in the late twentieth and early twenty-first centuries, who approached the world through the lens of nature. Take a Druid group, operating in the intermountain west of the U.S. from 2001 to 2015; instead of speculation or rumor about their activities, when their group records are archived you have, overnight, information on what they were doing, how they influenced their community, what type of community service they did, what rituals they performed, under what tradition, what gods were worshiped, how they viewed the world, what they thought about global conflict, poverty, wealth inequality, creative expression, and queer rights, and what inspired them in the early twenty-first century in the United States (Roe, 2005).

All of these elements and many more appear in the records because one group or individual decided that their experience, their life, their community, was important enough to preserve and did not assume that their culture and tradition would survive. How often have things changed, traditions and customs vanished? Or if bits and pieces of a long-dead culture surface and scholars speculate to fill in the gaps, based on the evidence, they may reach the wrong conclusion about the culture, beliefs, customs, and lives of those ancient people. Why not fill those gaps for them, so there is no debate?

You will want to consider when it is appropriate to start archiving your records. Where in life are you or your group? Youth, middle age, or at the end? Do you think it may be necessary now while things are ongoing so you do not have to do it all at once? Or are you going to state in a will that the documents be donated upon your death? It is never too late to start archiving, especially when you see shifts in the community, vanishing of traditions, or dwindling membership. You may want to get a start to ensure that your history from your part of the community is preserved. The rest of this article walks through the various considerations surrounding archives and many aspects of archives.

Archives and Secrecy

Some groups may be bound by secrecy. But if a group stops operation, or with an existing group's permission, you can archive their records. If not, their teachings and activity die with their members. No one will even know they existed perhaps or have the idea to carry on their traditions. Far too often though, with old or moribund groups a single individual may hold the records with no one else having access (which

is necessary for private archives of living traditions). But what happens when that last person holding them passes on?

One good example of working with esoteric traditions that still have a veil of secrecy is the archive of Israel Regardi's papers, which are held in private by the Hermetic Order of the Golden Dawn in Florida. They have published selected letters and documents online from their archives. While it is fantastic that the records exist, they are in the order's private archive and not accessible to others without permission (Hermetic Order of the Golden Dawn, 2010). This prevents the records from being archived at a public institution indefinitely. In some cases, as in the early days of the Golden Dawn, a secret tradition was necessary due to cultural stigma or misrepresentation of occult information. If Israel Regardi had not published his books on the Golden Dawn and broken his oath, the order and all of its rites and ceremonies would have died off. Much great history and tradition would have been lost, which would have been a tragedy considering the number of modern traditions that have roots in the Golden Dawn. Even secret mystery esoteric orders like the Masons and Rosicrucians keep archives at their headquarters. We need to find ways of negotiating between the secrecy in our traditions, and long-term preservation of our history.

Some may frown on others viewing their living tradition's secret documents. If they are so secret, so sacred, that the sacred living aspect would die and be defiled, and could not withstand the first set of uninitiated eyes that was to behold them, then do not archive them. But it is dangerous to assume that because it is alive and people practice it today, that it will continue to be in twenty years. Anything can happen to the tradition, to your documents, or to you in the near future—sudden death, house fire, decline in membership. Do not assume all will be well because friends and family participate or that they will take care of the records. Be proactive and do not let the mystery become a mystery and fade into the forgotten realms of history, never to live again.

Creating Your Own Private Archive

You can use all of the steps discussed in this article, including the filing system and the various perspectives examined, to arrange and store your own collection at home. You can do a simple version using files, a filing cabinet, or bins. You can also do a more professional version with acid-free folders and boxes (which is what

archives use), which will cost more, but will be better in the long run for the life of your collection. Companies such as Hollinger Metal Edge and Gaylord Archival sell the products online.

What is an Archive? How is it different than a Museum?

Museums are very similar to archives, as they essentially do the same thing, keeping history and preserving items. They, like archives, have a very specific and narrow focus, called "collecting scope" (Library of Congress, n.d.a). Museums are dedicated to a specific cultural, historical, or personal period, such as the World War I museum in Kansas or the National Museum of African American History and Culture in Washington, DC. Often more local museums cover natural history, state history, or a single person. Archives have a specific collecting scope but many will be flexible to allow for diverse collections to come in.

There is much overlap in the fields of libraries and museums, and even joint organizations. This is because some libraries, like the Marriott Library at the University of Utah, house many physical objects, nonpaper-based, usually three-dimensional objects called "artifacts" that would normally go to a museum (Ritzenthaler, 2010). But because the artifacts add to the story, they are kept with the paper-based collections (called manuscripts). It is much more informative and adds a wholeness to the story to see the actual typewriter that Wallace Stegner used to type his book manuscripts or the pen Emily Dickinson used to write her poetry.

Public vs. Private Archives

Most cities have at least one archive, usually housed within public institutions, like a college or university library. Historical societies may keep their own, based on what their interests are. So a state historical society will not gather documents from outside the state. Likewise, the Viola Da Gamba Society does not keep documents about guitars or piano but only about the gamba family of instruments.

Public archives are housed at public institutions, such as libraries, government bodies, public colleges, or universities. Private archives are held by private companies, organizations, individuals, churches, and private colleges and universities.

Public archives will allow anyone access to records, as they are usually required by law to have open access (although restrictions can be placed on photocopying, or

documents may be sealed). These public bodies will take great pains to provide proper care, as they are usually funded by donors, grants, and the government. The archive will have a set of rules, regulations, and procedures on how to handle, collect, process, and store the records to maintain accountability and integrity throughout the life of a collection. These archives usually belong to professional and national organizations such as the Society of American Archivists (2007), which sets the standards, clarifies professional ethics, and writes manuals on how to archive. Because of the integrity and the transparency of public archives, they are usually reliable and consistent in how they treat donors and their papers. Often they have a mix of high-value (like the Walt Whitman papers) and low-value collections (such as those of Ms. Jones Smith, a housewife).

Unlike most public archives, private archives can have a variety of practices in how and what they choose to archive. This is because private archives are not required by anyone except themselves, their institutions (like a private college or university), or their donors usually to be accountable for what they do with their collections. Private archives have freedom to deny access to collections, to be selective in their collecting area, or to handle collections how they feel is appropriate for their archive or their invested party. An organization's archive will serve that organization (such as the Catholic Church's archive).

Fitting Into an Archive's Mission

Many archives collect up to the state level, so they do not accept materials originating from outside that state. It would not be appropriate (and the archive would not even take it), for example, if you tried to give to the Indiana State Historical Society all your grove's papers from Eugene, Oregon. They would tell you to find an archive in Oregon. Because your grove's history is not part of the history of Indiana, it does not fit in with the rest of archive and does not make sense historically. The archive has to maintain space for own local history.

An archive will tell you if your collection fits better in a museum. If you have a set of T-shirts, for example, that are not connected to the rest of your collection, but come from a local convention, they may fit better in a local museum. It is really up to the archive whether they will take items as part of your collection. Usually archives that collect local, state, or religious history are going to be interested in your papers.

If you have a mix of materials from different regions that are connected or from an organization that has national membership, contact an archive to discuss options. Most likely you will want to keep them together, but a national archive in this case is also a viable option (such as the National Archives in the U.S.).

Once you find an archive that collects on your area (local history and/or spirituality), then you can discuss with them what you have and how to donate the materials. Usually once you donate to an archive, you sign a deed of gift that transfers ownership of the items to the archive. You would still have special access to your records to make changes (include that access in the deed) if needed, but legally the archive now owns the items.

If you cannot find a local or state archive interested in your materials, a last resort would be to contact the University of California, Santa Barbara, Special Collections as they have a specific collection called American Religions for all types of documents pertaining to religion in America. They are the archive that holds the Isaac Bonewits papers, among others (Online Archive of California, n.d.).

Who Wants Your Old Documents?

So who wants your old documents? Archives do! That's what they are all about. But you must be asking at this point, "Okay, so I'll donate, but why would anyone want to see my story, my life, and my perspective?" Because it is unique, it is you, and it is part of minority history and minority spirituality. It shows in the historical record that there were people who chose to live against the dominant culture, religion, and identities assumed by society. It states that there were people who chose to look back in time, to honor their kin, to reenchant nature, and to work for the betterment of themselves and their communities. It allows you to speak from the historical record instead of allowing someone else to speak for you and to assume things about you.

Such themes are of strong interest to historians and archivists as they help create the diversity in communities and show just how much was going on behind the scenes outside the dominant spirituality in a society. You may even encounter, for instance, a historian who is interested in textile history, who wants to know about Druid garb in the late twentieth century, asking questions such as, "What type of material were robes made from?" and "What were the trendy patterns?" Learning that Druid robes were white could lead to further questions such as, "What was the significance of white fabric in the Druid

community?" or "Was white just for one type of ritual, or did they wear seasonal colors and informal rites?" All of this is to say that your documents, your archives, are of interest.

Types of Documents: Primary, Secondary, and Tertiary Sources

Archives mainly contain and are interested in collecting primary documents: firsthand accounts, eyewitness reports, notes from a researcher in the field conducting original research, photographs and film (both of which capture an event, place, or person), manuscripts (a collection of the papers of a person or entity), book manuscripts (the original unpublished version), business documents, letters, transaction receipts, journals and diaries, and data that are unique (Society of American Archivists, 2007). These are the kinds of documents that are of most interest to an archive.

Primary documents are considered the reliable, verifiable origins of information. Researchers, writers, and historians use these types of documents to write books and TV programs, and piece stories together. The products they produce are called secondary sources since they include the authors' views, modifications, and interpretations based on the original source for a specific purpose (James Cook University, 2015). Anything beyond secondary (tertiary or third level) is unreliable (from the perspective of academic research) since it is too far removed from the original source of the information and is not directly connected to primary source documents (University of New Haven, n.d.).

What Can Be Archived?

Almost everything! Your records are primary source documents about your life and tradition. They do not have to be all about some aspect of Druidry, but because you live your life and identify as a pagan or Druid, that is what counts. Archivists like anything that is unique. The most obvious are those papers you have in your filing cabinet, such as these:

- Cards, letters, and other correspondence
- Scrapbooks
- Zines
- Maps
- Emails
- Community flyers or documents
- Photographs and negatives

- Publications, magazines, and newsletters
- Rituals and class outlines
- High school or college notes
- Art portfolio or sketchbook
- Journals, diaries, and field notes
- Datebooks
- Architectural drawings
- Magical items and textiles
- Blogs
- Computer files
- Videos
- Tax records
- Business records
- Personal files such as a birth certificate or passport
- Medical records
- Bills
- Receipts from purchases in person or online

Things Not to Include in Your Archive

Generally archives remove paper clips and metal clips from donated materials. Some leave staples as it is easier to keep papers organized. Regular school folders with pockets, plastic protective sheeting, binders, hair, bugs, organic materials, and liquids all should be left out.

Sensitive documents may not be appropriate. Leave out member records containing personal information. Membership applications, rosters, or attendance records may or may not be appropriate, depending of the level of inclusion. Some members of your grove may not want their name publicly associated with it.

Detailed medical records (such as blood type, disease status, individuals connected to you) would not be appropriate for an archive either. If your Social Security number is on a document, it can be cut out or redacted if the document needs to be included in the collection. This happens often when filing business paperwork (such as the state incorporation documents of an organization). Tax records provide information on your income or other activities that may be of interest to historians, but the sensitive information can be removed while maintaining the integrity of the document.

Understanding Paper and Preservation

Most archive collections will be in paper format. Different types of paper have been used in different periods of history. Premodern (1800) paper is very durable and is still in good shape today in book and manuscript collections. This is due to the use of recycled rags made from plant fibers of hemp and linen. It was later in the nineteenth century that wood pulp was introduced, along with chemical bleaching processes, which added acid to paper. Wood pulp was much cheaper to produce, and acid only added to instability and degradation (Ritzenthaler, 2010). Look at newspapers, printed on some of the cheapest paper around. It is high in acid and lignin (a complex cellular organic polymer), which degrades very quickly, becoming yellow and brittle, especially when exposed to light (Northeast Document Conservation Center, n.d.). The problem here is that newsprint and other paper from the late nineteenth through the mid-twentieth century is still acidic and getting brittle. The acid never leaves unless washed away by preservation processes (most big archives have a preservation section). The acid creates what is called a "slow fire," which is chemical in nature. Many books and manuscripts from the same period have this issue (Baird & Schaffner, 1999). The process will continue indefinitely from one sheet or book to another if the acid fire has a whole library to eat through. Archives use special paper to surround acidic materials (usually alkaline-based paper). With newsprint, they usually scan and reprint the clippings onto acid-free paper. For your own archive, use acid-free paper if at all possible.

Getting Started: How to Arrange Your Files

How to Organize Your Papers

Arranging and describing are processes of organizing files or documents within the collection so they can be identified and found (Roe, 2005). You can do this in preparation for donating to an archive, which will ensure that the files are in order and associated the way you would like them to be. This is called "provenance" or original order in archive terminology, which is the ethical rule on how to process collections (otherwise, if things get out of order the archivist has no idea what your intentions were or associations between items in your collection). You can also use these steps to create a private at-home archive.

You can group files according to chronology, which often makes the most sense, or by subject. Other systems exist but these two are easiest; a combination of the two

usually works best. You may group items of particular importance together, such as a series of outlines from classes you taught along with the flyers for the classes and the feedback comments. In this case, instead of distributing the outlines throughout a time period in the overall collection, you will want to group them all together in a single folder. This creates a file with all associated documents together in one place. If you have multiple folders, do not worry; just number them.

For example, correspondence almost always appears in chronological order. You can date letters by year or month depending on how many you have. You could also sort them by topic. Say you worked for a company from 1989 to 2001, and this correspondence is in with the rest of your correspondence from 1970 to 2016. You would most likely want to title the folders "Company B Correspondence 1989–2001." They would be separate from the overall correspondence instead of interspersed. This helps add a level of detail and tightens the accessibility of those items. It is much easier to find items with a specific title you can refer to than trying to find all the letters from a company in a set of files spanning forty years all mixed together.

A special subject grouping would be a collection of related materials. Say you have a poster from a Pagan Pride Day festival where you did tarot readings. You would want to group this with the contract you signed to have the booth, the article in your group's newsletter about how the festival went, the program from the festival, and the emails from your grove members who volunteered to staff the table. All these associated items show the varying levels of interaction in one historical event, who was involved, outcomes, and significance. Otherwise these items could be filed in different categories such as printed media, programs, newsletters, and correspondence.

Let's look at a sample record, arranged chronologically as well as by subject.

<u>The Albus Percival Wulfic Brian Dumbledore Papers: 1881–1997</u>

    Box 1: Community Documents, 1900–1997
    Folder 1. Raven's Moon Coven (undated)
          2. Odin's Bar (undated)
          3. Helen's Skyclad Hedonist Fellowship, 1920–1985
          4. Helen's Skyclad Hedonist Fellowship, 1920–1985 (2)
          5. Helen's Skyclad Hedonist Fellowship, 1920–1985 (3)

6. Pacific Circle, 1956–1990
7. Pacific Circle, 1991–1995
8. Gay Wizard's Spiritual Circle Newsletter, 1974–1989
9. Queer England Zine, 1989–1991

Box 2: Correspondence, 1900–1997
Folder 1. Personal Letters, 1900–1935
2. Personal Emails from Family, 1990–1997
3. Personal Emails from Minerva McGonagall, 1995–1997
4. Hogwarts Annual Holiday Cards, 1920–1962

Box 3: Pagan Pride Day Materials
Folder 1. Chicago, IL, USA, Pagan Pride Day, 1970, 1973
2. London, England, UK, Pagan Pride Day, 1984
3. Salt Lake City, UT, USA, Pagan Pride Day, 1985
4. Columbia, SC, USA, Pagan Pride Day, 1986–1990
5. Vancouver, BC, CA, Pagan Pride Day, 1992
6. Vancouver, BC, CA, Pagan Pride Day, 1992 (2)

This principle applies to other documents. Ritual outlines, reports, high school papers, college lecture notes, business and group records, emails (you will want to print, assuming you are giving to a print archive), vending contracts, expired passports (with all their travel stamps!), and all unique items can be arranged chronologically or by some special grouping if the items are related. You can choose to put together all rituals by year, all the contracts you signed, or newsletters you wrote for your grove. Each one of these and other areas can be divided into their own files and arranged chronologically. This is the least complex way of arranging the records (Roe, 2005).

Journals and Diaries
Journals and diaries contain written personal firsthand primary accounts of the lives of those who wrote them. Journals are a fantastic source of written accounts of current events, day-to-day living, cultural phenomena, scientific achievements, space adventures, and eyewitness accounts. People write mostly about things that happen to them, topics they find interesting, hobbies, or life-changing moments. The journals that AODA asks people to keep while working through the degree

system are just as valuable. They contain personal thoughts, questions, reflections, and our view of the world as AODA Druids. They are primary source documents about how druids lived their minority spirituality in the early twenty-first century. Journals are some of the most valuable and best sources of perspective and experiences in the historical record. You most likely would not want to give up your highly personal journals while alive, but they could be donated upon your death or after everyone mentioned in them has passed on. Of all the documents to include, these journals will be the crown of your collection, since they are so unique and contain the summation of your identities and life.

Date Books
Date books are unique as well, as records of events, meetings, classes, and appointments. They show the activities of an individual and provide historical perspective on that person's day-to-day life. Sometimes things get recorded there that are nowhere else. Say for example you had a planning meeting with the local Pagan Pride committee, then dinner afterward with an author in town for a book signing, and then drag bingo at a local gay bar. All these events in your date book create a very interesting day and story in the collection, and may be the only record of drag bingo!

Photographs
These days most pictures are digital. Many large archives have a separate division for photographs. Many also accept digital copies of pictures, but prefer print ones, as they will not print them out. If you have not already, start taking pictures of your events, rituals, workshops, and classes (if your tradition allows it). You most likely will not have to handle older photographs printed before the 1950s, but you can easily read about the different types of photographs and chemicals used in their processes of development over the last 200 years (which are many, thus my reference) on Wikipedia in the article "History of Photography."

Part of the reason why Druids and pagans are commonly absent from the historical record is that we have no proof of what we were doing, who was dancing around the fire, what we dressed up as, or where we held a rite during a certain time period. By having photographic evidence to add to the archival records, we can greatly increase the visualization and weave a more complete story of our history. The idiom a picture is worth a thousand words is true in this case. Since Druidry is a mystery to most folks, they will do much better with visuals to help them understand properly, for example, what a Druid rite looks like, or a how a robe should be fashioned, or what a Midsummer altar is adorned

with, instead of trying to visualize it all from a lengthy written or verbal description.

Talk with the archive in which you wish to deposit the photographs and they will instruct you how to identify them. A good method is to write up a document with all the relevant information for each photograph and write a number on the back of each one, lightly, in a soft pencil, corresponding to each description. Most people write on the back as a way of identifying their photos. While handy, archives cringe at this, as the writing can damage, deface, or even eat away at the paper (if marker/pen is used) and they will say, if you ever have to write on a photograph, use a pencil (archives never do anything they cannot undo).

You can group photographs similarly to paper records, grouping them chronologically or by event or subject. You will want to be as specific as possible, providing at least the following basic information for each photograph:

- First and last names (real names, but if that is not allowed, magical will do)
- Date
- Location

Those are the most crucial, but you would do well to provide a description of what is happening in each photograph to increase context, such as "this is a Druid ritual to Lugh at Central Park in New York on Beltane (May 1) 1989" or "Here we are sewing for fun at John Smith's house, making clothes for the poor." To help the flow better, you may want to use a numbering system like this:

Dancing Cranes Grove Photograph Collection
      1. Rituals
           a. Yule, December 21, 1994
                a.i. Left to right: Joe Smith, Raven Grimasi, Sara J. Parker, Elton John. Raven's house in Missoula, Montana, USA. Ritual performed by Sara to the god Osiris.

So using the pencil, you would write lightly on the back of this photo "1.A.a.i," which would indicate, according to the key written here, "Rituals. Yule, December 21, 1994." Then just continue down the list for rituals in sequence, 1.b, 1.c, 1.d, etc. Then move on to the next subject, such as community outreach, which you would then start with a new number. Following our sequence and logic, this would be 2. And then repeat

using a. So the first picture under the community outreach sequence would be 2.a, then 2.b, and so on.

The more information the better with photographs, as it can only help build the story. Never assume anyone will know anything about what you are describing, the people pictured, or what is taking place, so it is best to avoid abbreviations of names, places, events, subjects, or ideas.

Publications, Magazines, Newsletters, and Zines

Keeping all those issues of the magazine you read or newsletter you subscribed to is vitally important to building an archival collection. They are not unique, and fall under print media, but they are just as important as the personal papers.

Printed media like magazines and newsletters would go into the archive as part of your collection but would not be in the manuscripts area. Most of the time these types of items are removed but it is noted that they were donated by an individual. They will usually go into the archive's print area, such as the book collection (unless they are yours or your groups' newsletter, then they would stay with the collection most likely).

Collecting publications is important because if you look at older esoteric publications from the 1980s or earlier in the United States (if they are still around; many are lost), you can see a stark difference in what was being advertised, sought after, offered, and circulated compared to publications today. It is not just the content of what was being written, but the state of the community. These publications reflect the uniqueness and dialogue going on at a certain time period and the range of discussions or interests certain groups of people had. If you were reading a Catholic magazine from England in 1950, you would see different topics being discussed than you would see today. The same goes for a witch magazine or Druid journal you read in the late 1990s. The information may have similarities (awesome Celtic jewelry, ritual design, Imbolc poetry), but the communities then and now will be discussing radically different information because our issues are radically different (LGBT rights, queer deities, the Syrian civil war). These publications often are organized in chronological order and by title.

Zines may seem so minor that they almost go unnoticed. Some archives make it a point to collect them because they are unique. They are meant as a temporary message that is circulated underground for a small community. Usually fewer than 1,000

copies were printed. Most people tossed them or forgot them unless they fulfilled a particular need, such as the queer zines in the 1980s which supplied news and updates to those in the shadows before coming out. These zines are often organized in chronological order or by title or subject.

Newsletters provide a unique insight into a group or community. Did your grove put out a local newsletter or publish online the status of things, event outcomes, or give Druid messages to the rest of the grove? All this content is specialized information that can be archived. They are published directly by the organization or person, so function as a primary source (sometimes secondary if you are retelling news from elsewhere). They are a great way of tracking the history of a group or community from their own standpoint since the newsletters are produced by them. These newsletters are often organized in chronological order.

Collecting publications of these types allows you to capture articles and essays by authors who may not have ever written again, or who became famous. You can track changes in the community and the voices of the authors, what they believed or felt in a time period about a topic. Often the articles the authors wrote in those magazines and journals were unique and were not expanded to books or reprinted, so a part of their history and the community history is lost when the publications are thrown out.

By examining all the publications in circulation in a certain time periods, researchers and scholars can ask questions such as, "Why weren't there more Druid journals?" or "Where were all the heathens and what were they doing during the AIDS epidemic?" Even "where did pagans publish poetry during the Cold War?" These scholars can examine the state of the community and look at gaps, trends, activities, and statistics.

Sometimes the only way to capture the publications, though, is to print them yourself or to somehow capture a blog that a newsletter was published on (in blog format). This is frustrating and tiresome at times, but is well worth the project when it is all archived. Most web browsers have a setting in the print menu to save a page as a PDF that can be used to archive documents.

Scrapbooks

As much as I love them, scrapbooks are one of the things archives find most problematic. They are often highly acidic (the paper and glue), hard to store, and

hard to handle. They often contain different mediums of paper, photographs, history, and ephemera (material not intended to be archived, like a ticket stub), and other items. They are great, unique items worth archiving, but can take work to preserve. They usually are organized as is, kept together as a whole unit, and stored that way.

Field Notes

You may not realize it, but even the pagan and Druid communities have a field, which is defined as the place away from your home or office where you are working in real situations. The field category would include things such as vending at festivals, attending public rituals, classes, workshops, lectures, community events, parades, marches, and other happenings in the community.

The important idea here is to keep field notes on all the events that you attend in the community or that you are doing as a Druid in another community. Field notebooks are very specific, usually being used by the sciences. Most come in a small size, for pockets or bags, and are weather and waterproof.

Start taking notes! The notes can be simple observations about a ritual, the results and feelings about the tarot readings you did at a local festival, the panel on animal totems at a Furry convention, or any number of other situations you find yourself in within the pagan community or as a pagan doing something pagan or Druid in another community.

These notes function like a journal, but provide a specialized primary source because they are dedicated to the specifics of the field area, and do not include all the other personal entries a normal journal does. What is important is the observation aspect, the data you collect, the drawings or maps you include, the diagrams, the numbers you count for how many tarot readings you did, the miles of walking to the campsite, the altitude of the lake you camped at, and so on. This is an almost undeveloped area in the Druid community and can use serious development.

Art Portfolios

A portfolio could include all original art done by members, your group, commissions, paintings, sketches of nature, or anything else that is artistic. Paper flyers that are original or contain a graphic artist's work are included and can all be put together. Talk with the archive to discuss how they will store your different art media.

Architectural drawings and maps

Maps and architectural drawings are of great interest as they are unique documents. Architectural drawings are often unpublished and maps may or may not be. The maps I am suggesting here are festival maps, drawn maps of a nature area visited, river maps, and other unique unpublished maps. Often they are stored rolled in tubes but sometimes in flat map cases depending on the archive and its space for such items.

Annotated Books

Annotation is just another word for taking notes. It is specific to a text or book, as you do not annotate a lecture or a movie. When you write in a book, underline passages, or record your impressions in the margins, what you are creating in the process besides marginalia is a unique artifact. A published book is not special or unique for an archive. Annotations or marginalia create a dialogue and story around the item. The notes are evidence of a process that took place while reading and studying the book, so archives like to keep them with the personal papers as part of the story of a person or organization's record.

Cultural Documents

Often you will get items that are not related or produced directly by you. These are printed published community documents from events such as festivals, public rituals, workshops, or classes—the ticket stub from the Led Zeppelin concert or the flyer from the yoga class on the telephone pole. Perhaps you have a report on air quality from the state. A brochure from your local parrot rescue or the Facebook event from the local Goth club listing their next event. You even picked up some of the special dollars from the local comic convention. All these things, as odd or insignificant as some are, are critically important items called ephemera. They give depth and layers to the different communities we belong to.

These documents are usually not retained, but contain vital information on the life and times of the communities in a certain time period. They often go unnoticed in mainstream newspapers or publications, but later exist in people's files or trash bin. Sometimes they could be the only record an event took place, or that a band visited your town on tour.

Consider including them in a cultural section of your collection. You can ask the archive if they have an area such as a vertical file (a file system used for items that are

not suitable to be cataloged as books, manuscripts, or photographs but are kept for historical value) or if they should stay with your collection as a separate subject not related to paganism. The more you can add to history, the better. Do not dismiss these items because they do not relate to your history. Consider the fact that you may be the only person with those specific items.

At the University of Utah, I worked directly with cultural documents. I spent five years collecting on the culture of Utah and the West, adding these items and objects to the vertical file collection, which contained over 1,500 boxes and 10,000 subject files arranged by topic (e.g., music, restaurants in Utah 2004–2008, conventions in the West, community groups of Salt Lake City, and paganism in Utah). It was the largest and only active cultural collection in Utah, as no other library archive in the state was collecting those types of documents (Cureton, 2015). Often the University of Utah's vertical file collection contained records of events, such as festivals, band tours, restaurant menus, announcements, society meetings, newspaper clippings, reports, or brochures that were found nowhere else in the archives and were the primary sources for those topics (thus being of critical importance for research).

There is a great loss of cultural history because archives and libraries do not collect these types of documents. Sometimes they may come in with collections if a person was involved in a specific event or festival, in which case they would stay with the collection, but most often these documents fade from history and are lost.

Business and Magical Group Records

If you own or owned a business, these documents will be important. Pagan and Druid business owners are uncommon, so these types of records are a gem. Most likely you would donate them after your business closed. If you own a business currently and are entering year forty of operation, you can donate previous thirty years' worth of files.

Depending on what you want to archive, you will most likely have some of the following documents: emails, catalogs, receipts, advertisements, tax documents, contracts, vendor forms, and correspondence. There may be overlap in the titles with personal records, so they will have to be grouped under the name of the business. The sample organizational groupings discussed earlier can be applied here (box 1, folder 1, name/date; folder 2, name/date, etc.). You can just use a folder system if that is easier.

This organization system applies to group records from your grove or other magical organizations as well. It will be best to avoid confusion with other records you have, like personal and business, if you identify the records by their associations in this case. Your grove records, for example will all need to be arranged under the grove's name.

Vendor Catalogs

Pagan vendors are not common, so keeping catalogs adds invaluable data about the community in a certain time period. These catalogs can show what was popular, what was being produced, how ads were illustrated, what was being crafted, prices, accessibility of the items, where the companies were located, trends, and other important information. These can simply be grouped together chronologically.

How to Arrange Digital Files

We must not forget digital materials such as emails, online receipts from purchases, and photos uploaded to social media that exist only in cyberspace. The system of arrangement for physical files can be applied to digital files you will donate or for your personal archive.

Emails

It may be impractical to print thousands of emails, but you may not have to if the archive you are donating to has a digital space. You can save all of them to a flash drive or a cloud server for them to access. Like paper files, they also need to be organized. Since so much correspondence is done by email today, this is where the bulk of yours will be. You could do folders, using titles such as:

Folder 1: Personal correspondence, 2004–2016
      Subfolder 1. 2004
              2. 2005
              3. 2006
              4. 2007–2009
              5. 2010–2016

Do not forget about odds and ends such as email newsletters, updates from your favorite sewing store, or all those files you send through email. Emails that are non-personal, but not purely advertisement in nature contain a great deal of information on the culture of the day.

Blogs

Search engines send software robots called "spiders" out to collect data, or caches, on what web pages contain what words. They store these caches so when you search, all the relevant pages come up for the key terms (Franklin, 2000). Web crawlers in the archival world do the same thing, but instead take a snapshot of a site and archive it in a digital space (Library of Congress, n.d.b). You will want to consider crawling your own personal site, blog, or group site if you have one. The Internet Archive (https://archive.org/index.php), a nonprofit library organization, has what is called the Wayback Machine, which is a database that captures pages from around the web. You can input a site domain and if it has been crawled, it will come up with all the screen shots of your sites. If it has not, it is free to input your site and send the crawler to capture it. This is a great way to ensure all that hard work you put into building a site or blog and its contents do not just vanish into cyberspace. So often sites are lost, with no way of recovering or trace they even existed. So even if your paper records never make it to an archive, you can have this digital or transhuman presence (your digital content after death, which continues to exist).

Photographs and Videos

You can arrange videos and pictures the same way as print photos but include under each picture and video the appropriate, complete biographical information you would like. This is best practice just in case they get moved to another folder accidentally.

Folder 1. Dancer's Grove Photographs

    Subfolder 1. Rituals

        Sub subfolder 1. Yules

1. Yule 2010, left to right: John smith, Paula Deen, Elton John, December 21, 2010, Missoula, Montana.
2. Yule 2011, left to right: Brigham Young, Beyoncé, Freyja, December 20, 2011, Missoula, Montana.
3. Yule 2012, left to right: Wolfgang A. Mozart, Scott Cunningham, Ann Rice, Ice Cube, December 19, 2012, Missoula, Montana.

Computer Files

Almost all documents we create today will be on our hard drives. Most of it is never printed. You can use a similar system like the emails or paper files, once you determine what you would donate. Here is an example:

Folder 1-School Papers at Yale University
Subfolder 1. Freshman Year 2001
        2. Sophomore Year 2002
        3. Sophomore Year 2nd Semester Spring 2003
        4. Junior Year 2004
        5. Senior Year 2005
        6. Senior Project Summer 2005

Folder 2. Book Club Reading List Excel files
Subfolder 1. 2010
        2. 2011
        3. 2012

Folder 3. Scanned robe patterns
Subfolder 1. French design
        2. 1940's robe patterns
        3. Russian Robes
        4. Sewing club collective project pattern

Folder 4. Community Watch Meeting Minutes 2010
Subfolder 1. January-May
        2. June-December
     Sub subfolder 1. Updates to minutes
           2. Feedback for minute keeping in October
           3. Emails about Meetings
           4. Newspaper scan about our Community Watch 2011

What Can't Be Digitized?

Digital archiving has issues with longevity of storage with the current technology. A paper copy may change relatively little over centuries with proper storage and care. With digital items, you get degradation of data, storage media, and servers. If humans were

to suddenly vanish, the paper copies would still exist for a long period, but who would maintain the electronic equipment, provide electricity, plug in items, replace broken parts, migrate files to newer systems, update metadata standards, check for failures, and ensure that documents on one device are capable of being read on another (interoperability)?

Just think of how many files are still uncorrupted on your 3½-inch floppy disk today, which you stored in 2000. A mere fifteen years. Yet, you can still pull off the shelf your copy of *Harry Potter and the Sorcerer's Stone* from 1997 or *Lolita* from 1955 and read it like it was printed yesterday. This is why, in the field of archival science, the hard copies are called "enduring format." Though print has the best chance with the least work and care to survive the longest, anything worth archiving and preserving is considered to have enduring value.

Strangely enough, microfilm is highly durable and enduring. It does not require migration of formats and can be read, like photograph negatives, without equipment if necessary. It degrades very little over time. Now the technology is considered obsolete, and many microfilms have been digitized. There was also a loss of information with the storage medium since they did not capture color.

Most things can be captured in some way. Objects can be photographed with special 360 degree cameras, books can be scanned, papers can be digitized, and videos can be uploaded. But there is no way that everything in an archive can or should be scanned and put online. To digitize all materials in all libraries and archives would take thousands of years with current technologies. There simply aren't the funds, human power, and server space. There is also a "loss of information" when you digitize an item. Take the first edition of the works of Galileo. You can see them online, see the pages, but can you feel the parchment? Smell the leather binding? See the watermarks? Feel the gritty texture of the ink? Or feel the weight when you lift it? No, these little details get left out. For most people this is unimportant, but for many scholars these are the essential bits of information they go into an archive to examine.

The same principal applies to web crawlers. They can crawl sites and probe different tabs or structures within, but they will not be able to capture PDFs or videos.

Not digitizing items allows for their integrity to be protected from corruption or editing, which is why the hard copy is just as important to keep for verification. LOCKSS

is an open-source, library-led digital preservation system built on the principle that "Lots of Copies Keeps Stuff Safe" (Stanford University, n.d.). Never assume that because you have a copy that others do too. A library may toss a run of a magazine, only to find they were one of two libraries that had the entire run! Just because *People* magazine is highly popular and circulated does not mean it is being archived and preserved (treated to prevent further loss and degradation though chemical means or storage).

This philosophy of LOCKSS should apply to our Druid archives. If you are the only one with key documents from your grove or tradition, they are much more likely to be lost over time if they are never reproduced or archived. You have a better chance of ensuring the longevity of your tradition and history if multiple members have copies or the archive has copies of your documents. Though not eternal (as disasters do happen, such as earthquakes, fires, or floods), when an archive has copies, this is the best bet that your records will last indefinitely.

Objects, Magical Items, and Artifacts

As stated earlier, you can donate objects, known as realia, in conjunction with paper documents, especially if they are of significant, unique historical value. Say you were photographed using a wand at a ritual in 1991, but made a new wand the next year. That old wand can go with the ritual outline and photograph for that year in your collection. Perhaps you have a robe you used when you were of another faith, a Buddhist or Wiccan. Or the drinking horn from public rites you conducted during Super Bowl weekends from 2000 to 2010, your handmade tablecloth, the jewelry you crafted. All these items tell a story, tell who you were, your group, their interests or humor, and provide context to the documents and collection being donated. It is much more provocative to come in and see the New Year's Eve light bulb used by Edison in 1879 than to read about it or see a picture online.

Other types of objects you can consider include textiles, wrist bands, button pins, magnets, and ceramics. T-shirts or hats made for events can be donated as part of the story. If your grove did something unique like make mugs for Imbolc to drink coffee from or paint a plaster sugar skull for Samhain, all that can be archived with the collection to create a unique artifact history.

Putting It All Together

Simply follow the steps and outlines here and you will create a wonderful archive,

ready to donate. Take your time and consider everything you will include, why, and why or how it is all tied together. The story the collection presents is just as important as the documents. Always detail as much information as possible.

Spend time considering your subjects, context, and how you will group the records and title the folders or box them. It should make some sense, meaning the folders and boxes are not in random order. Think about how you would want to find your files in the future and that will probably be the best order. Unrelated folders can be put together at the end of the collection.

An archive will want some biographical or historical information as well to go with the collection so when others view it, they know why it is important and what it is about. Whether you decide to arrange the collection or let the archive do it, they will use what is called a finding aid, which is the index of the collection (Roe, 2005).

Example Collection
This example is from a real collection I arranged while working for the University of Utah Marriott Library. It is housed currently in their Print and Journal division of Special Collections, but is in the process of being transferred to manuscripts. The OCCAM (Orange County Circle of Ancient Magic, California) was a group that existed from the 1980s to 2012 in Southern California, until the person holding the records passed away. They are arranged by subject, chronologically and alphabetically. I had the privilege, through knowing a member who received the records in 2012, to be the archivist who arranged and described them for the archive.

OCCAM (Orange County Circle of Ancient Magic, CA) Finding Aid
Biographical Information
This collection contains the records from Ms. Barbara Podell and the Orange County Circle of Ancient Magic. Ms. Podell was born March 13, 1956 in California. She lived her life primarily in her home state of California. Ms. Podell graduated from UC Santa Cruz in 1978 with a BA in art history. She worked as a project manager for Northrup on B2 airplanes. She died October 20, 2012 in her home in Anaheim, California.

Ms. Podell had many interests from art history, dance, sexuality, and costume design to the occult, esoteric studies, and paganism. These records reflect primarily her interests in sexuality and the occult.

Historical Scope

The Orange County Circle of Ancient Magic was a group that existed from 1980–2012, when Barbara Podell passed away. OCCAM was a mix of various members from Southern California who came together to perform magic in various traditions from Wicca and Witchcraft, to Golden Dawn, Eucharist, and Norse. The primary purpose was the exploration of the occult and working in a group.

An interesting area of the collection is the history of the Pagan community in Southern California. Ms. Podell collected on a wide subject area and was able to capture ephemeral documents on the community and organizations to which she belonged, which are contained in box 9. Boxes 4 and 5 contain documents from various community organizations in which Ms. Podell participated. Box 10 contains vendor catalogs from this period. One unique community Ms. Podell collected on was the BDSM (bondage/discipline, dominance/submission, sadism/masochism) and sexuality community of Southern California. Those materials are housed in box 13

Contents

Box 1: Business Docs and Ephemera
        Folders 1. Calendar 1993
                2. Contracts
                3. Ephemera
                4. Expenditures, Dues, and Receipts
                5. OCCAM Collection Index
                6. Permission to Archive OCCAM

Box 2: Sabbat and Esbat (Moon) Rituals
        Folders 1. Rituals (Undated)
                2. Sabbat Rituals Prior to 1980
                3. Sabbat Rituals 1980–1989
                4. Sabbat Rituals 1990–1991
                5. Sabbat Rituals 1992
                6. Sabbat Rituals 1993
                7. Sabbat Rituals 1994–1995
                8. Sabbat Rituals 1996–1999
                9. Esbat (Moon) Rituals

Box 3: Other Rituals

Folders 1. Circle Casting and Releasing Rites
2. Eucharist Liturgies
3. Hagadah Ritual
4. Holy Mass Ritual 1996
5. Initiation Ritual 1990
6. Other Rituals
7. Planetary Rites
8. Quarter Call Rituals

Box 4: Community Organizations A–O

Folders 1. Ancient Keltic Church
2. Coven of Danu, Book of Shadows
3. Covenant of the Goddess
4. Fellowship of Isis
5. Hermetic Order of the Golden Dawn
6. Odinist (Norse-Asatru)
7. Order of the Pillars of Light
8. O.T.A. (Ordo Templi Astarte),Church of Hermetic Sciences
9. O.T.O (Ordo Templi Orientis)
10. O.T.O (Ordo Templi Orientis) 2

Box 5: Community Organizations P–Z

Folders 1. Pacific Circle 1990–1995
2. POW/SIG (Pagan, Occult, Witchcraft/Special Interest Group) MENSA
3. Servants of the Light
4. Raven's Moon Circle
5. Ravenwolfe Circle
6. The Circle of the Dragon and the Phoenix, Lessons 1999–2004
7. The Philosophical Research Society

Box 6: Reference Material

Folders 1. Astrology and Tarot Reference
2. Book of Shadows, Caer Calliach, Lord Greymantle and Lady Athena, 9 January, 1993
3. Essay: Basic Qabalistic Rituals 1988

        4. Evan McCallum Essays

        5. General Occult Reference

        6. Herbal Reference

        7. Poetry and Fiction

        8. Qabalah (Tree of Life) Reference

        9. The Wheel of the Year; The Music of Gwydion

Box 7: Correspondence

    Folders 1. General Correspondence (Undated)

        2. General Correspondence 1990

        3. General Correspondence 1991–1992

        4. General Correspondence 1993–1995

Box 8: Ed. Fitch Materials

    Folders 1. A Day with Ed. Fitch, 7 May 1994:
        Biographical Article with Notes

        2. Grimoire of the Shadows,
        Aidare Kelly and Ed. Fitch 1975

        3. Grimoire of the Shadows, Revised, Ed. Fitch 1991

        4. Norse Religion: The Way of the Rainbow Bridge,
        Ed. Fitch, July 1990

        5. Rituals by Ed. Fitch

        6. The Book of the Elders, Book No. 22, Ed. Fitch

        7. The Book of Shadows of the Outer Court, Ed. Fitch

        8. The Book of the Valkyr, Ed. Fitch, October 1990

Box 9: Community Publications

    Folders 1. A Witch's Brew by Adelma Simmons (Inscribed to Barbara
        Podell) 1991

        2. Community Journals

        3. Community Journals 2

        4. Community Newsletters

        5. Community Newsletters 2

        6. Community Flyers, Brochures, and Announcements

        7. Raising the Stakes: The Newsletter of Index 1994–1995

        8. The Hidden Path Magazine: The Voice of

Gardnerian Covens 1993–1996
Box 10: Vendor Catalogs
   Folders 1. Vendor Catalogs (Undated)
      2. Vendor Catalogs 1986–1991
      3. Vendor Catalogs 1992–1994

Box 11: The Roebuck, Ancient Keltic Church
   Folders 1. The Roebuck Book of Shadows
      2. The Roebuck General Materials
      3. The Roebuck Newsletters
      4. The Roebuck Training Circle

Box 12: Erotic Materials (Explicit)
   Folders 1. BDSM (Bondage, Discipline; Dominance, Submission; Sadism, Masochism) Reference
      2. BDSM (Bondage, Discipline; Dominance, Submission; Sadism, Masochism), Sex and Fetish Catalogs
      3. BDSM (Bondage, Discipline; Dominance, Submission; Sadism, Masochism), Sex and Fetish Community Flyers and Brochures
      4. Erotic Correspondence 1988–1994
      5. Erotic Magazines 1991–1996
      6. Erotic Stories
      7. Good Vibrations Catalogs 1994–1997
      8. Kinkycrafts 101, Do-It-Yourself S/M Toys, Lady Green and Jaymes Easton 1995
      9. The Sexuality Library Catalogs 1994–1997

Conclusion

As a member of a minority faith, you may have a unique practice. Each person practices differently. Groups vary widely. Just because two groves are doing Celtic pantheons with Lugh does not mean the rituals are the same, or their events, or how they teach their students, or how they influence their community.

While it may seem overwhelming and complicated, just take your time. It can be fun to go through all those old papers and photos, to organize them how you like, and

to consider that your collection has historical value (and to get some of that clutter out of the house).

Identify what you would want to donate to an archive, to which archive, what their collecting scope is, or if there is a university you like that would take your materials. Think local, donating to the region around you, especially if that is the history of the documents.

Remember, archives collect the documents that historians use to write history. You can change history. You can add your voice and the voice of the pagan and Druid communities to the historical record through your decision to save and archive.

References

Baird, B., Schaffner B. (1999). *Extinguishing slow fires: Cooperative preservation efforts.* ACRL Ninth Conference. Retrieved from http://www.ala.org/acrl/sites/ala.org.acrl/files/content/conferences/pdf/baird99.pdf

Cureton, D. (2015). *Diversity collections in archives: Capturing local minority cultural history through vertical file* [Power Point Slides]. Utah Library Association Annual Conference 2015.

Franklin, C. *How internet search engines works.* How Stuff Works: Tech. Retrieved from http://computer.howstuffworks.com/internet/basics/search-engine.htm

Hermetic Order of the Golden Dawn. 2010. Regardi Archives. Retrieved from http://www.hermeticgoldendawn.org/hogdframeset.html

Internet Archive. Retrieved from https://archive.org/index.php

James Cook University. *Primary, secondary, and tertiary sources.* December 8, 2015. Retrieved from http://libguides.jcu.edu.au/scholarlysources/secondary

Northeast Document Conservation Center. 4.4 Storage enclosures for books and artifacts on paper. Retrieved from https://www.nedcc.org/free-resources/preservation-leaflets/4.-storage-and-handling/4.4-storage-enclosures-for-books-and-artifacts-on-paper

Online Archive of California. Guide to the Isaac Bonewits papers ARC Mss 73. Retrieved from http://www.oac.cdlib.org/findaid/ark:/13030/c83x8c3p/?query=isaac+bonewits

OCCAM Papers. Special Collections Print and Journal Division. University of Utah, Salt Lake City, UT.

Ritzenthaler, M. (2010). *Preserving archives and manuscripts.* Chicago, IL. Society of American Archivists.

Roe, K. 2005. *Arranging and describing archives and manuscripts.* Chicago IL. Society of American Archivist.

Shilton, K., Srinivasan, R. (2007). Counterpoint: participatory appraisal and arrangement for multicultural archival collections. *Archivaria,* 61, 89.

Society of American Archivists. 2007. *What is an archives?* Retrieved from http://www.archivists.org/archivesmonth/2007WhatIsAnArchives.pdf

Stanford University. LOCKSS (Lots of Copies Keep Stuff Safe). Retrieved from http://www.lockss.org/

The Library of Congress. Collecting levels. Retrieved from http://www.loc.gov/acq/devpol/cpc.html

The Library of Congress. *What is a web crawler?* Retrieved from https://www.loc.gov/webarchiving/faq.html#faqs_12

University of New Haven. *What is a tertiary source?* Retrieve from http://libguides.newhaven.edu/content.php?pid=465151&sid=3809011

Blast from the Past: The Druids and Theosophy

Transcribed by J. Anthony Malerich.

J. Anthony Malerich has been a member of AODA since '08 and OBOD since '12. While his personal practice has moved in a different direction, he considers himself a bard, and remains in good contact with many druidic friends of both organizations. He currently lives and practices music in Japan.

Discovered by Donald J. Myers

Donald J. Myers
Assistant Librarian
Henry S. Olcott Memorial Library
Theosophical Society in America
1926 N Main St
PO Box 270
Wheaton, IL 60187
630-668-1571 x304
library@theosophical.org
www.theosophical.org
www.theosophy.wiki

Introduction by Trilithon Layout Designer

The following is a booklet printed in 1924 by the Theosophical Society[1] in the UK on the subject of the historical Druids and their similarities to Theosophy. By a stroke of good luck, the booklet was recently discovered by Donald L. Myers, the Assistant Librarian of the Henry S. Olcott Memorial Library of the Theosophical Society in America in Wheaton, IL. In an attempt to recreate the experience of seeing the actual booklet in its original format, the text and all of its contents have been layed out as accurately as possible to ressemble the source material as it was first printed ninety-two years ago (short of the delightful "old book smell"). We are gratefully indebtted to Donald for his remarkable contribution and hope that you enjoy this curious piece of historical writing.

Sincerely yours beneath the fruiting spicebush,
Paul Angelini
Layout Designer &
Grand Pendragon

---

1   So as to clear any confusion or misconeptions surrounding the use of the Swastika in the Theosohical Society seal, please refer to the following link: https://www.theosophical.org/on-line-resources/leaflets?id=1795

THE
DRUIDS
and THEOSOPHY

BY PETER FREEMAN
WITH A FOREWORD
BY DR. ANNIE BESANT

Y GWIR YN ERBYN Y BYD

DRUID SEAL

THE TRUTH AGAINST THE WORLD
(DRUID MOTTO)

SATYAN NASTI PARO DHARMA

T.S. SEAL

THERE IS NO RELIGION HIGHER

THAN TRUTH

(T.S. MOTTO)

THE
DRUIDS
AND
THEOSOPHY

By

PETER FREEMAN

Originally printed privately for Students,
now adapted, enlarged, and published
by permission

1924
PRINTED BY WILLIAM MCLELLAN & CO.
240 HOPE STREET
GLASGOW

Foreword

by

Dr. ANNIE BESANT

:: PRESIDENT OF THE ::
THEOSOPHICAL SOCIETY

"IN this little sketch of the Druid work and thought, Mr. Freeman unlocks a door which opens on long vistas of suggestive beauty, down which we would fain wander to gather the flowers of wisdom and tradition of which we catch a glimpse.

That the Druids held in trust secrets of science and mystic lore we know. Persecution by the ignorant and the superstitious slew, and drove into hiding the wise and the understanding, and robbed the lands of the Kelts of music and poesy, of art and grace, save that which was interwoven in the soul of the people and made them what they were.

This little brochure is but the opening of the door. May many walk through it, and enrich and beautify their land with the dust covered treasures they will find."

ANNIE BESANT.

THE DRUIDS
AND THEOSOPHY

The Gorsedd Prayer

"Grant us, O God, Thy protection,
And in protection, strength;
And in strength, understanding;
And in understanding, knowledge;
And in knowledge, the knowledge of justice;
And in knowledge of justice, the love of it;
And in that love, the love of existences;
And in that love of existences, the love of God;
God, and all goodness."

This prayer has been in constant and regular use for many centuries. When pronounced in the original Welsh it forms a powerful mantra.

The Ancient Bards or "Druids"

The Ancient Bards of Britain, otherwise known as the "Druids" of popular historians, have not always been well-spoken of by men of letters. Indeed, it has been almost the fashion among certain writers to represent these religious and ethical instructors as semi-barbarians, and of inferior capacity in spiritual knowledge.

This attitude, however, cannot be justified by evidence, but on the contrary it can be shown that the Druids have had a great and beneficent influence over the many nations and peoples in past centuries, particularly the Keltic civilization.

The Kelts

The Kelts were the Fourth Sub-Race, as the Teutons were the Fifth Sub-Race of the Aryan Root Race. The early history of their predecessors takes us back to Atlantis.

From the original Kelts migrating from Central Asia, many branches are found all over Europe, and now known amongst others, as the Greeks, Romans, Spaniards—and later—the Italians, French, Scotch, Irish and Welsh, Manx, etc.

The word Kelt comes from "Keli, the unmanifest concealed or hidden God."—*Morien.*

The Druids

The Druids were the acknowledged and recognised leaders and teachers of the Kelts for many thousands of years, though their power and influence probably attained its maximum in Ireland, Scotland and Wales (which included all England at this time), in the centuries preceding the Christian era. The Islands of Angelsey and Man were probably the last centres of Druidic activity.

We must, however, remember that that was an age of "Action" as the present is an age of "Thought," and Duty was enjoined rather than the Freedom of these more democratic days.

The Kelts were an idealistic, but emotional people, in contrast to the individualistic and intellectual Teutons, and undoubtedly the peculiar form of presentation of the "Mysteries" in the Druidic ceremonies and teachings, was more suitable to them than that of Christianity, and possibly some of the recent difficulties in Ireland may be directly traced to this question of "Religion."

Suppression of Druidism

The Romans eventually suppressed the whole Druidic organisation, especially in Wales, where their last headquarters were established. At the instructions of Suetonius Paulinus they "Cut down their sacred groves—destroyed their Temples and their Schools—burnt their Priests—punished adherents of their Faith, and suppressed their Teachings." Thus says a Christian book on "Faiths of the World": —"This idolatrous system disappeared as Christianity progressed, through all parts of the country, and before the zealous exertions of the Christian Missionaries, the barbarous rites and superstitions of the Druids passed away utterly and forever."

It is probably true that the exertions of these Christian (?) Missionaries were successful in destroying the form in which their teachings were given, as the modern Druids in Ireland or in Wales claim and know no link with this once great and beneficent organisation, but their Teachings still live and cannot die. Whether their statement as to their barbarous rites and superstitions is justified will hereafter be seen.

Druidic Sacrifices

"It is only candid to state, however, that human sacrifices have not only been denied, but it is supposed they were seldom even of the animal kind. The Gaelic language is said to contain no trace of such ceremonies—the word expressed by 'sacrifice' actually means 'the offering of a cake.'" —*Thompson*

No satisfactory evidence has ever been produced that the Druids themselves were ever guilty of the crimes and cruelties sometimes attributed to them.

In their decadent days, hordes of worthless brigands trading under the guise of Druids, and surreptitiously using their name, etc., may have done so, however.

Statements about Druidism

Of the Druids, Cowper wrote:—

> "Regions Caesar never knew,
> Thy posterity shall sway,
> Where his eagles never flew,
> None invincible as they."

and Pope:—

> "Hail Bards, triumphant born in happier days,
> Immortal heirs of universal praise."

And Matthew Arnold says: "There existed in the Island of Britain, before and at the time of its invasion by Julius Caesar, a class or caste of persons who, under the names of Druids, formed a powerful hierarchy. The Druids were the depository of great and extensive learning and possessors of civil power; acquainted with letters, arts and sciences, conversant with the most sublime speculations of geometry, in measuring the magnitude of the earth and of the world; philosophers of a sublime and penetrating spirit, adding the study of moral philosophy to that of physiology, skilled in mechanics, and acquainted with rhetoric and other polite arts."—*Studies of Celtic Literature.*

Further, in his introduction to the Everyman's Library edition of George Borrow's ever delightful little volume entitled Wild Wales, the editor, Mr. Theodore Watts-Dunton, writes most enthusiastically of "Druidism" as "that mysterious poetic religion which more than any other expresses the very voice of Nature." This is admittedly a large claim; but it is no doubt true in a sense.—*Ancient Bards Preface*.

Madame Blavatsky's *Secret Doctrine* contains many eulogistic references to their teaching and influence, and compares them with the Brahmins of India, the Magi of Persia, and the Orphic Teachers.

Activities of the Druids

The Druids generally:—

1. Were exempt from military service.
2. No Druid would engage in fighting.
3. They were never armed.
4. Their persons were regarded as sacred.
5. They paid no "taxes" or "tithes."
6. They accumulated no funds, or ever had any "wealth."
7. They always had a recognized right to speak first and last at all meetings.
8. Were always present at religious rites and festivals.
9. They nearly always lived in communities.
10. They always recognized the equality of men and women.
11. They were the interpreters of Religion—the Lawmakers, Teachers and Priests.
12. They had extensive powers which they used impartially in settling all disputes.

"So great was the veneration in which the Druids were held that when two hostile armies—inflamed with warlike rage, with swords drawn, and spears extended, were on the point of engaging in battle—at their intervention, they sheathed their swords, and became calm and peaceful, and would accept the impartial decision of the Druids on the dispute."—*Diodorus Siculus*.

Occult Knowledge: They had considerable occult knowledge of elementals, fairies, etc.—the use of talismans, occult forces, recognised the power of the sun, and had great faith in conducting their ceremonies in the "open air" and in "sacred places."

It was reputed that they could "Foretell the Future"—"Perform Magic"—"Cast Spells"—"Divine Mysteries"—and "Explain Dreams." The whole of their teachings were given orally, and none were allowed to be written. This accounts, to some extent, for the lack of so-called "evidence" of what they taught.

In one of the notes to his poems, Iolo vindicating the genuineness of the alleged primitive traditions very strenuously asserts that "letters cannot transmit knowledge so correctly as oral tradition."

Druidic Triads

Their method of conveying knowledge was in the form of "Triads" of which there were probably at least 20,000, dealing with every phase of life, and giving the answer to every question. A few of these have been handed down and are now available, and there can be no question as to their wisdom, simplicity, and value. They are generally regarded as the genuine remains of the Druidical Ages, but it being then considered unlawful to commit them to writing—accurate records of them are difficult to trace from the time they ceased to be handed on by word of mouth during the ceremonies of the Druids themselves. Further, the English translation does not probably convey the full meaning of the original Welsh or Gaelic.

A few examples of the Triads were:—

1. "Three eternal foundations of Ethics—Love to man, Justice to all, and Obedience to the Laws of Humanity."

2. "Of three things come Wisdom—of Truth, of Meditation, and of Suffering."

3. "Three good things to cultivate—Good Friends, Good Thoughts, and Good Humour."

4. "Three things to govern—Temper, Tongue, and Conduct."

5. "Three necessities of Transmigration—the least of all life, whence a beginning; the substance of all things, whence progress; and the formation of all things, whence individuality."

6. "Three things ever accumulate strength—Love, Knowledge and Righteousness; for there is an unceasing endeavour after them."

7. "Learn diligently what thou seest; keep diligently what thou learnest; and fear not to make known what thou knowest."

8. The duties of the Druid are:
    (1) To reform Morals and Customs,
    (2) To secure Peace,
    (3) To celebrate the praises of all that is good and excellent.

9. Three things to remember:
    (1) To act bravely,
    (2) That the Souls of men are immortal,
    (3) There is another life after death.

10. Three things to do:
    (1) To worship the Gods,

     (2) To do no evil,

     (3) To exercise fortitude.

11. The Three embellishing names of God:

     (1) The Soul of the Worlds,

     (2) The Father of Animation,

     (3) The Immensity of Love.

12. The Three embellishing names of the Stars:

     (1) The Eyes of Serenity,

     (2) The Candles of God,

     (3) The Gems of the Sky.

General Teachings

These included Astrology, Theology, Geography, Politics, Natural Science, and Art. The Druids certainly excelled in all forms of Art. The basis of all modern "verse" is probably due to them—all writings having been in the form of prose hitherto. They had their own musical notation—a little different from that of the present. They first introduced the violin and the harp. The Druids originated and developed the art of enamelling—to the surprise of the Romans, when they came and found it being carried on in Britain by those "uncivilised savages." They reduced design in art to its simplest form, and used four simple methods which were all probably symbolical, representing the four main Principles of Life.

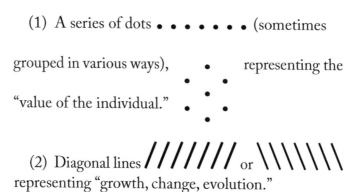

(1) A series of dots • • • • • • • (sometimes grouped in various ways), representing the "value of the individual."

(2) Diagonal lines ////// or \\\\\\ representing "growth, change, evolution."

(3) Zig-zag  "action and reaction" (Karma), and

(4) The ingrowing or outgrowing circle "Man's relationship to God and God's relationship to Man."

Many of the most beautiful designs of the Druid period can be reduced to these elementary forms.

Personality counted for little amongst the Druids. No names of their great teachers have been handed down to posterity. They erected no statues nor monuments, but believed men lived in their work, not in their names.

Religious Teachings

They had no special "Beliefs" nor "Faiths," no dogmas, no doctrines. Druidism was *not* a religion, but rather a religious system or philosophy of life, and all their teachings were inseparable from the activities of daily life. For this reason they gladly co-operated with the early Christian teachers in the introduction of Christianity into Britain.

St. David, the patron saint of Wales, although gaining his knowledge from Druidic sources, so efficiently organised Christian activities in the sixth century, that for the only time in our history Christianity, in this country, was a united body, and known as the British Church of Christianity.

St. Patrick, a little earlier than this, but coming also from Wales, where he was in charge of one of the

Druidic centres, including temples, colleges, etc., at Llantwit Major (S. Wales), undertook a similar work in Ireland, with conspicuous success, though probably encountering greater difficulties.

The Druids always used natural surroundings and conditions for their ceremonies. The 12 upright stones in a circle (the Gorsedd) (carefully oriented), represent the zodiac and typified the whole manifested universe—the stones themselves symbolising simplicity and stability—The "Legan Stone" (often weighing many tons), was probably made to move, and possibly represented the voice of God (Logos) to impress the multitude with certain teachings, but also used as a platform for the Arch-Druid.

It was on this stone that the mystic Fire was lit at the Midsummer Festival, after all lights and fires had been put out everywhere, all over the country.

During this ceremony, "the Mystic Fire of God" would descend on the altar, and the Arch Druid would then instruct his Druids; "Now take your brands fresh with the breath of God to light the hearths of men," and all fires would be re-lit by them in every home.

"Fire" and "Light" were regarded as a special "Gift of God," and this ceremony was performed to keep it in remembrance.

Worship with them, was a national institution, and everybody took part in their ceremonies. These were not held on Sundays, as is the custom in most religious services with us, but on such occasions as the solstices and equinoxes, times of full moon, Midsummer Day, etc.

Amongst other things they taught and practised were:—

1. The existence of One God, the Supreme Governor (not Ruler) of the Universe.

2. The Unity of all Life (all life was mutually dependent).

3. All beings and all forms of life were descended or "sprang from" God; (there is no reference to "creation" by God).

4. Immortality of the Soul, and Cremation of the Body.

5. Laws of Periodicity and Correspondences.

6.

7. Various planes or states of existence on a seven-fold basis.

8. Metamorphosis, metempsychosis, and/or reincarnation.

9. Sacredness of all life (many were probably vegetarians).

10. The Brotherhood of all Humanity; (a well-known Druidic motto says: "There is no Stability save in Brotherhood.")

11. The free and unlimited "Search for Truth."

12. The exoteric Truths for the people, and the esoteric Truths for students.

13. Existence of "Adepts," or Masters.

The Eisteddfod

The Eisteddfod (meaning "Sittings") probably dates back to the time when Wales was a self-governing and independent Nation, with its own laws (which Howell Dda systematised and have since become the basis of English common-law), their own educational institutions, and practising very largely a community life. At this time, the Eisteddfod was the House of Commons of the day, and their "sittings" always commenced with music.

When Wales fell under the more powerful military dominion of England, she was deprived of the privilege of making her own laws—but still kept on the Eisteddfod—which thereby became mainly a musical Festival, and has been so celebrated ever since even to this day.

The Druidic Order

The Old Druidic Order has, however, no connection between the present day activity which centres round the Eisteddfod, and has little in common with it other than the use of the "Gorsedd circle" (Caer—Sidi = Church—Star, representing the Kosmos and the Zodiac), the motto of the early Druids—"Y gwir yn erbyn y Byd." (The Truth against the World), and the symbol

It was divided into three degrees or orders:—
(1) The Druids—the teachers, and priests.
(2) The Bards—philosophers, poets, and prophets.
(3) The Ovates—the artists, the workers.

This priestly order was always held in great estimation. Nobles, and even princes, eagerly sought admission into it, and the more numerous the Druids were, the more prosperous would be the country. Dr. Henry says, "Many of the Druids seem to have lived a kind of collegiate or monastic life, united together in 'Fraternities,' as Morcellinus expressed it."

The Druids wore a flowing white robe with different coloured bands or scarves for the various degrees. They generally went bare-headed and bare-footed.

The Druids recognised the hierarchical basis of life, but the order was built on a democratic form. The Arch Druid being elected generally for life.

They had their annual conventions in each country, and bi-annual convocations for all Europe.

The Druidical "Secret Doctrine"

"Degrees were conferred by complicated ceremonies—and we hear for the first time of the "Secrets" and "Mysteries" of Bardism. Claims of the most extravagant kind are put forth for the Bards. And, "The Truth against the World" is represented not only as a motto, but as the basis and the character of every bardic work." (*Old History of Wales, p. 546, Woodward*).

"But the chief feature is the strange theosophic scheme which these two mystagogues (Iolo Morganwg and Dr. Owen Pughe) have developed out of the scanty authentic and traditional accounts of the Druids, and their mythological poems of the Middle Ages." (*ibid.*, p. 547).

"From this it is evident that there was a secret doctrine as well as a public one—and although it is not possible to say what the esoteric doctrine was, we may well believe with Caesar that it consisted of speculations concerning the World and the Universe—concerning Nature and the Deity." (*ibid.*, p. 54).

E. Renan traces the descent of Masonry from the Druids in his "Poetry of the Celtic Races."

Relationship of Druidism and Theosophy

Their symbol was

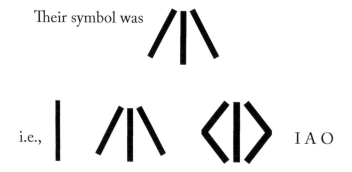

i.e., I A O

(the unpronounceable Name of God)

representing the three-fold nature of the Deity,

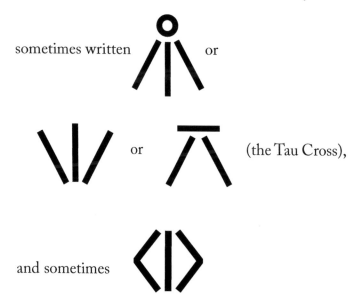

sometimes written   or

or   (the Tau Cross),

and sometimes

Another symbol was the Serpent and

the Serpent's Egg

One can see from both of these

 and  when conjoined,

a close connection with the Seal of

The Theosophical Society.

The word "Druid" is derived from, Dru = God (cf. Modern Welsh Duw; Gaelic, Draoi; French, Dieu; Greek, Δ; English, Deity), and "Vid" = "knowledge" (cf. Aryan root, vid = wisdom; Latin, video; Sanscrit, vidya; English, vision); in fact it is but another form of the words "Divine Wisdom," the Brahma-Vidya or **THEOSOPHY**.

From the above it does not seem unreasonable to assume that the Druids were to the Fourth Sub-Race, what the Theosophical Movement is to the Fifth, and that the same great fundamental teachings of life which inspired the Druids are now the ideals by which many try to live as Theosophists.

PETER FREEMAN.
St. David's Day,
1st March, 1924.

References

Myths and Legends of the Celtic Race (published by T. W. Rolleston-Horrap, 1912).

Tales about Wales (published by Hall, 1837).

The Ancient Bards of Britain, by D. Evans (published by The Educational Publishing Co., 1906).

Secret Doctrine, by H. P. Blavatsky.

Poetry of Celtic Races, by E. Renan.

The Ancient British Church.

History of Wales, by Woodward (published early 18th century).

Barddas, translated by Rev. Ap Ithel Williams (published by the Welsh M.S.S. Society, 1862).

The Philosophic Teachings of Catwg the Wise

On TRUTH

There is nothing easy but the seeing of Truth.

There is nothing difficult but the obtaining of Truth.

There is no wisdom but the love of Truth.

There is no learning but the knowledge of Truth.

There is no heroism but the speaking of Truth.

There is no love but in the expression of Truth.

There is no enemy but that of clinging* to Truth.

There is nothing wonderful but in obedience to Truth.

There is nothing more general than the praise of Truth.

There is nothing less general than the seeking of Truth.

There is no astonishment but the hearing of Truth.

There is nothing supreme over everything but Truth.

There is no attainment but the finding of Truth.

There is no wealth but the obtaining of Truth.

There is no effort that is good but the Search for Truth.

There is no peace but in the maintenance of Truth.

There is no good end but Truth.

There is no will of God but Truth.

The Letter of the Law and not the Spirit of Truth.

A Few Druidic Proverbs

Whoso possesses the grace of God, is rich.

Long the tongue, short the wit.

Vain is the advice not sought.

The fool loves the sound of his own voice.

Whoso loves wisdom will not practise deceit.

Truth is the eldest child of God.

Good for evil will take thee to heaven.

Often is the devil found in a garb of light.
The true home verily is heaven.

Happy is he whose life is pure.

Disagreeable is every Truth where it is not loved.

He verily is not good who cannot become better.

Whoso loves God is safe.

Early rising is the better half of the day's work.

The real friend will be seen in adversity.

Violence is insulting Truth.

Gentleness and patience will make the work perfect.

After leaping is too late to refrain.

AODA Groups Contact List

AODA supports three kinds of groups:

<u>Groves</u>,which perform initiations and provide regular ritual, ceremony, and support for members. They are led by a Druid Adept in the AODA and are officially chartered.

<u>Study Groups</u>,which perform introductory initiations (the candidate grade and first degree) and engage in regular ceremony. They are led by a Druid Companion in the AODA and are officially chartered.

<u>Home Circles</u>,which are able to be led by any AODA member. The principle of the home circle is simple: it is a group of people who meet regularly, learn from each other, and engage in a number of activities surrounding druidry. See the *Home Circle Manual* for more information (forthcoming, 2016).

<u>AODA Groves</u>

Delsarte Grove. Bremerton, WA
Led by Gordon Cooper, Druid Adept and Grand Archdruid.
Contact: <u>nwlorax@gmail.com</u>
Open to new members, performing initiations.

Grove of the Wise Fox, Chicago, IL
Led by Adam Robersmith, Druid Adept and Archdruid of Fire.
Contact: <u>druid@oakandthorn.com</u>
Grove of the Wise Fox is currently not accepting new members, but is available for initiations.

Star and Thorn Grove, Indiana, PA
Led by Dana O'Driscoll, Druid Adept and Archdruid of Water.
Contact: <u>danalynndriscoll@gmail.com</u>
Open to new members, performing initiations.

Three Roads Grove, Springfield, OH
Led by Lady Oceanstar, Druid Adept.
Contact: ladyoceanstar@gmail.com
Three Roads Grove is currently not accepting new members, but is available for initiations.

AODA Study Groups

Kawartha Study Group, Peterborough, ON, Canada
Led by Dennis Delorme, Druid Companion, sarezrael@yahoo.ca
Open to new members and performing initiations.

Ocean's Mist Study Group, Warwick, RI
Led by David P. Smith, Druid Companion, duir@cox.net
Open to new members and performing initiations.

AODA Home Circles

Home Circle, Minneapolis, MN
Led by Marcus Baker, AODA Candidate, animasaru@gmail.com

Home Circle, Sacramento, CA
Led by Jose Esparaza, AODA Candidate, anzuya312@live.com

Three Rivers Circle, Spanish Lake, MO (north of St. Louis)
Led by Claire Schosser, Druid Apprentice, cschosser@yahoo.com

Home Circle, Oakland, CA
Led by Adam Milner, Druid Apprentice, carmiac@gmail.com

Circle of the Seven Spirals, St. Augustine, FL
Led by William Herrington, vdc9119@aol.com

The Circle of the Great Aspens and Reeds, Kaysville, UT
Led by Brenda Holmes, brenda0951@yahoo.com

Awen, Oak, & Sage Home Circle, Salt Lake City, UT
Led by Daniel Cureton, <u>danielcureton@gmail.coom</u>

From the rising sun, three rays of light;
From the living earth, three stone of witness;
From the eye and mind and hand of wisdom,
Three rowan staves of all knowledge.

From the fire of the sun, the forge;
From the bones of the earth, the steel;
From the hand of the wise, the shaping:
From these, Excalibur.

By the Sword of Swords, I pledge my faithful service
To the Living Earth, our home and mother.

Awen, Awen, Awen.

Photograph by Grandarchdruid Gordon Cooper
Tree bole. Fauntleroy Creek Watershed, West Seattle, c. 1997.
(No Photoshop. Film, Rolleicord V, Verichrome Pan film, developed in D23.)

58981986R00133

Made in the USA
Charleston, SC
23 July 2016